Takashi Inoguchi
GLOBAL CHANGE
A Japanese Perspective

Jomo K.S. and Shyamala Nagaraj (*editors*)
GLOBALIZATION VERSUS DEVELOPMENT

Dominic Kelly and Wyn Grant (*editors*)
THE POLITICS OF INTERNATIONAL TRADE IN THE 21st CENTURY
Actors, Issues and Regional Dynamics

Craig N. Murphy (*editor*)
EGALITARIAN POLITICS IN THE AGE OF GLOBALIZATION

George Myconos
THE GLOBALIZATION OF ORGANIZED LABOUR
1945–2004

John Nauright and Kimberley S. Schimmel (*editors*)
THE POLITICAL ECONOMY OF SPORT

Morten Ougaard
THE GLOBALIZATION OF POLITICS
Power, Social Forces and Governance

Markus Perkmann and Ngai-Ling Sum (*editors*)
GLOBALIZATION, REGIONALIZATION AND CROSS-BORDER REGIONS

Leonard Seabrooke
US POWER IN INTERNATIONAL FINANCE
The Victory of Dividends

Timothy J. Sinclair and Kenneth P. Thomas (*editors*)
STRUCTURE AND AGENCY IN INTERNATIONAL CAPITAL MOBILITY

Fredrik Söderbaum and Timothy M. Shaw (*editors*)
THEORIES OF NEW REGIONALISM
A Palgrave Reader

Amy Verdun
EUROPEAN RESPONSES TO GLOBALIZATION AND FINANCIAL MARKET
INTEGRATION

International Political Economy Series
Series Standing Order ISBN 0–333–71708–2 hardback
Series Standing Order ISBN 0–333–71110–6 paperback
(*outside North America only*)

You can receive future titles in this series as they are published by placing a standing order. Please contact your bookseller or, in case of difficulty, write to us at the address below with your name and address, the title of the series and an ISBN quoted above.

Customer Services Department, Macmillan Distribution Ltd, Houndmills, Basingstoke, Hampshire RG21 6XS, England

The Political Economy of Regions and Regionalisms

Edited by

Morten Bøås
Fafo – Institute for Applied International Studies, Oslo Norway

Marianne H. Marchand
International Relations and History, University of the Americas, Puebla, Mexico

and

Timothy M. Shaw
Institute of Commonwealth Studies, School of Advanced Study,
University of London, UK

First published 2005 by
PALGRAVE MACMILLAN
Houndmills, Basingstoke, Hampshire RG21 6XS and
175 Fifth Avenue, New York, N. Y. 10010
Companies and representatives throughout the world

PALGRAVE MACMILLAN is the global academic imprint of the Palgrave Macmillan division of St. Martin's Press, LLC and of Palgrave Macmillan Ltd. Macmillan® is a registered trademark in the United States, United Kingdom and other countries. Palgrave is a registered trademark in the European Union and other countries.

ISBN-13: 9781–4039–2090–4
ISBN-10: 1–4039–2090–7

This book is printed on paper suitable for recycling and made from fully managed and sustained forest sources.

A catalogue record for this book is available from the British Library.

Library of Congress Cataloging-in-Publication Data
The political economy of regions and regionalisms / edited by Morten Bøås, Marianne H. Marchand, and Timothy M. Shaw.
    p. cm.
Includes bibliographical references and index.
ISBN 1-4039-2090-7
    1. International economic relations. 2. Regionalism. 3. Interregionalism. 4. Globalization. I. Bøås, Morten, 1965-II. Marchand, Marianne H., 1958-III. Shaw, Timothy M.
HF1359.P6554 2005
337–dc22   2005049997

10   9   8   7   6   5   4   3   2   1
14   13   12   11   10   09   08   07   06   05

Printed and bound in Great Britain by
Antony Rowe Ltd, Chippenham and Eastbourne

Contents

v

List of Maps and Tables

Maps

Tables

Acknowledgements

This volume began life as a revised edition of our co-edited late-1999 special issue of *Third World Quarterly* (20(5), October 1999, pp. 891–1070) on 'New Regionalisms in the New Millennium'. But it has ended up as an almost completely new collection with a quite different and distinct cast of contributors, chapters and concerns, reflective of the continued evolution of the field. So we thank our past and present editors for their support and patience through this journey (just two years between signing the contract and delivering the ms!): Shahid Qadir at *Third World Quarterly* and Jen Nelson at Palgrave Macmillan.

We are pleased to be able to thank two sets of colleagues for generous and invaluable assistance through the (unexpectedly long?!) life of this collection. First, we are most appreciative of colleagues from around the world who have been involved in a series of networks and meetings, starting in the late-1990s in Amsterdam and Oslo, which have informed both editors and contributors; especially those associated with British International Studies Association (BISA), European Consortium for Political Research (ECPR), International Political Science Association (IPSA) Research Commission no. 40 on 'New World Orders?' and International Studies Association (ISA) Section on 'Global Development', and now European Association of Development Institutes (EADI) Working Groups on 'New Regionalisms and Global Development' and on 'Governance'. And secondly, appropriate to a collection on continuing changes in regional and global arrangements, we have all moved posts over the new millennium: to Institute for Applied International Studies, Oslo (Fafo), Universidad de las Americas, Puebla (UDLA) and University of London, respectively. So we would like to thank all colleagues in both old Universities of Oslo, Amsterdam and Dalhousie respectively, and new institutions who have been accommodating of our occasional preoccupation with new regional dimensions and discussions. Also thanks to Henriette Lunde at Fafo–AIS for last minute editorial assistance.

As indicated in the introduction and conclusion, the volume is just one more station in a longish journey along the road of new regionalisms. One of the ways in which our preoccupations will be continued is through the REDESFRO network on 'Regionalism, Social

Development and Borders' which is being funded by the European Commission and coordinated by Marianne Marchand. The REDESFRO network will organize three summer schools in Puebla, London and Buenos Aires respectively starting in 2005 and provide an exciting venue for charting new directions to the study of new regionalisms. Finally, as always, thanks to children, parents, partners and pets, and others in our extended families, for putting up with this and related projects. Enjoy!

MORTEN BØÅS
MARIANNE H. MARCHAND
TIMOTHY M. SHAW

Notes on the Contributors

Ramses Amer, PhD and Associate Professor, is Senior Lecturer at the Department of Political Science, Umea University, Sweden. Major areas of research are security issues and conflict resolution in South-east Asia and the wider Pacific Asia, and the role of the United Nations in the international system. He is the author of 'The Sino-Vietnamese Approach to Managing Boundary Disputes', *Maritime Briefing*, vol. 3, no. 5 (Durham: International Boundaries Research Unit, University of Durham, 2002). He is co-editor, with Carlyle A. Thayer, of *Vietnamese Foreign Policy in Transition* (Singapore: Institute for Southeast Asian Studies; and New York: St Martin's Press, 1999). He has also contributed to international journals and to books and has written reports on issues of Southeast Asian Affairs and on the United Nations.

Claudia Sanchez Bajo is political scientist/sociologist with a PhD in Development Studies and research on regionalism and industrial actors. Her main tasks at present are being responsible for research and research coordination of ECG (European Association of Cooperative Groups), whose members are: Mondragon Corporacion Cooperativa and Grup Empresarial Cooperatiu Valencia (Spain), Groupe Crédit Mutuel and Groupe Crédit Coopératif (France), Consorzio Gino Mattarelli per la Cooperazione Sociale and Consorzio Cooperativo Produzione e Lavoro (Italy); and being representative in the EU of RECM (MERCOSUR Specialized Cooperative Conference), MERCOSUR organ grouping the cooperative confederations and the public institutions promoting cooperatives in Brazil, Argentina, Uruguay and Paraguay. She also works as a consultant on development and regionalism, entrepreneurship and human rights (e.g. in China), and has been lecturing at universities and parliaments, both in Europe and Latin America.

Mark Beeson is Senior Lecturer in the School of Political Science and International Studies at the University of Queensland, Australia. His latest book is *Contemporary Southeast Asia: Regional Dynamics, National Differences* (Palgrave Macmillan, 2004).

Mark T. Berger is Senior Lecturer in the Department of Spanish and Latin American Studies and the International Studies Program at the

University of New South Wales (Sydney, NSW, Australia). He is author of *Under Northern Eyes: Latin American Studies and U.S. Hegemony in the Americas, 1898–1990* (Indiana University Press, 1995) and *The Battle for Asia: From Decolonization to Globalization* (RoutledgeCurzon, 2004). He is co-author, with Heloise Weber, of *Rethinking the Third World: International Development and World Politics* (Palgrave Macmillan, forthcoming).

Morten Bøås is Senior Researcher, Fafo – Institute for Applied International Studies, Oslo. He has published extensively on African politics, the multilateral system, and regions and regionalization. His work has been published in journals such as *Third World Quarterly*, *New Political Economy*, *Journal of Contemporary African Studies*, *Current History*, *Global Governance* and *Global Society*. His most recent books in English include *New and Critical Security and Regionalism* (co-edited with James J. Hentz, Ashgate, 2003) and *Global Development and Institutions: Framing the World?* (co-edited with Desmond McNeill, Zed, 2004).

Benedicte Bull is Political Scientist and Research Fellow at the Centre for Development and the Environment (SUM), University of Oslo, Norway. Her main research interests include the politics of market reform and market governance in Latin America, regionalization, and the politics of multilateral aid. She is the author of *Aid, Power and Privatization: The Politics of Telecommunication Reform in Central America* (Cheltenham, UK and Northampton, US: Edward Elgar, 2005), and several articles published in, e.g., *Third World Quarterly*, *New Political Economy*, *Global Governance* and *Journal of Developing Societies*.

Sandra J. MacLean is Associate Professor of Political Science at Simon Fraser University, British Columbia, Canada. Her current research, which focuses particularly on the southern African region, is concerned with (global) governance in areas of human security, health and development. Among her recent publications are co-edited volumes, *Crises of Governance in Asia and Africa* (Ashgate, 2001) and *Advancing African Security and Development* (Halifax, Dalhousie University, 2002). Her work has appeared in *Third World Quarterly*, *Global Networks*, *Canadian Foreign Policy*, *Canadian Journal of Development Studies*, *New Political Economy*, *Journal of Contemporary African Studies*, as well as several edited volumes.

Ane Roald Mannsåker is currently a PhD student at the University of Oslo. She is working on a thesis on informal regionalism in the Gulf, with a focus on Iraq.

Marianne H. Marchand is Professor of International Relations at the University of the Americas, Puebla, Mexico, where she also coordinates the MA program in North American Studies. She is a member of the National System of Researchers (SNI). Her research demonstrates a great concern with the politics of change and (global) restructuring. In her work, Marchand looks to feminist and post-colonial theory and engages in critical explorations of the narratives and practices of development, globalization and regionalization/regionalism. She addresses the politics of change and how global restructuring often leads to increased marginalization and social exclusion. In 2003 she finished the national report to the Dutch parliament on the implementation of the UN Convention on the Elimination of all Forms of Discrimination against Women (CEDAW). In addition, Marchand recently received funding from the European Union to coordinate the REDESFRO Network on Regionalism, Social Development and Borders.

Kristen Nordhaug is Associate Professor at the Department of Geography and International Development Studies, Roskilde University, Denmark. He holds a mag.art. degree in Sociology from the University of Oslo and a PhD in International Development Studies from Roskilde University. His research focuses on issues of East Asian political economy and US – East Asian relations.

Timothy M. Shaw is Professor of Commonwealth Governance and Development in the School of Advanced Study at the University of London, where he also directs the Institute of Commonwealth Studies. He taught Political Science and Development Studies at Dalhousie University, Canada, for three decades and is visiting professor at Mbarara University in Uganda and Stellenbosch University in South Africa. His recent articles have appeared in *Commonwealth and Comparative Politics*, *Global Governance*, *Global Networks*, *Journal of International Development* and *Round Table*.

Ian Taylor is a senior lecturer in the School of International Relations, University of St Andrews, Scotland, and a Visiting Research Fellow in the Department of Political Science, University of Stellenbosch. His recent publications include *The New Partnership for Africa's Development: Towards Development or Another False Start?* (Boulder: Lynne Rienner, 2005), *Africa in International Politics: External Involvement on the Continent* (co-edited, London: Routledge, 2004), *Regionalism and Uneven Development in Southern Africa: The Case of The Maputo Development Corridor* (co-edited, Aldershot: Ashgate, 2003) and *Stuck in Middle GEAR: South Africa's Post-apartheid Foreign Relations* (Westport: Praeger, 2001).

List of Abbreviations

ADB	Asian Development Bank
AFC	Asian Financial Crisis
AFTA	ASEAN Free Trade Area
AMF	Asian Monetary Fund
ANC	African National Congress (South Africa)
APEC	Asia-Pacific Economic Cooperation
ARF	ASEAN Regional Forum
ASEAN	Association of South-east Asian Nations
BSAC	British South Africa Company
CACM	Central American Common Market
CAFTA	Central American Free Trade Agreement
CAP	Common Agricultural Policy
CBMs	Confidence-Building Measures
CET	Common External Tariff
COSATU	Congress of South African Trade Unions
DRC	Democratic Republic of Congo
EAEC	East Asian Economic Caucus
EAEG	East Asian Economic Group
EANICs	East Asian Newly Industrializing Countries
ECPR	European Consortium for Political Research
ECLAC	UN Economic Commission for Latin America and the Caribbean
EESC	European Economic and Social Committee
EZLN	Ejercito Zapatista de Liberacion Nacional
FCES	Mercosur Economic and Social Consultative Forum
FDI	Foreign Direct Investment
FTA	Free Trade Agreement
FTAA	Free Trade Area of the Americas
GDP	Gross Domestic Product
GPE	Global Political Economy
ICJ	International Court of Justice
IDB	Inter-American Development Bank
ILO	International Labour Organization
IMF	International Monetary Fund
ISI	import-substitution industrialization
ITG	Inter-institutional Technical Group (for Mesoamerica)

KDP	Kurdish Democratic Party
MEBF	Mercosur–European Union Business Forum
MDGs	Millennium Development Goals
MFN	Most-Favoured Nation
MOF	Ministry of Finance, Japan
NAFTA	North American Free Trade Agreement
NEPAD	New Partnership for Africa's Development
NGO	Non-Governmental Organization
NRA	New Regionalism Approach
OAU	Organization of African Unity
OECD	Organisation for Economic Co-operation and Development
PPP	Plan Puebla–Panama
PRI	*Partido Revolucionario Institucional* (Mexico)
PUK	Patriotic Union of Kurdistan
SADC	Southern Africa Development Community
SAP	Structural Adjustment Programme
SCIRI	Supreme Council for Islamic Revolution in Iraq
SICA	System of Central American Integration
SIEPAC	Central American System for Energy Integration
SMEs	Small and Medium Sized Enterprises
TBT	Technical Barriers to Trade
UDI	Unilateral Declaration of Independence (Rhodesia/ Zimbabwe)
UNDP	UN Development Programme
UPDF	Uganda People's Defence Force
WTC	World Trade Center
WTO	World Trade Organization
ZANU-PF	Zimbabwe African National Union-Patriotic Front Party
ZAPU	Zimbabwe African People's Union
ZOPFAN	Zone of Peace, Freedom & Neutrality

1
The Political Economy of Regions and Regionalisms: An Introduction to our Critical, Revisionist Inquiries

Morten Bøås, Marianne H. Marchand and Timothy M. Shaw

Since the publication at the end of the century of the *Third World Quarterly* special issue on 'New Regionalisms in the New Millennium' (Bøås, Marchand and Shaw 1999) the analysis of regionalization and regionalisms has evolved in various directions: from foci on accessions to the EU and FTAA 'light', for example, to several distinctive 'Commonwealths' – anglophone, francophone, lusophone, Russophone and Spanish – and onto a comparative edited overview of the 'new' regional politics of development (Payne 2004). Apparently, the field is sufficiently established that there is now even a 'reader' for it (Söderbaum and Shaw 2003).

So, the assumption that regional interactions and organizations focus not only on states but also on continuing linkages among a heterogeneous set of actors and realms is becoming increasingly accepted. Our position is that regional integration is not necessarily a state-led process. Regions are always in the making – constructed, deconstructed and reconstructed – through social practice and discourse. Not only states, but also non-state actors, participate in the process of constructing regions and giving each its specific content and character (Bull and Bøås 2003). This is the basic assumption, even assertion, of this collection. As such it presents a challenge to the conventional literature, which still tends to emphasize the state as the primary, if not only, regional actor and formal regional integration agreements as the only expression of regionalism and regionalization.

For the editors, this collection constitutes something of a crossroads. On the one hand, the chapters illustrate and reinforce quite nicely the points we made a little over five years ago, when they may have seemed more innovative, even controversial, than now. On the other hand, it provides (at least for us) closure of these earlier debates and a first step towards moving on and again rejuvenating the study of regions and regionalization. In our view, as indicated in the penultimate section of this chapter below and then again in the Conclusion, it is important to take on board insights from parallel disciplines/discourses such as critical geography, post-colonial theory and cultural studies, and post-structuralism in addition to international relations, international political economy, development and 'new security' (Söderbaum and Shaw 2003) to gain a deeper understanding of regionalisms' multidimensionality (Marchand and Bøås 2004).

The central objective of the present project has been to rethink debates on regions and regionalization, governance, development and change. Such an endeavour could be realized on the basis of the following concepts, to which we return in the second half of this overview and then again in the Conclusion:

- Space, spatiality and borders
- Ideas and identities (e.g. 'regionness' and regional identities)
- Governance and governmentality through institutionalizing, regulating and disciplining
- Networking and network logic (Marchand and Bøås 2004) (see section below)

In the next section of this introduction, we will briefly recapitulate the past debates on the new regionalism. This is followed by an overview of how the issues we raised more than five years ago are illustrated and advanced in this volume's chapters, which are either seriously revised and updated from their initial *TWQ* incarnation or novel post-*TWQ* contributions. Finally, as we approach the second decade of the twenty-first century, we will address some of the new directions in the study of regionalization in the last section.

Evolution of theoretical discussions about new regionalisms and regionalization

Since the early 1990s, particularly in the wake of the Cold War's termination, the regional level has increasingly become an important referent for students of international relations, international political economy and development as indicated by recent collections (e.g. Payne 2004, Söderbaum and Shaw 2003). The same trend is evident among governments and stakeholders from civil society and the private sector. Many actors are searching for regional solutions to problems and challenges apparently caused by the forces of globalization which are being perceived as too big to handle within the borders of the nation-state (Bøås 2000).

Initially, the discussions on regionalism and regionalization focused on the 'new' in new regionalism, trying to distinguish it from the 'old' regionalism of the 1960s and 1970s. Much scholarly energy has been devoted to studying in particular how regional processes relate to globalization: whether regional trade arrangements are stumbling blocks or stepping stones to ever increasing free trade, and whether regional integration can be interpreted as a way of 'negotiating' globalization or creating a social buffer against the potentially disturbing effects of globalization. Five years ago we (Bøås, Marchand and Shaw 1999:902) summarized the debates on regionalism and the articulation of different approaches to the study of regionalization and new regionalism as follows:

> First, there are various institutional approaches to regionalization, which have been influenced by the old functionalist and neo-functionalist approaches and more recent ideas about the role of institutions in international relations. Second, there are various (critical) IPE approaches, which see regionaliszation as part of larger world order transformations, especially the decline of U.S. hegemony and the end of the Cold War. Third, scholars such as Edward Mansfield and Helen Milner identify another set of explanations, which focus on domestic (political) factors and use, for example, strategic trade theory to account for the sudden keen interest on the part of policy makers, in regional projects. Fourth, there is the New Regionalism Approach/Theory (NRA/T), which has been developed over the 1990s by Björn Hettne and colleagues.

Since then the study of regionalism and regionalization has evolved both through case studies and theoretical discussions. There exists now ample agreement that globalization and regionalization can occur simultaneously. As processes of social transformation, they create winners and losers. Some groups of countries, but perhaps to a larger extent groups and communities within them, have gained from these processes. The starting point for coming to terms with the globalization/regionalization nexus must therefore be to acknowledge that the impact from both these processes is highly uneven.

It is also imperative that we understand the outcomes of the globalization/regionalization nexus as products reflecting diversity and not uniformity. Even the most sophisticated systems of modern communication and the development of integrated commodity and financial markets have not destroyed cultural, ethnic, economic or political diversity. Rather, the globalization/regionalization nexus has created a whole range of diversified patterns of interactions and responses at the local, national, regional and international levels. Some of these take place within the formal structures of politics and economics, but they can just as well be played out in the informal political economy. It is our view that one important but neglected issue in this field of analysis and praxis is the relationship between formal and informal regionalization: that is, formal regional agreements signed by states as well as those forms of regional interactions that mostly emanate from non-state actors and that are not covered by any formal agreement. In short, how compatible or nested are the two, or are there ambiguous, differing, fuzzy borders between them?

It is just as important to recognize that production and commodity chains, including brand management, are increasingly creating regionalized regimes of wealth accumulation, which (again) encompass formal and informal processes of regionalization. The post-Cold War era has changed the structure of the world from a single clean and quite transparent bipolar system to a set of intricate networks of strategic alliances and highly flexible markets. These developments cannot be seen in isolation from the formal/informal regional nexuses of 'new security issues', which defy easy control and containment, such as drugs, gangs, guns, mafias, migration, militias, networked terrorism and so forth, as they involve myriad actors.

This present volume intends to capture some of these recent developments through theoretically grounded case studies which will not only enrich knowledge about how regionalism and regionalization are articulated in practice, but also further theoretical insights, with relevance to a number of overlapping fields and discourses as indicated towards the end of this introduction.

New regionalisms contextualized

One of the important contributions of the new regionalisms approach has been its challenge to existing Western, in particular Eurocentric, bias in theorizing about regionalism and regionalization. This characteristic is clearly reflected in the contributions of this book. All chapters not only discuss regionalisms outside of a European context, but they also take a more encompassing view of regional processes, the actors involved and so on. For instance, Ian Taylor in his contribution clearly links formal and informal processes of regionalization. In his chapter he even illustrates how informal regionalism in Central Africa is actually challenging the formal state-led region-building project of Southern African Development Community (SADC). Taylor even goes so far as to suggest that we should include a new type of regionalization – that of malignant regionalization – based on a kleptocratic political economy that thrives on illegal activities and war profits (see also Duffield 2001, Reno 1998).

In some of the other chapters the interlinking of formal and informal regionalisms plays out rather differently. In the case of Latin America, regionalisms and regionalization involve myriad actors. As Benedicte Bull illustrates in her chapter on Mexico and Central America (or 'Mesoamerica'), the integration process between Mexico's most south-eastern states and Central America involves state actors, business elites as well as groups opposed to globalization (and, therefore, also neo-liberal regionalization). In other words, the interweaving of these actors and their projects sometimes works to strengthen the formal regionalization process. This is particularly the case when strong business groups are behind the formal project. Sometimes, though, the opposition of groups, such as the Social Hemispheric Alliance, has resulted in the watering down or even the barring of formal integration projects. This appears to be happening with the Free Trade Area of the Americas (FTAA) initiative, which has already turned into FTAA 'light', in part because of opposition by transnational groups and their success in (partially) convincing sympathetic governments such as Lula's Brazil.

In the (South-)East Asian and Asia Pacific context, all authors – Mark Berger and Mark Beeson, Kristen Nordhaug and Ramses Amer – argue and agree that regional projects are still primarily state-led. Berger and Beeson even challenge the notion that we can speak of a new regionalism in the Asia Pacific region. Instead, they assert that regional projects are still embedded in Cold War history and structures. Nordhaug, in turn, does not underestimate the importance of state actors but also sees the emergence of regional projects, which may include non-state actors in the future. Moreover, other authors have also pointed at the importance of regional non-state actors in the Asia Pacific political economy. These include networks of overseas Chinese businessmen and Japanese conglomerates which have moved part of their production abroad (Payne 2004, Perkmann and Sum 2002). Similar arguments are made with regard to South Asian capitalism and civil society (see Reed 2003, Quadir and Lele 2004).

What is interesting, then, in this particular region is the historic legacy of regional security-oriented organizations, which remain dominated by states, which are jealous of their recently acquired sovereignty and less inclined to involve other actors in the process. In terms of economic regional arrangements, there seems to be a co-existence of formal and informal processes, which are not clearly linked. Also, as Ramses Amer points out, economic and security dimensions are difficult to separate completely. What has occurred so far in terms of economic cooperation can be designated as a form of 'light regionalism', instead of a process, which leads to a deepening of regional integration through such instruments as harmonization.

Finally, the chapter by Claudia Sanchez Bajo sheds yet a different light on the interweaving of formal and informal regionalisms. Her contribution illustrates that Mercosur has become more institutionalized due to its interactions with the EU. The need to speak with a unified voice has actually triggered such deepening. This experience is not that different from the EU's own history of deepening regional integration.

A second dimension that the contributions to this volume illustrate very well is the plurality of regionalisms. Going beyond a state-centred approach involves recognition that other non-state actors also develop regional projects. As the contributions reveal, these projects may reinforce state-led projects or may provide alternatives and even opposition to such formal regionalism. In the chapter by Sandra MacLean on the Zimbabwean political crisis, it becomes clear that not only states but also non-state actors pursue different regional interests and projects. This has resulted, for instance, in the discordance between the reactions of neighbouring states toward Zimbabwe's crisis (in the form of the SADC's position voiced by its Council of Ministers) and the NEPAD partners' position on democracy and human rights.

In the context of Latin America, multiple actors also pursue distinct regional projects. Individual federal states in Mexico do not always side with the federal government on its Plan Puebla–Panama (PPP). For instance, the former governor of the state of Oaxaca, José Murat, has openly criticized the PPP. Moreover, many informal actors, including migrants and smugglers as well as the Zapatistas, have pursued their own regional interests, which do not necessarily coincide with the PPP. In other words, one sees not only an overlapping of regional projects and interests but also contradictory positions.

A similar dynamic is true for the Gulf region. As Ane Roald Mannsåker argues, dynamics in the Gulf and particularly the Iraq–Iran War cannot be properly understood without taking into account domestic Iraqi actors and their different regional interests. Important actors to take into consideration are the Kurds as well as the Shi'i majority, which, back in the early 1980s, were still marginalized under the regime of Saddam Hussein. In this context, ethnic as well as religious transnational ties play an important role.

What we can glean from these examples is that regional (transnational) networks, the existence of multiple regionalizing actors and thus the pursuit of different – sometimes overlapping, sometimes contradictory – regional projects need to be studied in terms of their interconnectedness. It is clear that the new regionalisms approach is sensitive to the contextual, multi-layered nature of regionalisms and regionalization.

As we transit from new regionalisms at the turn of the millennium to new strands or dimensions in the new century, we also need to bear in mind that the global community now consists of some 200 states, all too often poor, small and weak. But, unlike their predecessors in the era of decolonization in the 1960s/1970s, they are now confronted not by interstate bipolar blocs but by non-state corrosive and subversive forces: drugs, environmental change, mafias, people-smuggling, small arms, viruses and so on. Given their vulnerabilities, some such regimes seek security in regionalisms, which are therefore proliferating, whether they advance members' development or not. Scholars of regions and regionalization should pay more attention as to how difficult and hostile external environments frame approaches to the region by fragile states (see also DFID 2005).

Where to start with the rethinking on regionalism(s) and regionalization?[1]

Although much has happened since the publication of the special issue of *TWQ* five years ago, we also believe that there are important theoretical developments in the social sciences which have not yet been taken into account in the study of regionalism(s) and regionalization. These include, among other influences, the insights of post-colonial theory and cultural studies, in short the 'cultural turn'. To provide a first attempt to use such insights we will develop four concepts below. Together these reflect the direction in which we think the study of new regionalisms should be taken into the second decade of the twenty-first century.

Space, spatiality and borders

First, regions, and thus regionalism(s) and regionalization, are by definition territorial constructs. In the so-called age of globalization, where much emphasis is put on the deterritorialization of global flows, regions and the processes of regionalization imply the opposite: the (re-)territorialization of global/regional flows. Although the recent literature on regionalization has recognized the constructed nature of regions, it still considers them to be given and stable or static once constructed.

However, taking space and spatiality seriously involves a rethinking of how regional spaces and spatiality are being articulated. Regions are not necessarily stable or static once constructed. Moreover, regions are constituted and continuously articulated through the policies and practices of myriad actors (Perkmann and Sum 2002). In this respect, borders are important boundary markers and makers of regions. For example, the expanded EU boundary with the 'new' Eastern Europe has become an important border in the sense that it defines the 'other' Eastern Europe from the 'us' or the EU. Its construction needs to be continuously reiterated through a variety of border control practices. These practices in turn help to distinguish and differentiate the 'civilized' us from the 'barbaric' other, involved in organized crime, terrorism and uncontrolled migration. So, more than a territorial boundary, the border between the EU and Eastern Europe has become a cultural boundary.

A second element to take into consideration is that there are many overlapping and interlinked regions. Just as Arjun Appadurai (2001) suggested the existence of ethnoscapes, mediascapes, technoscapes and financescapes in the context of globalization, we can argue the same thing with respect to regionalization and regions. For example, it is clear that we now increasingly encounter regional financescapes in the form of a euro-zone, a yen area and a dollar-zone. Likewise, capitalist accumulation regimes have increasingly become regionalized leading to regionally based technoscapes which constitute the building-blocks for regional brands and supply chains as illustrated by the expansion of South African companies in Africa (Shaw and van der Westhuizen 2004).

Ideas and identities

A second aspect that does not receive much attention in the literature focusing on formal regionalism and regionalization is the construction of regional identities and the 'othering' of actors outside of the region. However, social constructivist approaches to the European Union (e.g. Wiener and Diez 2004, Risse-Kappen 1995) exemplify the need to include this dimension within the study of regionalism. The ways in which both micro- and macro-regional identities are being articulated and then related to the formation of governance structures, such as the emergence of a European polity, even emerging foreign and security policy, are important in understanding how regional imaginaries are being created.

Another interesting example of regional identity formation and articulation involves the emergence of regional transnationalized indigenous identities. The Mixtecas, an indigenous community from the state of Oaxaca (Mexico), have been very inventive in creating a transnational regional identity by, not only founding a bi-national political organization linking its US-based migrant community to their communities of origin, but also establishing common ground with other indigenous groups from Oaxaca in the US (in particular Zapotecas and Trikis) and North American Indians. After Arnold Schwarzenegger became Governor of the State of California, and established the policy that undocumented migrants may not have access to health services, North American Indians in the state made health services on their reservations available to their counterparts from Oaxaca. They did so on the basis of the argument that indigenous people are not migrants, but rather that people from non-indigenous descent are the migrants in the Americas. Moreover, they claimed a (transnational) regional indigenous identity based on solidarity among Indians and indigenous Mexicans.

Governance and governmentality

A third dimension that has begun to be taken seriously in the study of regionalism is 'governance'. However, governance usually relates to the creation of regimes of rules, norms and regulations in such areas as trade, the mobility of capital and the environment as well as 'new multilateralisms' such as the Montreal, Ottawa and Kimberley 'Processes'. In our attempt to move beyond current debates, we suggest that the concepts of governmentality and biopolitics should also be included. Foucault's ideas about governmentality and biopolitics have gained renewed attention since the events of 11 September 2001. Instead of trying to control territory, states appear to move towards controlling, regulating and disciplining population flows (as well as capital and goods flows). Examples of such direction in state behaviour are the Schengen agreements in the European context and the regionalization of US security policies.

The introduction of the Schengen Information System in Europe reflects a clear attempt to regulate population flows in a regional context. Potential visitors are now pigeon-holed into desirables, undesirables and Schengen area inhabitants. State performance is exercised at all ports of entry into the Schengen area, and people who are not part of this area are forced to wait in passport lines where the EU sign is not displayed. In practice, this means more scrutiny and longer lines.

The US Homeland Defense's (over)reaction to the 9/11 attacks on the World Trade Center (WTC) has triggered a policy of intelligent borders which extraterritorializes the regulation of population flows. For instance, one now passes through US immigration in major Canadian airports. This can result in absurd situations as experienced by one of the editors of this volume. While in the Montreal airport and carrying fruit bought in Canada (which was intended to be consumed in the airport, thus on 'Canadian' soil) the editor had most of the fruit confiscated by US customs intent on exercising extraterritorial, phytosanitary control.

Although to a lesser extent, even in the case of Mexico, the US has now convinced local authorities to use and deploy biometric border controls on its southern border as part of its intelligent borders policy. We can clearly see a regionalization of the control and regulation of population flows. Obviously, this is affecting existing undocumented migration from Mexico and Central America. On the one hand, the Regional Conference on Migration or the 'Puebla Process', which was established in 1996, implies efforts at regional policy coordination and a sharing of the 'problem of migration' – obliging sending states to assume responsibility and part of the burden of control and regulation. On the other hand, such increased regulation and attempts at control have led to a regionalization as well as professionalization of the 'migration industry': that is, smugglers, document falsifiers, (corrupt) officials, IT contractors, transportation companies and so on.

Networking and network logic

A final dimension that has to be taken much more seriously is that of transnational networks and network logic. These concepts, borrowed initially from sociology as well as migration and post-colonial studies on transnationalism, relate to fundamental transformations in society. Often these transformations are seen as an integral part of globalization processes, which have been engendered by a revolution in information and communication technologies. One of the societal transformations that this revolution has brought about is the introduction of network logic in society (Castells 1996). According to Castells, society now operates according to this logic – ranging from the network state, business and enterprise networks to a society based and functioning on networks and networking among individuals.

Its transnational dimension is increasingly being studied in relation to migration networks, which exercise transnationalism from below. Such networks not only help to orient recently arrived migrants but also allow diasporas to continue to have a presence in their communities of origin, often involving themselves in the economic and political futures of these communities. In many cases, such transnational migrant networks operate on a regional scale and thus reinforce and complement regionalizing tendencies. These migrant networks can and have become important regional actors especially on regional issues, ranging from security, human rights, the pursuit of democracy to regional trade and investment agreements. A better understanding of their functioning and their connections to regionalisms and regionalization is therefore important.

Conclusion

We conclude this section by briefly juxtaposing orthodox and new approaches to regions and regionalization. The former still privileges the state, the formal, the institutional and the economic incentives to market integration. There is nothing wrong with such studies and such approaches. However, we also believe that if the study of regionalism is yet once more to uncover new ground it must move into the 'unknown'. It must seek to occupy new positions and uncover novel contradictions and challenges. This is why we argue for a more poststructural turn, a 'cultural turn' which privileges space and spatiality, identities, governmentality and the logic of networks and networking. Together these dimensions pose important implications and ramifications both for theory and for policy, not just of states, but also for a wide range of 'non-state' actors (see ILO 2004, UN 2004a). If new regionalism is to remain as a relevant theoretical contribution to global studies broadly defined, this is the way that scholars should go.

Note

1 This section relies heavily on the Marchand and Bøås presentation at the Fifth Pan-European International Relations Conference of the ECPR Standing Group on International Relations, The Hague, September 9–11, 2004.

2
Between Bush and Bolívar: Change and Continuity in the Remaking of Mesoamerica[1]

Benedicte Bull

Introduction

Regionalism in Latin America has traditionally revolved around two competing visions: the Latin American-led regionalism originating in Simon Bolívar's Pan-American dream, and US visions of a cooperating Latin America originating in the Monroe Doctrine (Hurrell 1995, Kirby 2003). Currently, the most important expressions of the two competing forms of regionalism are Brazilian-led Mercosur pursuing a multidimensional regionalism on the one hand, and the US-led neo-liberal project of creating a Free Trade Area of the Americas (FTAA) on the other.

Parallel to these forms of regionalism, there are a series of projects reconfiguring regional spaces, partly in response to the two above-mentioned forces, but partly also being driven by other concerns. One such project is the current efforts to integrate the south-eastern part of Mexico with Central America into a new *Mesoamerica*. The main instrument for doing so is the Puebla–Panama Plan (PPP), a major development plan launched by Mexican President Vicente Fox in 2001 as a means to develop the most impoverished parts of Mexico, while also increasing the integration between Mexico and the Central American countries. The area included in the plan has a strategic location and plentiful resources: two oceans, extensive coastlines, soil varieties, vast forests, rich biodiversity, abundant water, minerals and oilfields. But it is also poor: the south-eastern states of Mexico had in 1994 five times higher poverty levels than the north-east and forty times higher than the federal district (Lustig 1998), and Central America includes two of Latin America's poorest countries (Honduras and Nicaragua).

This chapter analyses how, by whom, and for what purpose the Mesoamerica area is being reconfigured, renamed and redefined. The starting point is the argument that regions are constructed and reconstructed through social practice. Regions are not static units, but are shaped by both formal and informal practices, ranging from political projects pursued at the highest governmental levels, to informal networks and diverse kinds of motion. The argument made here is that Mesoamerica is currently being constructed by a series of different 'regionalizing actors' (Neuman 2003). As part of a political project, regionalizing actors attempt to create a certain spatial and chronological identity for a region and to disseminate this to the maximum number of outsiders. In the case of Mesoamerica, some of these pursue projects aligned with a neo-liberal globalization project, some represent formal attempts to create buffers against globalization, and some represent counterforces against globalization. These compete in their attempts to give the region a new meaning and new borders, but somehow they all contribute to the construction of Mesoamerica.

The reconstruction of Mesoamerica

Most formal regional integration projects in the area in question have been based on the idea of *Central America* as a region. Central America includes the five countries that were formerly a part of the Central American Republic (1924–38): Guatemala, El Salvador, Honduras, Nicaragua and Costa Rica. These countries also made up the Central American Common Market (CACM) established in 1962, and they became the parties to the renewed treaty of cooperation leading to the establishment of the System of Central American Integration (SICA) in 1991. Belize and Panama were later included in SICA, which thereby came to encompass the area known as *Middle America,* which is nevertheless often referred to as Central America (Bull 1999).

The PPP attempts to construct a larger region, called Mesoamerica. This includes the eight south-eastern states of Mexico,[2] the five Central American republics, Belize and Panama. The physical means to construct Mesoamerica are twenty different projects under the heading of eight 'Mesoamerican initiatives,' aimed to construct infrastructure, facilitate commercial exchange, and improve natural management and human development in the area.[3] The PPP includes planned investments of US$10–25 billion. It aims to build a 288-kilometer dry canal (a highway and railway network), which will cross Mexico's Isthmus of Tehuantepec that divides the Gulf of Mexico and the Pacific Ocean.

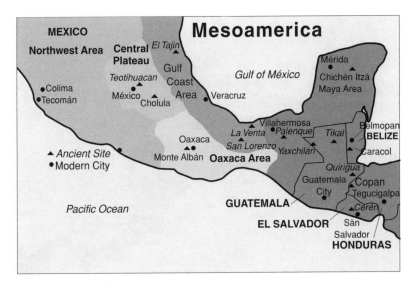

Map 2.1   The 'old' demarcation of Mesoamerica, including what is now Mexico City and the southern parts of Mexico, Guatmala, Belize, El Salvador and parts of Honduras

There are also plans for integration of electricity and telecommunication networks, and a biological corridor through Mesoamerica. In addition, there are several projects that may be called 'secondary PPP projects'; namely, projects that may be possible due to investments under the PPP, although they are not directly included in the plans. These include a set of smaller roads, hydroelectric dams and oil and gas pipelines.

However, PPP does not only attempt to construct a region through connecting it physically, it also attempts to construct a region through discourse. Mesoamerica is an ancient label for an area depicting an interrelated set of high cultures in pre-Columbian times situated in an area including what is now central and southern Mexico, Guatemala, Belize, El Salvador, and parts of current Honduras (Lockhart and Schwartz 1983:33). During colonial times, Mesoamerica was included in the Mexican orbit, wherein Mexico City (then Tenochtitlan) was the main city, whereas the southern part of Central America fell within the Peruvian orbit (see Map 2.1).

Compared to the historical Mesoamerica, the Mesoamerica of the PPP excludes large parts of central Mexico, but adds Nicaragua, Costa Rica and Panama, that fell outside the ancient Mesoamerican cultures.

Map 2.2   The 'new' demarcation of Mesoamerica, excluding Mexico City, but including Nicaragua, Costa Rica and Panama

Thus, the Mesoamerica of the PPP is a new invention, mixing and matching formerly established regions. It cuts Mexico in two, transgresses different Middle American regions, and brings Panama closer to the north (see Map 2.2).

For what purpose is this new Mesoamerica constructed, and how may it change the area between North and South America? These are the questions that will be discussed in the following section.

The free trade agenda: towards a borderless 'Americas'?

One main driving force of Mesoamerican integration has been to the neo-liberal project to create a Free Trade Area of the Americas (FTAA) by 2005, envisioned to extend the integrated economies of the NAFTA countries towards the south. The free trade proponents view Mesoamerica as an integrated part of a hemispheric free trade system. It is to become a sub-region within an increasingly borderless Western hemisphere, envisioned as governed by market relations in 'a frictionless world of shared meaning' (Mittelman 1996:205). The free trade agenda is driven by key actors of the different states, including the US, but also transnationally oriented business elites. The vision is to foster industrialization and economic growth in the region through attracting national and foreign investors that may take advantage of the lowering of trade barriers under the coming FTA (GTI 2001).

Within a hemispheric free trade area, the niche for Mesoamerica is primarily to attract more assembly industry (mainly maquiladoras operating in the textile industry), producing for export to the US market. Increasing employment in the maquila industry is an explicit goal of the PPP, and it was even more explicit in the forerunner of the PPP 'The March towards the South' (see below), which aimed to create 36,000 new jobs in the maquila industry in southern Mexico by 2002 (Sandoval Palacios 2001).

The advantage of southern Mexico and Central America compared with northern Mexico as a site for investment is lower wages. The Mexican administration has therefore argued that the future for investments in maquila industry lies in the south-east, as the wages there may be less than half than in the north (Moro 2002). In parts of Central America the wages are even lower. For example, in the textile industry the average hourly wage in Mexico is $0.52, while it is $0.43 in Honduras, and $0.25 in Nicaragua (Maquila Solidarity Network 2003). However, in order for big business to be interested in establishing production plants in the scantily developed areas of Mesoamerica, better infrastructure is needed for local operation and for transportation of goods to the US market. Moreover, border controls must be made more efficient to reduce transaction costs. These are the kind of issues that the PPP seeks to address.[4]

Understanding the driving forces of the PPP will therefore have to include explanations of the Mexican and Central American elites' interest in free trade agreements. The interest of the political elites in regional agreements in these countries has been explained by three major factors:

(i)   changes in the organization of production, leading managers to seek a regional rather than national home base;
(ii) attempts by neo-liberal elites to block a potential roll-back of neo-liberal strategies; and
(iii) developments in Europe and East Asia (Marchand 2001).

For the Central American leaders the latter was essentially a matter of attempting to compete with East Asia in the attraction of investments that seek to take advantage of abundance of cheap labour

(Bulmer-Thomas 1998). Currently, China is the main competitor with regards to investments in the maquila industry.

However, the close link between the PPP and the FTAA process has also been among its main vulnerabilities as there have been great uncertainties with regards to the feasibility of FTAA in its original proposed form. After the free trade agreement between the US and the Central American countries (CAFTA) was signed in January 2004, this has become the main backdrop of PPP.

The US motivation for signing CAFTA is essentially twofold. First, Central America is a significant market for the US: total US exports to the region is US$9 billion, which is roughly the same as US exports to India, Indonesia and Russia together. Although the Central American countries have lowered trade barriers to much of these exports bilaterally and through the SICA system, tariffs are still applied to some US exports. Secondly, the US strategy is to establish principles for the multilateral FTAA agreements through a set of subregional and bilateral agreements. These now include CAFTA and the US–Chile FTA. One important principle set down in these agreements is reciprocity. While the former agreements regulating the relationship between Central America and the US gave unilateral preferences to the Central American countries and allowed 74 per cent of this products to freely enter the US market, CAFTA will give market access only in return for similar access given to US products in Central America.

CAFTA may also be regarded as a follow-up to the FTAs signed between Central America and Mexico, Canada and Chile, respectively. The Central American countries have had a dialogue with Mexico about an FTA since January 1991, when the Declaration of Tuxtla Gutierrez was signed.[5] The main topics of the Tuxtla process have been economic cooperation and facilitation of the free trade agreement, and also unification of efforts to protect the environment, and the fight against organized international crime. Costa Rica signed an FTA with Mexico in 1995, Nicaragua in 1998, and at the end of 2001, after nine years of negotiations, an agreement was signed between the Northern Triangle of Central America (Honduras, Guatemala and El Salvador) and Mexico.

But how borderless will the free-trade Mesoamerica really be? That question will get different answers depending on whether you talk about people, goods or capital. But in all cases, the process of dismantling borders will be paralleled by the strengthening of old borders and the creation of new.

One sector in which old borders will be maintained is agriculture. CAFTA opens up a significant increase in US agricultural exports to Central America, without including any moderation of US trade-distorting subsidies. The differences in productivity and efficiency between the highly modern US agriculture propped up with US$170 billion subsidies may uphold an effective border against Central American products entering the US, and about a million corn and rice producers are left vulnerable to continued importation of subsidised US grains.

The main sector intended to 'mop up' surplus labour is, as mentioned, assembly industry. However, new borders here are also created as the agreement includes rules of origin that denies free entry to the US for goods produced with inputs from countries that do not enjoy preferential trading rights with the US. Only Nicaragua was able to negotiate a partial exception to this rule, which will constitute an effective border against many of the goods produced in the Central American maquila industries.

With regards to capital, the Central American countries are already rather wide open in terms of allowing foreign investments, but CAFTA will improve the conditions for possible investors through making the legal framework more predictable. The US has made, as standard in bilateral agreements, the principle that gives companies the right to demand compensation from governments in host countries that adopt legal regulations that have possible negative consequences for their profits. It was given a particularly extensive formulation in NAFTA's Chapter 11, and has entered into CAFTA in a slightly modified form. Thus, some of the borders that the agreement challenge most efficiently may be those set to limit for example the negative environmental effects of industrialization by host governments.

In sum, the ongoing 'reconfiguration' of the Mesoamerican region will mean that the division of labour between different regions that is currently developing under NAFTA will be extended to include also Central America. The result may be that certain industry sectors will be moved south, creating some low-skilled jobs, while the employment in the agricultural sector decreases. One analysis commented on the agricultural agreement under CAFTA in the following way: 'The signal to Central American farmers was to prepare themselves for the journey north as part of a new wave of emigration' (McElhinny 2004:2). But for these people, an entirely different map is being applied. This is the one drawn up in the security agenda.

The security agenda: strengthening the southern frontier

Understanding the remaking of Mesoamerica requires that we also take into account security issues. Security is here understood in the constructivist sense, as issues that have been 'staged as existential threats to a referent object by a securitizing actor who thereby generates endorsement of emergency measures beyond rules that would otherwise bind' (Buzan, Wæver and de Wilde 1998:5). It is, in other words, not claimed that the security issues of the PPP are existential threats to the people of the PPP Mesoamerican area, only that they are treated as such by core actors. The referent objects involved here are primarily the United States, secondarily the federal government of Mexico. The existential threat is flows of migrants from the south. However, access to core resources, such as oil and water, has also been treated as a security issue.

Free trade issues have been closely connected to migration control ever since the Commission for the Study of International Migration and Cooperative Economic Development was established in the US Congress in 1986, related to the approval of the Simpson-Rodino Law (the Immigration Reform and Control Act) (Sandoval Palacios 2001). In its report from 1990, the Commission argued that 'The United States should approve the applications for funds presented by Mexico and the international financial institutions to improve the infrastructure in inland areas with capacity to host maquiladora activities'. This was recommended because 'the Commission is convinced that – through stimulating economic growth – the expansion of commerce between the countries of origin and the United States is the most efficient remedy for the task that we have been set to study' (quoted in Sandoval Palacios 2001, p.3). The Commission not only linked free trade and migration, but it also acknowledged the need to look beyond the Mexican border, as the second largest immigration flows to the US comes from Central America, particularly Guatemala, Honduras and Nicaragua. To stop the use of Mexico as a transitory country of immigrants on their way to the United States, it was considered crucial to develop integrated economic activities that included the Central American countries.

From the start it was recognized that the PPP was also an integrated part of the strategy to cut off migration flows from Central America. During the meeting where the PPP was agreed upon with the Central American presidents, Fox made it clear that migration issues were at the core of PPP (*La Jornada*, Mexico, 20 June 2001). Guatemala has therefore achieved a strategic position, reflected in Bush's invitation of Guatemalan President Alfonso Portillo to Washington DC on 5 July 2001, at which occasion Bush called Guatemala 'the first border of the Plan Puebla–Panama', emphasizing the need for limiting migration from Central America through Mexico (*Prensa Libre*, Guatemala, 6 July 2001). The Central Americans have only reluctantly approved of the plans.

Whereas the whole PPP can be viewed as a plan to encourage possible migrants to stay, there are also specific measures included in the Mesoamerican initiative for human development to create a joint information system for migration in the area in order to improve control of migratory flows (IDB 2002).

However, the strategy to control migration is not limited to encouraging economic activities in order to dishearten potential migrants. It also includes a vast expansion of military control at the southern border between Guatemala and Mexico, part of which goes through Chiapas. The most comprehensive effort to seal the southern border was presented by the Mexican government in the Plan South (Plan Sur) presented 1 July 2001. The Plan Sur is a law enforcement initiative directed at stopping Central Americans from traversing the 620-mile stretch of rain forest that Mexico shares with Guatemala and Belize. The plan involved increased vigilance of elite military and police forces deployed along the border from Chiapas to the Tehuantepec Isthmus (*La Jornada*, 19 June 2001). As a consequence, the number of Central American deportees increased to approximately. 200,000 in 2001, as compared to 150,000 in 2000. However, the plan was not only directed towards stopping immigration flows; it was characterized by Mexican Secretary of Governance, Santiago Creel Miranda, as 'an unprecedented effort to cut off the flow of immigrants, drugs and arms to the country from Central America' (interview *Washington Post* 18 June 2001 quoted in Sandoval Palacios 2001:5).

Plan Sur was announced soon after the Action Plan for Cooperation about Border Security, agreed between the Mexican and US governments on 22 June the same year, increasing the US military presence, primarily along the northern border. More importantly, however, it was conducted parallel to negotiations between the Mexican and US government over amnesty for Mexico's illegal immigrants living in the US (New California Media Online 20 August 2001).

After the introduction of Plan Sur, accusations soon arose that the Mexicans were doing the 'dirty work' for the US. This was rejected by Mexican officials who argued that the plan was introduced to protect the 'national security' of the Mexicans, not serving the US. In either case, it is clear that the Mexicans reproduce the security discourse used by the Americans with regards to the northern border (Sandoval Palacios 2002).

PPP may also serve US security in another sense: namely to secure access to key natural resources. Mexico has become an increasingly important supplier of oil to the US market as Venezuela's production has plummeted. The PPP area not only borders with oil-producing Colombia and Venezuela, it also contains alternative oil reserves to their increasingly unreliable supply. The Mexican states included in the PPP account for 65 per cent of Mexico's oil reserves and 95 per cent of its current oil production (*Chiapas al Día*, Mexico, 29 October 2002). Moreover, Guatemala has announced oil reserves in the Peten jungle to be made available to foreign investors. Thus, construction of infrastructure in those areas may be of crucial importance.

However, the PPP does not only include security agendas of the US, but also those of the federal government of Mexico. The south-eastern parts of Mexico including the Guatemala/Mexico borderlands have traditionally primarily been of concern to the Mexican federal government, related to environmental degradation of the area, its centrality as a corridor for migration, and as a buffer against Central American guerillas (Herzog 1992). The Mexican government has periodically launched plans to address these issues. In 1983, two major plans, Plan del Surestre and Plan Chiapas, were launched in order to build infrastructure in the region and control the different peasant movements that had started to organize against the federal government (Harvey 1998).

There is a clear connection between the PPP and former development plans in the region. The immediate predecessor was the 'Marcha Hacia el Sur'[6] (The March towards the South) a plan formulated by the former PRI (Partido Revolucionario Institucional) government of President Ernesto Zedillo. It was based on an essay published by Santiago Levy in July 2000 called 'The South Also Exists: An Essay about Regional Development in Mexico' (Call 2001; 2002a).[7] In spite of the shift of government, and the arrival of President Fox in 2001, Levy kept a key governmental position, this time as the head of the Mexican Institute for Social Security. Fox's innovation related to the former plans was to include Central America in the regional vision. Thus, the main difference between PPP and earlier plans is that the former plans mainly tried to seal the border to avoid the entry of Guatemalan guerilla groups into Mexico, whereas PPP aims to connect Mexico with

Central America, but at the same time to control the entry of unwanted migrants (Harvey 1998:151–3).

PPP is also closely linked to the Chiapas conflict. Owing to what is presumably 'inspection and vigilance of the natural areas' in order to eliminate organized crime, the presence of the Federal Preventive Police (Policía Federal Preventiva – PFP) has increased during 2002, not only in Chiapas, but also in other provinces in the PPP area. The purpose is stated as both to protect the natural areas against bio-piracy and other crimes against nature, and generally to put in order these zones of 'high ingovernability'. According to the director of the Mexican Federal Protector of the Environment (PROFEPA): 'If one does not recuperate these areas of high ingovernability, no private investors will come' (*El Universal*, Mexico, 25 December 2001). Such increasing control over the southern areas of Mexico is clearly not only done in the security interests of the United States, but also in the interests of the federal government of Mexico that aims to strengthen central state control over the Zapatista nerve centre.

A further issue for the Mexican government is access to water. Owing to the needs of agribusiness, water scarcity has become a major problem. Thanks to their tropical location between the Atlantic and Pacific oceans, the Central American nations and the Mexican states of Tabasco, Campeche and Chiapas all experience significant rainfall, whereas the northern Mexican states are dry (Moro 2002).

In sum, it is not only the security concerns of the US government that affect the plans, but also those of the Mexican government which seeks to increase control over the southern provinces. While the discourse of the free trade agenda implies a geopolitical imagery of a borderless area stretching from the Panama Canal to Alaska, the map implicit in the security agenda is one with increasing vigilance along the northern and southern borders of Mexico and heavily militarized belts around them. Thus, rather than the borders being removed, they are indeed being reinforced.

However, there are also obstacles against the security agenda, and against concerted efforts to halt migration in particular. While issues of migration control and Latin America in general was high on the agenda in the early days of the Bush administration, it was soon overshadowed by the anti-terrorist agenda. With the severely reduced interest from the North in reaching an agreement on migration issues, and the related resignation of Mexican Minister of Foreign Affairs, Jorge Castañeda, the PPP lost some of its driving force. However, that does not mean that the PPP is dead, as there are several other agendas that are being pursued through the same plan. One of them is the developmentalist agenda.

The developmentalist agenda: a Mesoamerica with increased state cooperation

The developmentalist agenda overlaps with the free trade agenda, but it is to a larger extent based on state-led developmentalism than dependence on the private sector. The rhetoric of all key actors promoting PPP emphasizes its potential in transforming a large but inert pool of human and natural resources to a growth area through modernization, and thus follow the path of other regions in the world. As Fox (IDB 2001) argues:

> We believe that, based on pre-existing bonds and similarities, we can create a vast chain of development. Southern and south-eastern Mexico have a great wealth of natural resources, and exceptional endowment of human talent and, regrettably unacceptable levels of poverty and marginalization, against which we are hastening to launch a direct offensive. The sum total of the determination and talents of Mexico and the Central American nations will enable us to forge a zone of exchange and cooperation on the same level as others that have been created around the world.

Also, within the Fox administration there are actors that place stronger emphasis on state-led modernization projects than on free trade, but the main sources of the developmentalist initiative can be identified as SICA and the IDB. After two decades of deadlock, the Central American integration process received new impetuses in the early 1990s. In 1991, the Tegucigalpa Protocol was signed outlining the judicial basis of the functioning of SICA. Under the renewed General Treaty of Regional Integration signed in 1993, free trade has been introduced between the signatory countries (with certain exceptions).[8] Moreover, a common policy towards third parties has been introduced, and the tariff barriers towards third parties are reduced to an average of 7.5 per cent.

However, the Central American integration process had far higher ambitions than merely creating a free trade area. The goal has always been a parallel political and social integration and these ambitions reached a climax in the Nicaragua Declaration of September 1997, where the states express the political will to initiate a gradual and progressive process to create a Central American Union as the ultimate state of association in a community as laid down in the Tegucigalpa Protocol.

In spite of achievements with regards to free trade, the process generally failed to lead to the expected political integration (Cerdas 1998; Bulmer-Thomas 1998; Bull 1999). Among the obstacles have been: recurring conflicts between the Central American states, a lukewarm attitude of Costa Rica that could have played a leadership role in the process, and scarcity of funds for implementing joint projects. Furthermore, the skewed distribution of benefits, favouring the stronger economies of Guatemala, El Salvador and Costa Rica over Honduras and Nicaragua, has halted the process.

Soon after the idea of a PPP was launched, Vicente Fox took steps to ensure Central American support for the plans. He met Central American business leaders and politicians, emphasizing the need for constructing regional integration 'from below' through establishment of the infrastructure and the legislation required for large production plants to give people jobs and spur economic growth. In late November 2001 the IDB and ECLAC were brought on board, creating the Inter-institutional Technical Group (ITG, GTI in Spanish) to coordinate further work with developing a regional development plan. In the following months, the Mexican Presidency and the SICA parallel prepared projects to be included in a joint development plan. On 15 June the Presidents of Mexico and Central America gave their approval to the PPP.

One of the great hopes of the Central Americans with regards to the PPP was that Mexican leadership would pull Central American integration forwards, and that the Mexican presence would ensure funds for different development projects. As Salvadoran President Francisco Flores expressed at the meeting in June 2001: 'The presence of Fox is crucial in order to achieve an agreement about financing of the plan' (*La Jornada*, Mexico, 14 June 2001).

However, including SICA has also meant a change in the nature of the plans. Although the revival of CACM and the creation of SICA have been based on 'open regionalism' in which the emphasis has been on a gradual opening towards integration in the world economy (ECLAC 1994), it is nevertheless an example of a traditional state-led integration project. Also the projects prepared by SICA carry the features of state-led integration. Recent efforts of SICA are also to a great extent donor-led, and therefore the projects prepared bear the clear marks of being driven by the priorities of the donors, primarily European ones. This is clear for example in Mesoamerican initiatives for Sustainable Development and Disaster Relief, reflecting the agendas agreed upon in consultative meetings of donors in Stockholm (1999) and Madrid (2001) related primarily to reconstruction after Hurricane Mitch.

Admitting the IDB a central role in the process also means including a political actor with its own agenda and with its own institutional structure and purpose affecting the content of the regional project of Mesoamerica. IDB is not only a loyal servant of the regional governments, but also an institution seeking to carve out a role for itself. One of the ways IDB traditionally has done that is by actively fostering regional integration, and presenting itself as 'the integration bank' (Bull and Bøås 2003; IDB 2002). IDB President Enrique Iglesias repeatedly emphasizes the need for joint Latin American efforts and the Latin American cohesion and common identity (Iglesias 1997). Recently, his rhetoric has extended to include Mesoamerican unity (*La Vanguardia*, Mexico, 1 July 2002).

However, whereas IDB has portrayed itself as an integration bank ever since its establishment, and has, as the other multilateral institutions, pursued market-oriented policies over the last fifteen years, its institutional structure is still primarily geared towards cooperation with governments. Funds channelled to regional projects and towards the private sector are dwarfed by the amount and forms of funding directed towards states. Thus, although private sector participation is encouraged on all levels, the IDB engagement in the PPP process strengthens the statist features of the plan. This has meant that parts of the private sector, traditionally impatient with bureaucracies and no less so when they are international, have become disillusioned with the plan.

However, donors and international financial institutions, first and foremost among them the IDB, have been able to keep up the focus on the plan, even when the enthusiasm of the regional politicians has faded. After a strong interest during the first two years of his administration, by late 2002, Fox stopped investing much political capital and energy into the PPP (Call 2003). The same was true for the Central American presidents. Nevertheless, ongoing development projects have continued, and the IDB in particular continues to support them. Thus, a new 'regionalizing actor' has taken over much of the task of constructing a Mesoamerica.

What is the Mesoamerica of this agenda? It is based on classical concepts of modernization, aiming to bring the area of Mesoamerica out of poverty through investments and industrialization originating in the

North. Although the aim is to make the South and the North more 'like', the process is based on a notion of Mesoamerica as a backwater in need for 'development'. In other words, the PPP is about to construct a new South. It is this attempt to impose an identity on the area that the opponents of the PPP resist.

The anti-development agenda: fighting the construction of a new south

When the PPP was announced, Sub-commandante Marcos of the Ejercito Zapatista de Liberación Nacional (EZLN) immediately denounced it and promised that it would be a huge failure. He was joined by representatives of 109 peasant, labour, environmental and indigenous organizations in Tapachula, Chiapas in May 2001. The resulting declaration of Tapachula denounced PPP as 'savage colonialism'. After this, the anti-PPP groups have developed into a regional movement. It includes the general anti-globalization movement (in Latin America particularly anti-FTAA) but also different community groups, peasants movements, and so on.[9] Civil society groups have organized three large-scale gatherings – May 2001 in Chiapas, November 2001 in Guatemala, and July 2002 in Nicaragua – each including between 250 and 350 groups. Moreover, on 12 October 2002, the 510th anniversary of the first invasion of the Americas, a series of interlinked demonstrations from Mexico to Panama were held to protest the PPP and the FTAA.

Although the civil society movement lacks a shared agenda, one may argue that they pursue what James Mittleman calls 'transformative regionalism' (Mittleman 2000). The protest movement uses global anticapitalist discourses, and slogans well known from recent mobilizations against global capitalism (e.g. 'People before the PPP'). But the global discourses are given a local or regional expression, primarily through harking back to the world-view of the inhabitants of the ancient Mesoamerica. What is crucial for the anti-PPP movement is not only to oppose the development projects that PPP includes, but also to reject the new division between North and South and the conceptualization of the South that it entails. As Barta (2001:1) says in his introduction to a book on alternatives to the PPP:

South is the profound planet. Christened and labeled by the expansive and colonizing North that defined the top and the bottom of the world map. South is a geographical concept, but also a symbol.

It is an allegory that links the lavish nature with social poverty, luxurious and opulent vegetation with inert, lazy and barbarian humanity; that associates the midsummer sun with a strident character, with the liberation of the oppressed impulses, with the feminine and free, with the imagination and the dreams, with the inconsistent, with the revolution, with the utopia … we talk also about the colonization of the images of the northerners of the third world culture, the spiritual frame of a South that exports paradigms and utopias in the same way as they used to export precious woods.[10]

The anti-PPP movement thus tries to develop a local and historical foundation for the struggle. The Maya cosmology and its view of the relationship between human beings and nature, particularly the perspective on the 'sacred earth' (Marcos 1995) is emphasized as a platform for rejecting the entire philosophy of the PPP. Thus, the Mesoamerican initiatives directed at environmental management are also rejected, as they allegedly reveal a different attitude towards nature than the one that is familiar to the peoples of the region (Barta 2001).

Within the anti-PPP movement's discourse, the Maya way of living is portrayed as threatened by imperialist actors from the North. It is emphasized that PPP is essentially a means for big business located in northern Mexico and the United States to exploit the oil resources, the biology and natural resources and the human resources of the areas. The inclusion of the project to create a biological corridor through Mesoamerica is viewed as another means of controlling and managing resources for the exploitation of multilateral companies, rather than traditional use by indigenous groups.[11]

The anti-PPP movement also opposes PPP because it runs counter to the San Andres accords agreed between the EZLN and the federal government (Castro Soto 2002). The accords explicitly recognized the ideas of territory and collective management of natural resources (aside from strategic resources such as minerals and oil) and established legal mechanisms to ensure autonomy. After a long legislative process, a constitutional reform that eviscerated the original accords was introduced in 2001, but it was rejected by the EZLN. Thus, in spite of President Fox's argument to the opposite, the accords failed to end the Chiapas conflict peacefully (Moro 2002).

For the Zapatistas, the PPP does not represent anything new but a continuation of Mexican federal government's strategy to redraw the map and deny its responsibility for the Chiapas region. They argue that the government aims to include Chiapas in Mexico when they want to get something from it, and include it in Central America when there is a question of giving something back (Molina 2000:149). As Sub-commandante Marcos proclaimed in 1998:

> Mesoamericanism? It is not fair that they part with us; it is not fair that they keep us apart in a political dependence, but in a miserable economic independence. It is not right that we should be closer to Central America at the time of exploitation; at the time of exploitation we are closer to the North, the centre and North of the country.

The resistance agenda is a demand not for taking control over the state, but for reforming it. The resistance movement contests the terms of political representation, including clientilism and patronage. In the Mexican case this has translated into a pervasive challenge to clientilism and regional or sectoral bossism, for example, *caciquismo* (Harvey 1998). Whereas the elites promoting the PPP see it as a sign of modernization of state practices, for the resistance movement, there are no signs that PPP will change any of the key practices that they have resisted for years.

Call (2002b) identifies four strategies applied by the anti-PPP movement:

(i)   insist on being included in the PPP planning and implementation process, and refuse to accept the plan otherwise;
(ii) gather information on PPP projects from a wide variety of sources and disseminate it as widely as possible;
(iii) fight the most destructive elements of the plan with direct action; and
(iv) document and promote alternative development strategies.

However, increasingly, the tendency today is 'just to say no.' Disillusionment with the quality of representation in, for example, consultations organized by the IDB have led to a rejection of further cooperation or attempts at cooptation.

Thus, what seems to emerge is a 'corridor of resistance'[12] created by organizations that reject the imposition of mega-projects allegedly constructed to suit big capital, but also rejecting the geopolitical imagining that they claim lies at the bottom of the plans. According to the researcher of Global Exchange's Chiapas office, Ryan Zinn: 'The overall opposition to the PPP is widespread, strong, and potentially the single unifying force not only among diverse national environmental, indigenous and labor movements, but regionally as well. Cross-border organizing throughout Mesoamerica has never been as strong and coordinated as it is now' (Treat 2002:4). Through the rhetoric emphasizing the common heritage of the Mesoamerican people, and through forming cross-border alliances, it may ironically be the opponents of the PPP that will make the Mesoamerican region a political reality.

Concluding remarks

The process towards the construction of a Mesoamerica is currently being shaped by the political projects of states, business, civil society groups and international financial institutions. They have different visions of what Mesoamerica should be and what kinds of borders should demarcate it. The political process leading to the creation of a new Mesoamerica is characterized by a nesting of different agendas. In this chapter, four different agendas have been identified. However, they are closely linked and are either complementary or existing in opposition to each other. The Mesoamerican integration process is also linked to globalization and macro-regionalism, in the Americas also called neo-Panamericanism (Prevost and Campos 2002).

The future of the Mesoamerican region will depend on the interaction between the different regionalizing actors, what alliances are formed and how these affect the content of the political agenda. However, the future of the PPP also depends crucially on funding for the different projects. Therefore the international financial institutions and other donors play a crucial role. Regionalism in the poorer parts of the world operates under quite different premises from those in the richer parts. As a consequence, foreign states and international organizations affect the agenda for the regional process. The deep involvement by the IDB and the interest in particular of the European donor community in the SICA process could help move the process forward. However, it is equally likely that the different donors will attempt to move the plan in their desired direction, and that the PPP through attempting to 'become everything to everyone' is reduced to a set of development projects with little coherence or connection.

However, even if the proponents of the PPP should fail to implement a majority of the projects envisaged, this does not mean that Mesoamerican regionalism is dead. By now the term Mesoamerica has left the pre-Columbian shadowlands for good, and entered into the common political discourse. Although the Zapatistas have opposed the use of the term, it is only the President of Costa Rica (the potential but often reluctant leader of a Central American integration process) Abel Pacheco who has attempted to rename it, calling it *Grand Central America*, and thereby drawing the nucleus of the project further South (*Notimex*, Mexico, 1 July 2002). Most of the opponents have adopted the term Mesoamerica while attempting to give it a content different from the PPP's.

The strength of the new realism approach to regionalism is that it points to the multiple meanings and contents of regional configuration of spaces, and that it makes us question how and for what purposes borders and boundaries are created. The PPP is not merely the regional expression of the neo-liberal project aimed to subject new areas to the logics of global capitalism. Neither is it a 'natural' and 'historic' region waiting to be reunited under the leadership of Fox. Rather, the discussions about the PPP have created Mesoamerica as a political space upon which different actors compete to impose their agendas. The outcome of this competition will affect the future map of Mesoamerica.

Notes

1 Earlier versions of this chapter have been presented at Tercer Congreso Europeo de Latinoamericanistas, Amsterdam 3–6 July 2002, Nordic Political Science Association/Nordic International Studies Association's Tri-annual Joint Congress, Aalborg 15–17 August 2002, and the British International Studies Association's 27th Annual Conference, 16–18 December 2002. I would like to thank Morten Bøås, Karin Dokken, Johannes Dragbæk, Björn Hettne, Marianne Marchand, Isidro Morales, Kristen Nordhaug, and Fredrik Söderbaum for comments on earlier draft versions of the chapter.

2 Campeche, Chiapas, Guerrero, Oaxaca, Puebla, Quintana Roo, Tabasco, Veracruz, and Yucatan.

3 These are: the Mesoamerican initiative for facilitating commercial exchange, the Mesoamerican initiative for road integration, the Mesoamerican initiative for energy interconnection, the Mesoamerican initiative for integration of telecommunication services, the Mesoamerican initiative for human development, the Mesoamerican initiative for sustainable development, the Mesoamerican initiative for prevention of disasters, and the Mesoamerican tourism initiative.

4 Among the initiatives aimed to support FTAA are: the *initiative for facilitating commercial exchange*, aiming to reduce barriers to free trade through reduction of non-tarrif barriers and harmonization of the free trade agreements in the region; the *initiative for road integration* consisting of the construction, rehabilitation and improvement of three highway 'corridors' through the region: the Pacific Corridor connecting Puebla with Panama, the Atlantic Corridor connecting Mexico, Belize, Guatemala, Honduras and

El Salvador, and inland road systems in Mexico; the *initiative for energy interconnection* attempting to unify three initiatives that have been under planning and implementation since the 1970s: the Central American System for Energy Integration (SIEPAC), and the interconnection between Guatemala and Mexico: the *integration of telecommunication services*, aiming to connect various pieces of fibre-Optic networks under construction in Central America, and to integrate the regulatory frameworks for the telecommunication sector; and finally, *the initiative for human development*, including labour training programs, particularly focused on tourism and maquila industry.

5　In February 1996 the Declaration of Tuxtla II, which included a more concrete action plan and an agenda for further meetings, was signed in San José, Costa Rica. Tuxtla III was held on 17 June 1998 in San Salvador with the objective of consolidating and strengthening the mechanisms of dialogue. Tuxtla IV was realized in Guatemala 25 August.

6　Alluding to a reversal of the Marcha hacia el Norte (the March towards the North) which the migration flow from Central America and Mexico towards the United States is often called.

7　'El sur también existe: un ensayo sobre el desarrollo regional de México'.

8　There are exceptions to the free trade for wheat, coffee, alcoholic beverages and petrol products. As a consequence of the integration process, intra-regional trade expanded five-fold between 1990 and 2000. Its current value is now US$2,626 million.

9　An important node to the network is RMALC (the Mexican Network for Action against Free Trade), but it includes also Mexican NGOs and research groups with transnational linkages such as CIEPAC (Centro de Investigación Económica y Política y Acción Comunitaria), research/advocacy networks such as Global Exchange, Washington-based NGOs such as the Washington Office for Latin America (WOLA) and the Bank Information Centre (BIC), and a host of smaller peasant organizations, community groups, indigenous peoples organizations and environmental groups in the region.

10　Translated from Spanish by author.

11　Mesoamerica is unique in its variety of endemic plant and animal species because of its situation as a bridge between the northern and southern parts of the hemisphere. It holds just over ten per cent of the world's living species. The creation of a biological corridor is motivated by the fact that most of the protected areas within the separate Central American states are too small to constitute an adequate range for many animal species (Carriére 2000).

12　The term is from Maquila Solidarity Network (2001).

3
European Union–Mercosur Interregionalism: Negotiations, Civil Society and Governance

Claudia Sanchez Bajo

Introduction

Interregional free trade negotiations between the EU and Mercosur were leading, in the middle of the first decade of the twenty-first century, to the first ever association agreement between two custom unions. It would result from an interregional relationship between a bloc of more developed countries and another of less developed ones, and thus constitute a significant case. After an evolutionany period of more than ten years and with negotiations coming to a close, the analysis of the main issues and outcomes in this early instance of inter-regionalism deserves scrutiny.

EU–Mercosur interregionalism has undergone several phases under a changing global environment. While optimism was widespread in the first half of the 1990s, towards the end of the twentieth century the relationship between the two blocs was stagnating, with an increasing gap between the rhetoric of formal interregionalism and its contents. At the beginning of the twenty-first century, while the agricultural blockage remained, a new global context arose with the cumulative effects of the successive crises that took place after the end of 1997, such as financial crises in different regions of the world, the Argentinean economic collapse and political implosion, the difficulties of the WTO Doha round, the aftermath of September 11 with the second Iraq war, and the US-led war against terrorism. Still, although the EU–Mercosur negotiations seemed to stall, interregionalism did advance as predicted in 1997 when it was announced that the association agreement would be signed at the end of 2004.

The concept of interregionalism must be seen as a novelty in a multi-tiered system of international relations. Its rise must be linked to the proliferation of regional organizations under the auspices of what, since the mid-1980s, is known as the 'new regionalism' (Rüland 2002). It was conceptualized amidst economic globalization to connect regional integration with trade liberalization so as to advance a world system of open economies. In this way interregionalism, embedded within economic globalization, has emerged as a component of world governance.

And, as interregional organizations are increasingly interacting with each other, they develop actor qualities of their own (Ibid.). Indeed, as EU–Mercosur negotiations have spread over several years, one should ask whether there have been any side effects. In order to seek empirical evidence of possible effects and actor qualities, this chapter explores the evolution of EU–Mercosur interregionalism. Has it remained an exclusively intergovernmental process? Has civil society participated with any influence or role in the negotiations? And what about the values and visions of such interregionalism?

After a brief comparison with the EU, the chapter explores EU–Mercosur interregionalism diachronically and the role of civil society by type of actor. In the last part of the chapter, the relation between interregionalism and governance is discussed.

Mercosur and the European Union

Mercosur, the Common Market of the South, was established by Argentina, Brazil, Paraguay and Uruguay in 1991 and became a customs union in January 1995, following the EU model. Mercosur is the fourth largest economic group in the world with Brazil as its largest member, accounting for about 75 per cent of regional GDP and 80 per cent of the population. It adheres to the UN Economic Commission for Latin America and the Caribbean's (ECLAC) concept of 'open regionalism', whose main requisites are: commercial liberalization, harmonization of standards, and flexibility in its regional institutional regime. In its first years, the high level of trade growth was impressive. Intraregional exports increased almost five times between 1990 and 1997, from less than 10 per cent in 1990 to almost 25 per cent of total Mercosur exports in 1997 (IDB 1998). Yet, Mercosur remained with a low level of institutionalization and harmonization of rules (Veiga 1995). Between 1995 and January 1999, it incorporated new associate countries (Chile and Bolivia), and experienced cumulative impacts from several financial crises (Mexico in 1995, Asia in 1997, Brazil in 1998).

After Brazil's currency devaluation in January, Mercosur suffered a serious paralysis and regional trade decreased by 26 per cent in 1999. Although it renewed growth by 17 per cent in 2000, it diminished again later with Argentina's troubles (ECLAC 2000/2001). Until 2003, Mercosur experienced the multiplication of sectoral conflicts and the break in the common external tariff that weakened its position at negotiations (Milner, Elliot, Bellos and Goni 2001; Krauss 2001). It was the removal of Argentina's currency board that allowed for Mercosur's rebirth (Gerschenson 2001). Yet, regional trade suffered again with Argentina's crash.[1]

Three dynamics underline Mercosur revival: Brazil's support for Argentina after its economic and political implosion, including the integration of entrepreneurs in Brazilian missions and chamber;[2] the emergence of a new policy agenda based on development, poverty and human rights, transparency and justice; and the surmounting of Mercosur's 'ideological crisis' with Lula's presidency in Brazil after January 2003 and Kirchner's in Argentina since May 2003. With their Buenos Aires Consensus they agreed on the need to institutionalize Mercosur further and beyond economic issues, favouring South American integration and building a development model based on growth and 'social justice' (a term equivalent to the EU's 'social cohesion'). Since 2003, under the leadership of the Lula and Kirchner governments, Mercosur has rediscovered the quality of convergence. An elected Mercosur Parliament is under consideration and an Argentina–Brazil commission has been set up to explore the possibility of a common currency. The social dimension has begun to receive more attention. The Olivos Protocol for the solution of legal and commercial conflicts has been implemented since the start of 2004, creating the Mercosur Arbitral Tribunal.

In order to fully understand the interregional relationship, one should always keep in mind the power asymmetry between the EU and Mercosur, which stems from differences in development, institutionalization and power at the international level. Whereas for Mercosur the relationship may affect some change in that asymmetry, for the EU the relationship has had a lower degree of salience. The EU and Mercosur were already two customs unions when they began to relate to each other, and both centred on bilateral axes of decision-making (France–Germany and Argentina–Brazil); but they are intrinsically diverse. Mercosur decision-making is based on the rule of consensus and intergovernmentalism. Its institutions do not exercise either delegated or transferred powers from member states.

In comparison, the EU is the most institutionalized regional economic union in the world. With the 1986 Single Act, it became a common market in 1993. By 2004, the EU was a monetary and economic union facing the challenges of enlargement towards Central and Eastern Europe. On 1 May 2004 another, ten countries joined, nine with a relatively low level of development. Not only does Mercosur remain oblivious to the latter, but some of its members also have an enormous proportion of their labour force in agriculture compared to the EU. The reform of the Common Agricultural Policy (CAP) is already taking place, but can the EU afford to rapidly liberalize agriculture, as that may induce significant migration flows within the EU? At present, the EU is facing crucial decisions in terms of institutions and model of development; some favour the so-called Washington Consensus while some EU states still resort to policies more akin to the EU social-market integration model.

The process of negotiations and their wider environment

Rüland (2002) was one of the first to propose a research agenda on interregionalism and has described seven functions it performs: balancing and bandwagoning, institution-building, rationalizing, agenda-setting and controlling, identity-building, stabilizing and development. He also recognized that these functions have been more theoretically deduced than contrasted to empirical evidence. Among the difficulties, there are the methodological issues of measurement and the impact of interregionalism on developed countries, as in the case of EU regionalism. In the case of EU–Mercosur interregionalism, evidence is traced throughout the historical period, without measurement.

The process of interregional negotiations between the European Union (EU) and Mercosur has had two major objectives: a transcontinental free trade area, and an interregional association with a strategic character. Two main phases can be distinguished in this interregional relationship. Between 1991 and mid-1999, there was a first phase in preparation for the launching of formal free trade negotiations. Since 2000, formal negotiations have taken place, regaining dynamism after the end of 2003.

One of the interesting phenomena to observe is how civil society in Mercosur turns to interregionalism and promotes the further institutionalization of Mercosur. While some civil society actors, namely entrepreneurs, had a significant role in relation to the process of formal negotiations, others, such as trade unions and cooperatives, have begun to organize themselves interregionally, while contrasting visions of regional integration have been advanced.

EU–Mercosur interregionalism from 1991 to 1999: the preparatory phase

EU–Mercosur relations have their roots in the very first day of the latter's creation in 1991, which was warmly welcomed by the former. In 1992, the two blocs signed a Framework for Institutional Cooperation. In December 1995, they reached a Framework for Cooperation Agreement. In May 1998, a complete 'photograph' of products and services was presented. In 1999, negotiations were announced and were expected to be concluded by 2003, whilst the relationship was embedded in a broader Latin American–EU relationship through the first Summit of Heads of States in Rio de Janeiro.

In 1992 the signing of the Inter-Institutional Cooperation Agreement provided the basis for EU support to Mercosur's institutional development, funding its institutions, study trips to the EU itself and training. In December 1994, the Joint EU–Mercosur Declaration established three mechanisms to develop the ensuing Framework for Cooperation: one for political consultation, another to promote investment and a third one to negotiate trade liberalization. It was this Joint Declaration that openly established the goal of an interregional association between the EU and Mercosur. In the first half of 1995, an initial negative reaction occurred in the EU: the European Farmers' Confederation rejected this and similar initiatives in favour of free trade in agriculture. Its strategy has been to lobby EU institutions and national governments against such an association. Years later, at the World Social Forum in Porto Alegre, it would get in touch with Mercosur farmers but without building any interregional coordination.

During the first phase, the most important document agreed upon was the Interregional Framework for Cooperation Agreement signed in Madrid on 15 December 1995, directly linked to Mercosur becoming a customs union. The choice of a customs union versus a free trade area was settled by the Ouro Preto Protocol at the end of 1994, giving Mercosur the capacity to act with one voice. The same day that the Protocol came into force, the Interregional Framework was signed in Madrid. Two weeks later, on 1 January 1995, Fernando Cardoso assumed the presidency in Brazil, and Mercosur became a customs union and a subject of international law. The EU had made known in advance its preference for a Southern Cone regional organization with one voice, and the dates coincide sufficiently to hypothesize a close relationship between the choice of institutionalization as a customs union and interregionalism.

The 1995 Framework was not a trade treaty in itself, but it led to the preparation of a draft for an interregional association agreement. It covered trade (agricultural, food, industrial, and customs as well as intellectual property and services), economics (investment, energy, transport, science and technology, and environmental protection), and a system for exchange of information. It was based on the principles of reciprocity and community of interests. As of June 1997, the Framework also included the participation of Chile and Bolivia.[3] Cooperation on technical norms (agro-industrial and industrial ones in particular) and on customs were covered, as well as business cooperation, focusing mainly on networks and SMEs. Investment issues focused on SMEs and on achieving a stable and secure legal environment. Trade liberalization was no longer the main motive but rather world economic restructuring and globalization; intra-firm and industry trade coordination eased through both harmonization of norms and/or standardization and legal security, a major aspect related to governance, as explained in the last part of this chapter.

Yet, the values framing this relationship were not just economic. Socio-historical relations between the two regions are profound and migration, democracy and human rights, as well as environment and social rights are mentioned in the Declaration on Political Dialogue. The latter included the support to the concept of 'open regionalism' and the goal of conforming to WTO norms. It also established a council for ministerial dialogue, a joint-committee and a trade sub-committee with three working groups, which started to work in November 1996. As political dialogue began to be implemented, a first agreement was signed between the European Parliament and the Mercosur Parliamentary Commission. In May 1997, the interregional working groups began to prepare a complete report on trade flows with a 'photograph' of institutional practices and regulations over competition, anti-dumping, technical standards, norms of origin and import licences. Their work was carried out during 1997 and 1998, the objective being to attain a broad mandate to negotiate an interregional free trade agreement.

Thus, the Framework Agreement, in reality, was the preparatory stage for trade liberalization, and its time-frame lasted until 2003: 'If there is a political decision, negotiations on liberalization could begin [in] 1999 ... and last until 2003' (Eurosur 16 June 1997). This statement is relevant because it was actually implemented as agreed, even though declarations and analysis during the second phase led to an over-whelming perception of a doomed attempt.

Expectations over the impact of trade liberalization remained limited on the Mercosur side. This had less to do with the fact that implementation would start years later (around the year 2005, the same year proposed by the US government for the Free Trade Area of the Americas – FTAA), than with the recognized difficulties over negotiating some 'sensitive' products. This concern was addressed in both the Joint Declaration of December 1994, and the *Considerandum* and Article 4 of the 1995 Interregional Framework Agreement. In compliance with the WTO, no sector was exempted a priori. Yet, agriculture was not truly included, 'as that would amount to already entering into trade negotiations, which is not our brief ... [it was] stressed at the European Commission' (ibid.). Particularly sensitive for the EU were agricultural products, which totalled 55 per cent of all Mercosur exports to the EU in 1994, and its Common Agricultural Policy (CAP). In fact, the classic north–south divide, revealed in the interregional trade structure, has been the main source of conflict in the EU–Mercosur relation.

In 1995, the Agriculture General Directorate of the European Commission expressed its objections to the Agreement. To overcome these objections, Mercosur countries prepared a study showing that only 16 per cent of trade between the EU and Mercosur had to do with 'sensitive' products (i.e., subject to quotas under the CAP: meat, cereals and dairy products). A liberalization schedule of ten years was compatible with the WTO, so that the CAP would not be immediately compromised. Further, they argued, trade was complementary and if agricultural exports to the EU were more important in 1994 than industrial ones, their growth rate was stagnant. For the first time, the industrial sector appeared to be more significant than the agricultural one.

The leverage of advancing negotiations towards agricultural liberalization as a bloc was a main expectation on the Mercosur side. Furthermore, by 1996, Brazil's increasing balance of trade deficit and the longer-term issues of FDI localization and maturity were souring the expectations of the Brazilian government. In 1997 Brazil had a 50 per cent increase in its trade deficit over 1996 (US$ 8.4 billion). Bilateral relations with the EU also suffered. First there was a major row concerning the automobile sector. In 1997, it was about textiles.[4]

In July 1998, most agricultural ministers in EU countries rejected the immediate start of negotiations with Mercosur, obtaining an adjournment of a few weeks. France and Germany advocated a delay arguing

Table 3.1 Participation by sectors in Mercosur–EU trade (in US$ thousand)

EU imports from Mercosur

	Agricultural Sector	Industrial Sector	Total
1994	9,367,038	7,755,065	17,122,103
Percentage	55%	45%	100%
1995	9,766,219	9,838,495	19,604,714
Percentage	50%	50%	100%

EU exports to Mercosur

	Agricultural Sector	Industrial Sector	Total
1994	933,490	14,446,103	15,379,593
Percentage	6%	94%	100%
1995	1,551,878	20,434,819	21,986,697
Percentage	7%	93%	100%

Source: EUROSTAT (supl.2/96) in Relaciones Mercosur–Union Europea-1995-Support Documents.

that identical issues would be negotiated in the Millennium Doha round of the WTO as from 1999. Besides, together with Belgium, they privileged the CAP reform within the EU 2000 Agenda. Additional concerns were the entry of Eastern European countries into the EU, which would increase estimated costs by US$ 4 billion. The European Commission presented to the Council a draft mandate on 26 July of 1998. The approval of the start of negotiations with Mercosur provoked the threat of a veto from the French government to a final EU endorsement, which needed a unanimous vote (*El Cronista Comercial* 1998). Nevertheless, the European Commission expected that, during the 1999 First EU–Latin American Summit, an agreement would be signed, which indeed happened.

The EU disagreement surrounding the start of negotiations visibly reflected an intra-EU divide between industrial interests, that favoured a deeper relation with Mercosur, and agricultural interests which opposed it. The latter pressured at the national level and at the EU level. However, no European government, with the exception of France, took a negative stance at the EU level (Sucesos Mercosur 1998). And EU industrial exports to Mercosur comprise 94 per cent of total EU 1994 exports to that region (*Eurostat* 1996). The European Commission, on its part, was careful to listen to sectoral demands, such as those from EU producers of wines and spirits, when entering interregional negotiations.

France agreed to allow the opening of such negotiations from July 2001 only one week before the opening of the 1999 first EU–Latin America Summit in Rio de Janeiro. Britain and other smaller EU countries sided with France. Conversely, Spain and Portugal wanted to accelerate negotiations, while Germany acted as a broker. The compromise was that 'negotiations will be conducted and closed taking due account of the results of the WTO round and the timetable foreseen for the free trade zone in the Americas' (*Reuters* 1999).

The long-lasting rivalry between the USA and the EU concerning Latin American markets, and the use of such rivalry by Latin America to strengthen its negotiating stance, should be kept in mind. Many believe that cooperating with the EU strengthens the Latin American stand in trade negotiations with the USA. In effect, Mercosur has been engaged in a double strategy. Brazil, as the most important Latin American trade partner of the EU and Germany, presided at the 1999 EU–Latin American Summit, with Argentina (then the closest US ally within Mercosur) playing a key role in the negotiations for the FTAA in the same period. But the second refusal of a fast track to the US President undermined this option.

This aspect provides evidence of the balancing function of EU–Mercosur interregionalism. On the one hand, Mercosur was seeking public support from the EU to reinforce and protect itself from exogenous pressures, in particular those from the USA and its proposed FTAA. On the other hand, the EU proposed a broad range of issues for cooperation, including technology transfer, business and social aid, while contributing to Mercosur's institutional consolidation. For the EU, two documents clarified its strategy: the Agenda 2000 approved in 1997 and a 1999 document prepared by European Commissioner Manuel Marin (the most influential European official during this phase of the process) and approved by the Commission on 9 March that stated EU political and economic objectives towards Latin America. Politically, these included conflict prevention, democratization, arms proliferation, the fight against terrorism and illegal drug traffic and conflict prevention, the economic objective being trade liberalization. Lying behind these was competition with the US for markets, including its bids for public works lagging behind in Latin America, and standards.

In June 1999, marking the end of this first phase, the first EU–Latin America Summit in Rio de Janeiro with 48 heads of states gave momentum to interregionalism; but it also meant a U-turn in EU strategy towards Latin America. The former was to deal with the latter as a whole, in correspondence to the US proposal for a continental free trade area. This time, on the EU side, there was evidence of interregionalism balancing and bandwagoning in international relations, particularly in regard to EU positioning in relation to the US and the latter's project of a continental free trade area. The gathering could not announce a precise date for the start of EU–Mercosur negotiations, but only vaguely declared that they would start at some point in the future. The main achievements of the Mercosur countries was to present their first common position and to obtain EU agreement in defining the future negotiations as a 'single undertaking', thus ensuring the inclusion of agricultural products. This aspect of the agenda-controlling function endorses Tussie's statement (1998:95): 'the leading edge of liberalization lies in regionalism'.

EU–Mercosur interregionalism from 1998 to 2004: formal free trade negotiations

In the 1990s, the EU–Mercosur relationship was shaped, on the one hand, by ongoing world economic restructuring and financial liberalization and, on the other hand, by a strong faith within Mercosur countries in unfettered progress following structural reform, open markets and privatization. But by the turn of the century, those high expectations seemed drowned in uncertainty. Corruption and economic mishandling were provoking revolt while the old themes of debt, poverty, exclusion and unemployment were back. While Mercosur was in crisis, at the end of 1999 the European Commission resigned and a new one, with a quite different vision, came into office. The 'new' EU opted for bilateral free trade agreements with countries which had already signed one with the US, namely Mexico and Chile, while the WTO talks collapsed in Seattle.

Yet, the EU remained the first trading partner of Mercosur countries, ahead of the United States and Japan. Between 1998 and 2000, as shown in Table 3.2, total EU participation in Mercosur trade averaged 25.9 per cent, and was particularly important for Brazil and Argentina.

Negotiations towards interregionalism began in 2000, with thirteen rounds before May 2004. The first one took place in April 2000 in Buenos Aires, with an agreement on general principles and the establishment of three technical groups on trade and three working subgroups on specific issues. The two guiding principles were that negotiations should cover all sectors and be based on reciprocity. Since then, many thematic working groups have been formed, meeting every few months both in Mercosur and in Brussels. Mercosur officials from

Table 3.2   Participation of the EU in Mercosur trade 1998–2000 (annual average, in percentages)

	Exports	*Imports*	*Total*
Argentina	18.6	26.3	22.6
Brazil	28.5	27.9	28.2
Paraguay	26.2	12.4	16.2
Uruguay	17.4	19.4	18.5
Mercosur	25.0	26.7	25.9

Source: ECLAC, Montevideo office, based on information from BCU, INDEC, SECEX, Paraguay Central Bank.

Central Banks, for example, have developed common working practices: they meet regularly, exchange information and communicate online. Interregionalism has had the function of institutionalizing patterns of communication and decision-making within Mercosur.

In June 2000, the second round worked on three areas: exchange of information, non-tariff obstacles, and objectives for each area. In November 2000, in Brasilia, the third round focused on technical data and a written draft on economic cooperation, political dialogue, preamble and institutional framework.

The fourth and fifth rounds took place one after the other. In March 2001, in Brussels, cooperation and business facilitation were the focus of attention, while in July 2001, in Montevideo, the EU unilaterally made an offer on goods, services and government procurement. An agreement was reached on customs, competition, statistics, and scientific and technological cooperation. Regarding the dispute on agricultural subsidies and protectionism, the EU asserted the multi-functional character of agriculture.

The sixth round, in October 2001 in Brussels, was the occasion for Mercosur to present its counter-offer. Just one month before, in September, trade negotiations for the FTAA had been launched, and the EU appeared more demanding than before. The chapters on cooperation, science, telecommunications, transport and energy were drafted, while Mercosur's offer to the EU was rather limited (33.1 per cent of all industry imports from the EU) as if matching the EU's offer in agriculture imports from Mercosur.

The seventh round, took place in April 2002 in Buenos Aires, just before the second EU–Latin American Summit of Heads of States in Madrid. Even though the draft of the chapters on political dialogue and cooperation were completed, a general disappointment could be felt. Yet, soon after, in May 2002, the work of the seventh round became apparent through the adoption of a package on business facilitation measures adopted during the Madrid Summit. This package supported entrepreneurs' activities through customs, conformity and sanitary standards, and e-commerce regulation, following requests from the Mercosur–EU Business Forum. Furthermore, both the EU and Mercosur 'agreed to discuss the business facilitation action plan at each negotiations round and expressed their willingness to make rapid progress where possible' (MEBF 2003).

But by 2002, the hopes stemming from the interregional relationship had vanished (Sberro 2002). In contrast to the 1999 Rio Summit momentum, the relationship remained at a standstill after the Madrid Summit. The major outcomes were the signature of a bilateral free trade treaty between the EU and Chile, and the above-mentioned package for trade and business facilitation. Since 1998, trade between the EU and the Mercosur has been losing market share: 'exports from Mercosur to the EU reached $20.7bn in 2002, only marginally higher than in 1998, while Mercosur imports from Europe have slumped, falling last year to $15.4bn, just over half the level achieved in 1995' (Lapper 2003). By contrast, in the past decade, though, Mercosur exports to the US nearly doubled and the US had become a marginally smaller trading partner than the EU (Ibid.). The rhetoric of strategic alliance and interregionalism suffered from a broadening gap between discourse and reality. The only formal outcomes for Mercosur were a Mercosur–EU Memorandum of Understanding signed in June 2001 and a work programme to speed up negotiations for interregional free trade to be carried out from July 2002 to the end of 2003.

Given Argentina's protracted crisis, Brazil's importance in interregionalism grew farther. Already by 1999, Brazil was among the 15 most important commercial partners of the EU:[5]

> In 2001, the trade exchange between the EU and Brazil totalled US$ 29,688 billion. As first commercial partner of Brazil, the EU received, in that year, 26.84% of Brazil's exports and was the origin of 25.9% of all imports by Brazil ... the EU stands out as the first foreign investor in Brazil. Until 2001, [EU FDI in Brazil was] equivalent to 43.8% [of total FDI].[6]

The first return to real progress in interregionalism took place in July 2002, at a ministerial meeting in Rio de Janeiro under the presence of European Commissioners, Chris Patten and Pascal Lamy, the two most important EU decision-makers during this phase. The EU offered Mercosur a tariff proposal that included agricultural goods. Within ten years, 90 per cent of goods and services would be free, with sensitive goods remaining subject to quotas. Agricultural subsidies were not to be discussed, waiting for the WTO round. The EU requested Mercosur to maintain its common external tariff (CET) as it was.

Mercosur created a negotiating working group in order to reach a common position. This group named Enrique Iglesias, President of the Inter-American Development Bank (IDB), as its main advisor. Mercosur submitted its offer, accepting to negotiate all tariffs but claiming that liberalization had to deal with tariff as well as non-tariff barriers, and defending its freedom to modify its own CET. Major difficulties remained: agriculture, non-tariff barriers to trade and access to the EU single market. Given the structure of Mercosur exports, these are vital for the region to maintain a positive trade balance.

Three rounds of negotiations were organized and a ministerial meeting planned for the second half of 2003, with the expectation that a final agreement could be reached by then in Brussels. In November 2002, the eighth round in Brasilia focused on market access as well as methods and modalities for negotiating goods and services, TBT, competition, rules of origin, customs and dispute settlement. In addition, the EU had bilateral discussions with Argentina, Brazil and Uruguay on wines and spirits. A decoupling of sectoral issues could be observed, with different treatment – bilateral, interregional, regional and global – linked to the search for governance by sector.

At the beginning of 2003, European Commissioner Pascal Lamy visited Brazil for three days and met with ministers, economists and Brazilian entrepreneurs, closing the visit with a meeting with the new President Lula da Silva. Both regions had to hand in new proposals now that the EU had reached a common position for the WTO talks. The EU proposal for the WTO foresaw a decrease of 45 per cent in export subsidies until 2012, of around 55 per cent in internal aid to production, and 40 per cent in tariffs. Yet, it excluded many products such as tobacco and oil seeds; and the proposed cuts depended on the alignment of all developed countries on maximum sums at the WTO. According to Brazil's Foreign Ministry, actual reductions could be less than 25 per cent (Osava 2003).

In March 2003, the ninth round in Brussels discussed the new Mercosur offer, and made progress in investment and public procurement. On 27 March 2003, a much higher-level meeting took place in Athens. This was a ministerial meeting on political dialogue between the European Union, Mercosur, Bolivia and Chile. It included, along with all ministers of foreign relations from Mercosur member and associate countries, George Papandreu (President-in-Office of the European Union), Javier Solana (Secretary-General of the Council and High Representative for the CFSP of the EU), and Christopher Patten (Commissioner for External Relations of the European Commission). Expressing concern about human rights and poverty, they focused on the UN and Iraq. They took a further step in institutionalizing interregional coordination within the UN. The EU offered support for technical cooperation on a regional basis for Mercosur for the design and implementation of monetary, exchange rate and financial policies, while Mercosur representatives pledged further institutionalization of Mercosur.

On 23–7 June 2003, Asuncion hosted the tenth round of negotiations. This meeting took place after the Mercosur Presidential Summit of 18 June in the same city, with the new presidents of Brazil and Argentina participating. The EU noted that there was a new initiative for consolidating the customs union and the internal market was tabled. It also recognized that Mercosur is a political initiative, which must encourage civil society participation. The creation of a Mercosur Regional Parliament was also proposed. This is one of the many examples of the fact that the EU does not impose its own model on Mercosur, but that there is cross-fertilization without reproducing an EU-like Mercosur.

In November 2003, an EU–Mercosur trade ministerial meeting approved in Brussels a new work programme with a schedule of five more negotiation rounds and two more meetings at ministerial level with the goal of closing all talks in October 2004.

The eleventh round of the EU–Mercosur Bi-regional Negotiations Committee in Brussels in early December 2003 exchanged points of view on agricultural modes. Other issues included a common text on all areas including services, government procurement and investment, competition and intellectual property rights; business facilitation; sustainable development; wines and beverages and phytosanitary issues. There was also an exchange of views on the WTO talks. Around the eleventh meeting, European Commissioner Pascal Lamy formally visited Mercosur countries to convey his personal commitment to interregionalism. Although things would not happen exactly as planned in the rounds that took place in April and May 2004, the breakthrough did take place. The EU had decided to change its strategy towards Mercosur and opted out of formal negotiations based on reciprocity. Why and how did this happen?

The growing social discontent and new political landscape within Mercosur

Not all events within Mercosur can be described here due to space restrictions, but apart from Argentina's economic collapse, between 2001 and 2003, Argentineans, Paraguayans and Bolivians threw out their governments without breaking their democratic systems. These plus other events encouraged the EU discourse towards Mercosur on social inclusion and poverty-reduction policies. But it took responses to the US-led war in Iraq and the failure of the WTO meeting in Cancun in September 2003 for the Commission to truly reconsider its negotiating stand towards Mercosur.

The war in Iraq and the international system

Since the second war in Iraq, the international system has been strained, affecting UN organizations, humanitarian aid and the scope of international treaties and law. The US inclination towards unilateralism as well as extremist ideologies are upsetting multilateralist mechanisms for concerted action at the world level. Peace and war are no longer readily distinguished, as war operations can be both military and 'non-military' and armies public and/or private. In the war against Iraq, the EU presented a divided stance, while Latin American countries demonstrated a subdued but balanced standpoint vis-à-vis the United States, remaining in favour of international law and peace negotiations, standing firm about the lack of evidence of weapons of mass destruction. Mercosur leaders were well coordinated about the matter (Lapper 2003). Without them, it would have been more difficult for those governments unconvinced by the pro-war faction to make a case for international institutions. Global governance and multilateralism constitute shared interests between Mercosur and the EU, including the issues of the International Criminal Court, the WTO negotiations and the UN system, including Millennium Development Goals and the High Level Review on global security.

The failure of WTO meetings

Multilateralism again appears to be in trouble, first with the general collapse in Seattle and then with the uncompromising stands of various nation-states in the Doha round launched in December 2001. Multilateral WTO agreements represent the minimum requirements on which to construct further regional development. As the stakes are raised, developing countries become more vocal for their interests. In addition, civil society actors mobilize strongly to bring up issues of general interest to the negotiations. The WTO failure in Cancun attested to such developments, as well as to the minimal groundwork done by developed countries to address the growing concerns of less developed ones. After the second failure at Cancun, the European Commission took over the role of unblocking the process and building alliances, in which both the EU and Mercosur believed that they could benefit compared to a world of unilateralism (Jonquières 2003). Given current circumstances, regionalism continues to be the most likely path in the near future and its enlargement is constantly sought, whether in the EU with ten newcomers or in Mercosur with its recent 2003 agreements with Peru and the Andean countries and closer relations with Venezuela. Accordingly, EU and Mercosur countries continue to face the most decisive and wide-ranging trade negotiations in history.

Interregionalism and an open multipolar system

However, in order to keep the world system open and multipolar, interregionalism emerges as the logical strategy to accompany regionalism. Partly due to the EU's role in building alliances to unblock the WTO round and partly to Mercosur countries' role in the Cancun failure, EU–Mercosur negotiations regained dynamism. In 2003 and 2004, the European Commission addressed a set of global developments in the manner described below.

Mobilizing other institutional bodies in support of negotiations

The EU has continuously supported Mercosur institution-building, and this is always welcomed by Mercosur. The European Commission drafted the 2002–2006 Regional Indicative Programme for Mercosur worth 48 million, destined to support Mercosur institution-building and civil society.[7] In order to build support from civil society, the EU welcomed the activities of the two regional economic and social consultative bodies – the European Economic and Social Committee (EESC) and the Mercosur Economic and Social Consultative Forum (FCES) – and entrepreneurs through the MEBF, and the setting of an interregional forum for trade unions.

Introducing a discourse on social cohesion

The EU adapted its discourse to the changing landscape in Latin America, legitimized by the EU Lisbon strategy. It targeted the whole of Latin America but implementation is mainly by regional integration arrangements such as Mercosur. EU social cohesion policy was defined in June 2003 in the EU–IDB Joint Seminar on Social Cohesion in

Brussels and channelled through the IDB. Their collaboration, formalized in a 2002 Memorandum of Understanding (IDB 2002), covers four areas: consolidation of democracy and human rights; poverty reduction; regional integration; and information technologies. Routing the EU expertise on regionalism through multilateral banks like the IDB is part of its 2000 development policy. The IDB thus took a step further in interregional governance.

Building a coalition upon which the WTO round would restart

As mentioned before, interregional negotiations regained dynamism after the WTO failure in Cancun in mid-September 2003. Already on 23 September, there was belief that a two-tiered WTO should help clear the way (Leader 2003). On 30 April 2004, a meeting took place in London with Robert Zoellick (US trade representative), Pascal Lamy (EU trade commissioner), and certain countries such as Brazil under condition of exceptional secrecy. This meeting was followed by another one at the OECD two weeks later. The two-tiered WTO was born (Jonquières 2004).

The logic of interregional activity

As Mercosur countries improved their capacity for coalition-making at the global level, interregional bargaining became more active. At the same time, the interests of EU small- and medium-sized agricultural producers may have had their stance weakened partly due to their lack of interregional activity. While large industrial and service interests made interregional alliances and built a Business Forum, smaller producers stayed out of such strategies with their Mercosur counterparts despite similar concerns like biodiversity versus genetically modified crops and food security (Brown 2004).

The EU–Mercosur negotiations have thus achieved most in the pillar of political cooperation, although many technical details of commercial negotiations remain uncertain. Interestingly, while EU strategies helped to stay the course without always obtaining the sought-after consensus or 'technical' solution, both political will at the highest level and commitment to reach agreement by October 2004 have remained firm.

There are probably three aspects that sustain political will: the need to bargain with the USA, world governance, and the idea that the chance should not be missed before the new European members took office on 1 November 2004. A larger EU bureaucracy may cause complications, and the process of rearticulating EU identity and values may take time. If the EU turns inwards, Mercosur may decline in importance for the EU and vice versa. Yet, societies in both regions do have shared visions of regionalism and development. Bottom-up interregionalism(s) continue to prosper seeking direct and fair relations.

The rise of civil society in EU–Mercosur interregionalism

Civil society strategies have helped to institutionalize interregionalism. The European Commission is engaged in improving possibilities for civil society actors to actively contribute to further integration and to EU–Mercosur relations, as one of the three main objectives of its Regional Programme for Mercosur 2002–2006. The Commission organized three conferences: October 2000 in Rio de Janeiro, February 2002, in Madrid and April 2004 in Mexico (EU–Mercosur 2002). Moreover, the European Commission has played an active role in financing the participation of various non-state actors in both Mercosur and interregionalism.

On the other hand, interregionalism is not disconnected from globalization, regardless of whether it is critical or not towards the type of globalization that has predominated so far. Many civil society actors are concerned with economic globalization, human rights and public common good. They are turning towards universal concerns, transcending their geographic delimitation, sharing common values and beliefs. On the one hand, they build upon regional bases and then reach out further. On the other hand, international umbrellas or coalitions support their moves and integrate them into world strategies. In the case of EU–Mercosur, both regions strongly favour regionalism and the EU–Mercosur rapprochement. When studies on regionalisms explore institutionalization, factors such as actors' interests and ideational visions about regionalism enter the analysis. Both visions and discourses are powerful engines for consensus-building and public policy-making.

Entrepreneurs

Entrepreneurs have been by far the leading and most highly regarded civil society participants in EU–Mercosur interregionalism by public authorities. The Mercosur–EU Business Forum (MEBF) was the first to exist and the most active, with gatherings lasting several days, in which top EU and Mercosur authorities participate. Its official declarations and policy recommendations are taken seriously into account by public negotiators. Integrated by large holdings present in both regions and active in industry and services,[8] it supports the idea of reform in agriculture. The MEBF has made sure that negotiations remained on track, requesting, in particular, business facilitation plans for harmonization and standardization, and the inclusion of services and investment in interregional negotiations.

Trade unions

Compared to all other regional integration arrangements in the Americas or the negotiations between Chile or Mexico with the EU, Mercosur stands out for the relevant participation of trade unions (Zapata 2003). The terrain for trade union interregionalism has thus been favourable. Zapata offers two explanations for Mercosur trade unions' impact: the Brazilian organization combining professions and territory, and the strong articulation with both political parties and system in both Argentina and Brazil.

Trade unions have worked to institutionalize EU–Mercosur interregional relations, demanding that labour rights, ILO conventions and the social dimension be included in any future agreement. When the Commission organizes conferences to inform civil society organizations on the evolution of interregionalism, the latter lobby for further institutionalization and more effective participation. There is an EU–Mercosur Trade Union Forum, and a 2003 strategy document with important implications for interregionalism by the European Trade Union Confederation.

Social economy actors

The actors of the social economy, composed of cooperatives, mutual funds, NGOs and foundations, have only had a recent impact on interregionalism. These actors have participated through institutional representation in both Economic and Social Consultative bodies of Mercosur and Committee of the EU, in what is called the 'third' sector, and in all three Civil Society Encounters organized by the EU. In May 2003, taking into account the Commission's declared interest in social cohesion, and given the interregional meeting of the EESC and the FCES, the two cooperative umbrella organizations for all cooperatives within the EU and Mercosur signed a cooperation agreement to exchange information and to promote cooperation for democratic and inclusive socio-economic development. In April 2004, after one year's work, the two cooperative movements presented their first interregional document to the third civil society gathering in Mexico. In its official final declaration, they obtained the recognition of their existence and their role in society and economy in the two regions.

Civil society and interregionalism

There have been a series of civil society initiatives directly connected to interregionalism, whose aims are not just to influence negotiations but also to further their own visions of regionalism and interregionalism. Their struggles are also embedded at the world level. Civil society actors have taken continuous steps to institutionally coordinate their interregional strategies through forums, conferences, projects and formal communications to the EU–Mercosur authorities. They have done so on the basis of their socio-economic identity, receiving more or less support from EU and Mercosur public authorities. On the public side, and in particular from the European Commission and EESC, there has been warm support and financial encouragement for an institutionalization process that organizes, channels and represents parts of civil society. This is something in which the European Commission in particular has excelled, so furthering regionalism within the EU itself (Greenwood 2003).

Governance and interregionalism

If the ultimate results of EU–Mercosur negotiations remained uncertain with a bottom-line agreement and a two-step approach, to what purpose has the whole exercise been about? My hypothesis is that it might have served two main purposes: global governance and common standards. As far as political governance is concerned, the interregional exercise will have served to promote the institutionaliza- tion of Mercosur and its actors, and by building Mercosur as an actor, to enhance political dialogue at the global level. Before exploring the connection between governance and interregionalism, let us first explore the concept of governance and its relation to regionalism.

Defining governance in relation to regionalism

Schmitter (2001) connects governance to regionalism, and Abbott and Snidal (2000) relate governance to standards. Governance denotes a co- government arrangement between public and private actors that opens up a profound conceptual change concerning political power and how public–private relations are effected (Schmitter 2001). Probably the most outstanding function of such governance arrangements has been the definition of standards. Deep integration – standardization and harmonization of norms and rules – is vital for formal regionalism.

Governance is distinguished from government in three aspects: first, by its mechanisms and proceedings. Government refers to polyarchy, subject to periodical elections and mutual control among several institutions. Secondly, by hierarchy: government should remain at the top of any governance arrangements. Finally, by number: while there is the expectation of only one government in a given territory, governance arrangements are multiple and segmented, private as well as public–private ones (Schmitter 2001). In general, analysis of governance is applied below and beyond the nation-state, on to regional and world levels. Its major normative principle is efficiency and the preferred conditions of those in favour of governance arrangements are autonomy and voluntary self-rule.

There are two sides to the issue of governance: political and economic. For Abbott and Snidal (2000), political science has a new object of study: defining standards. Both standards themselves and the institutions, by which they are created, administered and enforced, are subcategories of governance. These result from the interactions of states, firms and other international actors seeking to resolve diverse global issues. Schmitter (2001) thinks of a *politeia*, which is non-national and non-statist, capable of generating valid and enforceable decisions. For him, governance practices would be more helpful in solving Europe's deficit of legitimacy than reforming conventional governmental institutions.

The debate about governance stems from a crisis of legitimacy of political regimes and institutions as well as from the need for more flexible and efficient mechanisms based on comprehensive information. Governance arrangements are expected to legitimize government and to render policy-making and regulation more efficient. However, the lack of enforcement mechanisms and sanctions, universality, transparency and cross-controls within the system in which such arrangements operate, and the probability of encapsulating public policy, are yet to be studied.

In the EU, governance is a priority and the object of a White Paper published in July 2001. Here governance is defined as the 'rules, processes and behaviour that affect the way in which powers are exercised at European level, particularly as regards openness, participation, accountability, effectiveness and coherence' (EU 2001:428). The White Paper on Governance explains that such co-regulation has already been used for internal market standards for products and the environment, stating that its exact form – namely, the combination of juridical and non-juridical instruments and the origin for the policy initiative – vary according to sectors.

Standards are crucial to both regionalism and governance in ensuring deep market integration. In addition, as the EU explains, the adoption of standards and regulation based on, or compatible with, EU practices, facilitates trade and access of its products to those regulated markets. Harmonization and/or mutual recognition of standards make regimes 'trade friendly': they then warrant 'business facilitation' (EU 1999). It should be added that trade costs are lowered while local certification is enhanced. Common standards reinforce the place of those who abide by the regime as sites of production. Finally, harmonized regulation facilitates intra-industrial trade, allowing for economies of scale, advancing those who comply in the process of economic globalization. As Fontagne, Freudenberg and Unal-Kesenci (1996:11) explain:

> the globalization of the world economy passes through the reorganization of processes of production along a rather regional, even global basis ... The importance of economies of scale, that imposes the reduction in the number of units of production, and the need to standardize the processes of production ... combine themselves in order to determine the new modes of articulation of products and processes of production.

Conclusion: governance and EU–Mercosur interregionalism

When issues in world governance become pressing, such as reviving multilateral negotiations or coordinating positions in UN Councils, EU–Mercosur interregionalism appears to help with several functions: balancing, agenda-setting and, to some extent, stabilizing. At such moments, interregionalism seemed to receive a push from top EU negotiators in order to bypass bottlenecks. These developments can take place because there has been an evolution in Mercosur capabilities to act as an actor in its own right.

Mercosur's efforts to multiply its world linkages intensified its interests in further institutionalization. And the EU has played an influential role given its longer existence and greater institutionalization, since many in Mercosur tend to view it as an inspiring model. Mercosur member states are concerned about sovereignty issues and reject ideas of supranationality or a heavy bureaucratic structure requiring finance. Institutional differences apart, there is a perception that

Mercosur has most affinity with EU regionalism. The EU–Mercosur relation has been influential in Mercosur's institutional trajectory: its choice of a customs union, the inclusion of a consultative economic and social forum, the ideas of a monetary union and a regional parliament brought up again in 2003. The choice to become a customs union was not an easy one for Mercosur (Bajo 1999), which helped to show its commitment to 'open regionalism', to multilateralism and, most importantly, to be recognised as a subject of international law, so enabling it to engage in international negotiations, such as those with the EU, the FTAA or the WTO Doha round. This choice endorsed Mercosur as a global actor.

EU–Mercosur interregionalism has privileged four areas of action: trade, cooperation, 'business facilitation', and political dialogue. During negotiations, the EU gave priority to the defence of its sectoral and national economic interests, until the issues of governance came to the fore. In the meantime, the other areas changed notably. EU cooperation either supports Mercosur macroeconomic coordination and standardization, or has been decentralized to a large extent. More focused and sectoral, it now responds partly to market demands and partly to the needs of national governments, channelled through local authorities and private actors. The EU may now act through intermediary institutions that do not embody EU values as such, like the IDB.

Entrepreneurs have promoted the issues of standards and business facilitation, related to both governance and deep market integration. The definition of common norms and standards reflects world trade and is essential in economic globalization.

Other civil society actors recognized that many issues can no longer be addressed by nation-states alone. The EU has provided some consultation in general and more regular dialogue with selected actors. But the political arena has remained mostly circumscribed by formal interstate bargaining and coordination on world issues. Ideational visions about regionalism also played a part. Many were expecting a different model from that proposed for the US-led FTAA, but the relationship turned into one closer to that proposed by the US. In response, various civil society actors have become more critical of the EU–Mercosur interregional agreement (CEO and TNI 2003). So there is divergence: civil society is becoming sceptical, while Mercosur countries have grown more confident at the multilateral level.

The political pillar has been the key to differentiate Europe from the US. On the Mercosur side, Brazilian foreign minister Amorim asserted that 'this is much more than a trade accord; it is a strategic objective ...

We give enormous priority to the EU. Our strong cultural relationship and political affinity lead us to give this accord a high priority' (Colitt 2004). For various reasons, the EU offers an interesting example to Mercosur beyond the issues of regional economic space, institutional-building and competitiveness. The EU is, with all its limitations, an example of constructing an international power based on peace and law. In Vasconcelos's (2003) words, 'the EU acts in the international sphere as an eminently civilian power through a long-term strategy of inclusion which relies on the full panoply of instruments of soft power'.

Yet, the EU was losing soft power by letting certain economic considerations determine its relationship with Mercosur, therefore risking the loss of important allies in building an international order that reflects its ambitions (Vasconcelos 2003). Also, for Sberro (2002), the EU was making a strategic error by concentrating on economic demands to the point of forgetting the political objectives of the relationship. Then, the Iraq war and the WTO round, by making apparent the many shared elements in the EU and Mercosur approach to world governance, plus the socio-economic imperatives within Mercosur, helped the EU to reconsider some of its positions. Interregionalism thus interacted with other salient processes: new regionalism, economic globalization and world governance. It has moved ahead through shared visions and values as well as interregional economic interests, in particular industrial and service sectors. It is unclear whether interregionalism had any impact on the EU but it has certainly promoted Mercosur as a global actor.

Notes

1 There was a fall of 61 per cent of Brazilian exports to the other three Mercosur member states in only three months. Imports were reduced by 25 per cent. Argentina, accounting for 18 per cent of Brazil's exports in 1998, could only purchase 3.6 per cent of the total.
2 Many entrepreneurs either moved to Brazil or opened a second shop, business or production site in that country, which in turn led them to integrate Brazilian industry and trade organizations as well as commercial initiatives abroad. ECLAC noticed such trend, even when trade was seriously decreasing. See ECLAC (2000/2001).
3 Agreed in the Mercosur Presidential Summit of 20 June 1997, in Asuncion.
4 Under Provisional Measure No. 1569, on 25 March 1997, Brazil suddenly imposed barriers to different products, including textiles, with the aim to protect its monetary stability and reduce its trade deficit. The barriers were

also implemented for its Mercosur partners. This measure was criticized by the EU and the WTO.

5 'União Européia – Brasil, as diversas faces de uma parceria', CD-rom by the EU Delegation in Brazil, section 'Apresentação'.

6 Ibid, section 'Economia'.

7 The RIP supports the completion of the internal market of Mercosur, Mercosur institutions and sectoral policies and civil society actors' contributions to integration and to EU–Mercosur interrregionalism. Stronger support was given to veterinary and agricultural standards as well as the subregional economies.

8 Examples are Arcelor, Repsol, Vivendi, Carrefour, Volkswagen, Siemens and Basf.

4
APEC, ASEAN+3 and American Power: The History and Limits of the New Regionalism in the Asia-Pacific

Mark T. Berger and Mark Beeson

Introduction: 'East Asia' or the 'Asia-Pacific'?

The post-Cold War era has seen a growth in regional economic integration and increased levels of transnational political interaction.[1] By the 1990s both non-state-centred and state-centred regional processes of integration had emerged as increasingly important components of, and responses to, processes associated with 'globalization'. Indeed, some observers have argued that regional initiatives provide important mechanisms with which to take advantage of the opportunities and mediate the pressures generated by globalization (see Oman 1994). In the post-World War II period generally, and since the end of the Cold War era in particular, global processes have been driven primarily by the United States: state-led regionalism reflects attempts by elites to accommodate this central geopolitical reality. In short, whether it is in the economic, political or even in the strategic sphere, there are powerful incentives for state and non-state actors based within regions to cooperate to their mutual advantage.

Yet, such observations raise questions about how regions should be defined and which nation-states and peoples should be considered 'authentic' members. In some parts of the world, most notably Western Europe, regional identity reflects long-standing processes of economic and political integration, which have been facilitated by shared political and even cultural practices (Gillingham 2003). In the 'Asia-Pacific', by contrast, not only are processes of regional integration and coordination of more recent vintage, the very definition of the region has been a far more highly contested and far more incompletely realized project (Dirlik 1992). Indeed, the term Asia-Pacific only gained widespread currency in the 1990s and continues to be used alongside the narrower and more long-standing notion of 'East Asia'. Such definitional imprecision has been compounded by continuing tensions within and between the western and eastern shores of the more nebulous Asia-Pacific region, something that has made the establishment of a coherent regional organization inherently problematic. The failure of the Asia Pacific Economic Cooperation (APEC) forum to realize the hopes of its advocates is a powerful reminder of just how difficult regional political and economic cooperation can be, especially when it tries to encompass countries as diverse as those in APEC (see Ravenhill 2001).

The failure of APEC was, therefore, predictable (see Beeson 1996, Berger 1999). Set up in 1989, APEC reflected both a naive belief amongst some sectors of the region's elites that economic reform could be insulated from politics, and a general lack of US interest in an organization that provided few benefits to successive administrations in Washington where there has been a growing predilection for bilateral or unilateral approaches to foreign policy (Bell 1999). What is of greater long-term significance than APEC's faltering progress, however, is the contradictory impact of US hegemony on regional processes. US indifference to APEC and outright hostility to more specifically East Asian organizations in the 1990s, provided a catalyst for the development of what may yet prove to be a more significant and enduring regional entity: ASEAN+3 (the Association of South-east Asian Nations plus China, Japan and South Korea).

This chapter explores the limits of the new regionalism in post-Cold War East Asia initially by focusing on the Cold War history of the region, and then by considering the changing character of US hegemony in the post-Cold War era. We emphasize that in the context of the complex shifts and continuities of the past five decades there are far more serious constraints on the new regionalism in the Asia-Pacific than in Europe, or the Americas, where regionalization and regionalism is arguably most advanced (Wallace 2000). We examine the development of APEC and ASEAN+3, paying particular attention to the role of the United States, which has played a pivotal role in shaping regional outcomes. Finally, we consider the prospects for a distinctive East Asian form of regionalism grounded in a much narrower conception of regional identity. We conclude that while there are limits to the coherence and unity of ASEAN+3 in the context of the continued salience of US power in the region, APEC has now clearly been displaced by ASEAN+3 as the most significant embodiment of the new regionalism in the Asia-Pacific.

The Cold War in East Asia and the rise of ASEAN

The various meanings and the shifting boundaries of 'Asia' have a long and complex history. Meanwhile, against the backdrop of decolonization and the Cold War, East Asia was often used to refer to North-east Asia at the same time as the Eastern Asian region was increasingly subdivided into North-east and South-east Asia.[2] At the end of the 1940s, North-east Asia emerged as the pivot of the particularly complex territorial and geopolitical intersection of the People's Republic of China, Japan, the USSR and the United States. The Cold War divisions between North and South Korea, and between the Chinese mainland and Taiwan that were solidified in the 1950s, remain in place to this day. These geopolitical and geoeconomic imperatives have had a profound influence on the shape and limits of regionalism in North-east Asia where the US developed major bilateral relationships with Japan, South Korea and Taiwan. A major consequence of Washington's strategic engagement with the North-east Asian region during the Cold War was a network of primarily bilateral security alliances, which in the long term served to inhibit intra-regional cooperation (Berger 2004).

As already implied above, the idea of South-east Asia as a distinct historical, political, economic and geographical unit is also of relatively recent origin. While usage of the term can be traced back to the nineteenth century, it only gained currency amongst scholars, colonial officials, policy-makers and nationalist leaders in the 1930s and early 1940s. While the 1950s saw the emergence of the South East Asian Treaty Organization (SEATO), its membership was never regionally focused and it played a minimal role in regional and international politics. Meanwhile, the deepening of the Cold War in South-east Asia in the 1960s prompted the emergence of the Association of South-east Asian Nations (ASEAN). While ASEAN was a response to security concerns on the part of the governments involved, the organization also placed a major emphasis on economic collaboration. The emergence of ASEAN flowed from the conjuncture of local, regional and international initiatives. By the mid-1960s, anti-communist governments in South-east Asia had a shared concern with local insurgencies in their respective nations, even though they differed with regard to the level of support they wanted to provide for escalating US involvement in

South Vietnam. They were also concerned to establish a framework for regional negotiations in the wake of *Konfrontasi* between Indonesia and Malaysia in the early to mid-1960s (see Jones 2002).

Following a series of meetings behind closed doors in 1966 and early 1967, the governments of Indonesia, Malaysia, the Philippines, Singapore and Thailand formally promulgated the ASEAN Declaration in Bangkok on 8 August 1967. In formal terms the organization's main goals were economic and social cooperation; however, a key implicit objective was political cooperation and the founding document also embodied a desire to shape the regional order. These latter concerns were reflected in the organization's declared commitment in November 1971 to make South-east Asia a Zone of Peace, Freedom and Neutrality (ZOPFAN). Despite such grandiose declarations, ASEAN did very little for almost ten years after its initial establishment in 1967. The organization did not have its first summit meeting until February 1976. In the 1980s, ASEAN opposed Vietnam's occupation of Cambodia; however, Vietnamese withdrawal and the end of the Cold War undermined the organization's united front against Vietnam. The early 1990s saw a reorientation: Vietnam joined ASEAN in 1995, Laos joined in 1997 and Cambodia eventually joined in 1999 (Burma – Myanmar – also became a member in 1997). By the end of the 1990s its membership encompassed all of the nation-states in South-east Asia (Brunei had already joined in 1984). Politically and economically this has created difficulties: an enlarged ASEAN has had more difficulty in achieving consensus, while the Asian financial crisis contributed to the organization's apparent disarray (Funston 1998). This period also saw the promulgation of a formal commitment to an ASEAN Free Trade Area (AFTA), something that has proved difficult to achieve and reflects the generally competitive nature of the ASEAN economies. More positively, beginning in January 1992, ASEAN initiated a security dialogue with nation-states beyond South-east Asia – the People's Republic of China, Russia and the US, as well as other Asia-Pacific governments – culminating in the launch of the ASEAN Regional Forum (ARF).

Generally, the end of the Cold War and organizational expansion has carried ASEAN into uncharted territory. The organization has always emphasized mutual respect for, and reinforced the sovereignty of, member nation-states and it has no commitment to political integration along the lines being pursued by the European Union (EU). These concerns and practices, as well as a desire to move towards a 'more rules-based association' were reflected in the public comments in

2001 of Rodolfo C. Severino, Secretary-General of ASEAN. He observed that 'regional agreements may need national legislation to carry them out ... This would help strengthen the national legal systems of the member-states as well as the rule of law in the region as a whole' (Severino 2001). Whether ASEAN's members will be prepared to move in this direction and grant the hitherto small and powerless ASEAN Secretariat greater authority remains a moot point. To judge by the experience of its principal rival for regional institutional authority – APEC – this would seem unlikely.

The Post-Cold War Asia-Pacfic and the rise of APEC

The establishment of APEC in 1989 underscored the important relationship between economic cooperation and geopolitical and security considerations. The Cold War had inhibited a more expansive regionalism in at least two ways. First, nation-states in South-east Asia were wary of an organization that might have 'security overtones' and thus (in the context of the Cold War) limit its membership to capitalist economies, while the US was opposed to an organization in which the USSR might have a forum for the discussion of security questions (Ravenhill 2001:85). Against the backdrop of the end of the Cold War and the dramatic economic transformation of Asia over the preceding decades, APEC emerged as the major institutional expression of the idea of a form of regionalism based on the idea of the Asia-Pacific. It represented a forum for the articulation and accommodation of a revised and reconfigured version of various long-standing geopolitical and geoeconomic visions for the region. Neo-liberal narratives on economic development and international relations increasingly represented the Asia-Pacific as destined to become an ever more integrated region of prosperous free-trading nation-states (Linder 1986).[3]

But APEC was challenged from the outset by Prime Minister Mahathir Mohamed of Malaysia: as an alternative to APEC, Mahathir proposed the establishment of a trading bloc, initially called the East Asian Economic Group (EAEG), which would exclude the United States, Australia and New Zealand and all other 'non-Asian' nation-states. Apart from concerns about the possible formation of economic blocs in the post-Cold War era and the need to respond in kind, elites in Asia were also uncertain about the US approach to security issues after the Cold War. At the outset Washington was preoccupied with the situation in Europe, but in a 1991 visit to East Asia, George Bush's Secretary of State, James Baker reaffirmed a US commitment to the region emphasizing the continued importance of Washington's bilateral security arrangements (see Baker 1991). These arrangements maintained, in a somewhat revised fashion, the basic bilateral politico-military architecture of the Cold War (Berger 2004).

This did not necessarily mean that the US actively opposed regional and multilateral initiatives, but it was the Australian government that had taken the lead, with the active encouragement and involvement of the Japanese government, in the establishment of APEC less than two years before. Although Tokyo was as interested in trade cooperation as it was in trade liberalization, APEC quickly emerged as a forum for the latter. From the outset APEC was portrayed by many of its supporters as being committed to 'open regionalism' in contrast to the preferential trading practices that characterize the EU and NAFTA.[4] The idea of open regionalism was in keeping with the US-led globalization project and widely-held view that APEC could play a key role in the international diffusion of economic liberalism (for example, see Garnaut 1996). This vision was readily apparent at the first major meeting in Seattle in late 1993, and the second major meeting in Bogor, Indonesia in November 1994. On the final day of the Bogor meeting, the leaders from the eighteen member countries agreed in principle to the virtual elimination of tariff barriers and obstacles to capital flows within the APEC region by the year 2020 (2010 for developed nations and 2020 for developing nations). Subsequently, however, the difficulty of implementing this agenda has been made more difficult by powerful protectionist forces within East Asia and by the US's own growing preference for bilateral trade deals (Ravenhill 2003).

By the mid-1990s the idea of a new East–West synthesis for which the US–Japan alliance served as the explicit or implicit cornerstone had become widespread. For example, in 1995, Tommy Koh, former Singaporean representative to the United Nations, argued that the new 'Pacific Community' would be founded on a fusion of values and practices drawn from Asia and the West (Koh 1995:107–18; see also Mahbubani 1995:107). In this regard, APEC was emerging, prior to the Asian crisis, not as just an organizational attempt to facilitate trade liberalization and advance the globalization project, but as a possible embodiment of a new vision of the Pacific Century that ostensibly synthesized East and West. This view was particularly apparent at the annual APEC summit in Osaka, Japan, in November 1995. The Japan meeting produced an 'Action Agenda' which eschewed binding trade agreements in favour of what Fidel Ramos (president of the Philippines) called the 'Asian Way'. This amounted to verbal assurances by all member governments that they would make every effort to meet the economic liberalization goals of APEC. The representation of this result as evidence of the 'Asian Way' at work was significant. The emergence of APEC was indicative of an attempt to promote a form of neo-liberalism that sought to accommodate ostensibly Asian ideas and practices against the backdrop of the continued resilience of US hegemony. This process was also apparent at the World Bank, which played a very significant role in trying to reconcile the East Asian Miracle with the influential neo-liberal narratives on globalization in the 1980s and 1990s (Berger and Beeson 1998).

Prior to 1997 the dominant neo-liberal narratives on the Pacific Century rested on the assumption that the rise of East Asia and the end of the Cold War had produced increased opportunities for greater regional integration and the spreading and deepening of economic prosperity and political stability. APEC was grounded in these optimistic visions and directly implicated in the view that the economic trends that were carrying the region forward were going to continue indefinitely, delivering prosperity to an ever-growing number of people. This celebratory view of the Pacific Century was dramatically challenged as the financial crisis, which ostensibly began in Thailand in July 1997, rapidly engulfed the region (Higgott 2000).

The Asian financial crisis and the decline of APEC

Within months of the fall of the Thai baht in July 1997, commentators such as Kishore Mahbubani (a prominent advocate of the new East–West synthesis) were warning that the crisis could 'split' the Pacific Ocean 'down the middle' and create 'an east–west divide' (cited in Hatcher and Dwyer 1997). As long as the various leaders who attended APEC's annual summits were only being called upon to agree to relatively distant trade liberalization targets (so distant that even those leaders who measured the length of their tenure in decades would probably not be in office when the deadline was reached), the meetings had proceeded with few serious problems. By the time of the meeting in Vancouver in November 1997, however, the Asian financial crisis presented APEC leaders with a serious and immediate problem, and, not surprisingly, the 1997 APEC meeting produced little of substance. In fact, by the time of the Vancouver summit, the organization had already become irrelevant.

The prominent role the IMF began to play in the management of the Asian financial crisis provided the United States with the opportunity to pursue economic liberalization and deregulation far more effectively than could ever have occurred with APEC. In the second half of 1997 as APEC drifted to the sidelines, the IMF embarked on major efforts to restore financial stability to the region via loan packages to the governments of Thailand, Indonesia and South Korea. IMF loans were conditional on the implementation of a range of austerity measures and liberal economic reforms. The IMF set out to remake the financial systems of the various countries and was able to demand far-reaching regulatory reforms of a sort that were completely beyond APEC's consensual, voluntaristic approach (Beeson 1999). These included the shutting down of a range of banks and financial institutions, the liberalization of capital markets, and allowing foreign capital to embark on hostile acquisitions and mergers.

The overall approach taken by the IMF reflected the dominant neo-liberal perspective that the crisis flowed from the efficiencies and distortions that were characteristic of the various state-centred approaches to capitalist development that prevailed in East Asia ('crony capitalism') (IMF 1997). Of course, this view was challenged at the outset from a number of quarters.[5] Not surprisingly, Prime Minister Mahathir was quick to dispute IMF explanations, at the same time as his government sought to avoid IMF support and interference. Mahathir and a number of other politicians and commentators placed the blame for the region's problems at the door of foreign currency speculators. He also criticized the IMF's approach – something that was in keeping with the observations of numerous other government officials and regional ideologues that had questioned the relevance of Western ideas and practices to the region, and championed distinctive 'Asian' values in their place (Berger 2003:210–11).

The idea of an Asian renaissance and the resurgence of Pan-Asianism provided an important backdrop to Mahathir's promotion of an East Asian Economic Caucus (EAEC). Mahathir sought to establish an exclusive Asian trading bloc on the grounds that Malaysia and other countries would lose out in any larger grouping such as APEC that included countries such as the United States. While Mahathir's initiative flowed from concerns about the membership and orientation of APEC, as well as the rise of NAFTA and the EU, it also represented an attempt to curb the growing flow of Chinese-Malaysian capital to China by linking China more tightly into a regional economic cooperation network. The EAEC proposal, which the ASEAN secretariat had put forward at Mahathir's instigation, envisioned a caucus that enjoyed considerable independence within the framework of APEC and was made up of the governments of ASEAN plus Japan, South Korea and China (ASEAN+3). This line-up reflected the perception in ASEAN that Japan and South Korea were the driving economic forces in the region. The exclusion of Hong Kong and Taiwan from this list also catered to Beijing's sensitivities. At the same time, Mahathir's vision remained focused on Japan as the leading economic power in the region, and a major economic force internationally: he foresaw the Japanese government acting as the 'voice of Asia' at meetings of the G7 (Hook 1996:194–5; Berger 2003:211–12).

Japan's economic malaise throughout the 1990s and into the twenty-first century has meant that the government and Japanese corporations have been unable to play as significant a role in the region in the post-Cold War era as many inside and outside Japan had anticipated. The Japanese government's general acquiescence to the US and the maintenance of the bilateral ally–client relationship of the Cold War era shifted somewhat following the Asian crisis. There were early efforts by Tokyo to play a more significant role in handling the crisis. In September 1997 at a G7 finance minister meeting, Japan's Finance Minister, Hiroshi Mitsuzuka, first proposed the concept of an Asian Monetary Fund (AMF) as a means of countering economic instability without the conditions attached to the IMF packages (Dwyer 1997).[6] While Mahathir was attacking currency speculators at the annual IMF–World Bank meeting in Hong Kong in mid-1997, the Japanese government again floated the Asian Monetary Fund idea, proposing that upwards of US$ 100 billion be set aside and that the institutional infrastructure to administer it be created, in order to be prepared for any future crises of the kind that was destabilizing South-east Asia (*The Economist* 1997:15). Significantly, other East Asian leaders, particularly those of Singapore and Malaysia, made clear their frustration with the IMF's approach to the crisis (*Pacific Rim Review* 1997).

The Asian Monetary Fund proposal was notable in that there were to be no conditions attached. It would have maintained the restrictions on foreign ownership of financial institutions and sustained the economic practices that East Asian elites associate with rapid capitalist development. However, the idea of an Asian Monetary Fund was defeated at the November 1997 APEC Finance Minister's meeting in Manila and the end result of the ASEAN summit in Kuala Lumpur, the following month, was a weak endorsement of the IMF's plan for the crisis. Despite this trend, Mahathir did not abandon his pan-Asian vision. With the Malaysian government in the lead, a number of governments appeared to be drifting in the direction of capital controls by the end of 1998 (Wade and Veneroso 1998b:20–1, 30, 41–2).

The rise and future of ASEAN+3

In the medium-term, however, the Asian crisis and the failure of a number of proposed regional initiatives like the AMF had actually given renewed life to East Asian attempts to develop regional political institutions and crisis management mechanisms. If one thing became clear to East Asia's political elites during the crisis and its aftermath, it was that East Asia remained highly dependent on, and vulnerable to, external forces over which regional leaders had little control. At one level this was apparent in the region's exposure to massive flows of short-term capital in and out of the region. At another level, however, the crisis made clear that, without an effective regional organization which could take responsibility for responding to, or attempting to manage economic instability, the region would continue to remain dependent on external actors like the IMF and the US – with all that that implied for national sovereignty and independence. Unsurprisingly, then, renewed interest has been expressed in developing some sort of pan-Asian organization of a sort championed for so long by Mahathir. It is significant and revealing that Mahathir – the advocate of currency controls and an outspoken critic of the 'West' – appears to have been at least partially rehabilitated and to some extent vindicated in the aftermath of the crisis. The war on terrorism also strengthened Mahathir's ability to contain his domestic opponents at the same time that his relationship with the US improved somewhat. Mahathir quickly moved to align his government with the war on terrorism after September 11, arresting suspected terrorists under his government's Internal Security Act and garnering praise from Washington (Wain 2002:19–20). While the style of Mahathir's successor, Abdullah Badawi, is noticeablly different, the substance is not, so Malaysian support of pan-Asian cooperation looks set to continue.

But an examination of the emergence of ASEAN+3 highlights how difficult it will be for East Asia to develop an authoritative and independent regional entity along the lines envisioned by Mahathir. Optimists like Richard Stubbs (2002) argue that there are a number of factors which are encouraging the development of East Asian regionalism:

(i)   common historical experiences like nationalism, and the events of the Second World War and Cold War;

(ii)   common cultural traits associated with authoritarianism and hierarchy;
(iii) the importance of the developmental state;
(iv)   distinctive East Asian forms of capitalist organization, especially Japanese and those associated with the 'overseas Chinese';
(v)   cross-cutting investment patterns throughout East Asia, especially those associated with Chinese and Japanese capital.

While there may be serious doubts about how encompassing or significant some of these features actually are, or how much they reflect a common historical experience, Stubbs does draw attention to some potential commonalities that could be deployed by elites to generate greater unity in a region that is still characterized by considerable diversity. In this context, it is important to note that the widely felt sense of resentment about the way the Asian financial crisis and its aftermath unfolded, especially about the activities of the US and the IMF over which it exerts so much influence, provided an important source of regional mobilization and identification and the basis for subsequent policy initiatives by East Asian elites (Higgott 1998).

In contrast to Stubbs's reading of the prospects for East Asian regionalism, Douglas Webber argues that the ASEAN+3 initiative is unlikely to amount to much. Noting ASEAN's low levels of intra-regional trade, its diminished leadership credentials in post-crisis East Asia, and its notorious lack of an effective capacity with which to implement and/or enforce policy, Webber (2001:365) concludes that 'the vast intra-regional political–systemic disparities pose an extremely high obstacle to the development of much closer inter-state cooperation'. And yet Webber also notes two other distinguishing qualities of East Asia's putative regionalism: that ASEAN+3's rise has been stimulated primarily by the actions of the US generally and the IMF specifically; and that the 'distinguishing' characteristic of 'East Asian regionalism' is the fact 'its initial focus has been less on trade than on money' (2001:359–60).

Both of these observations are important and merit further explication as they tell us much both about the contradictory course of East Asian regionalism and about the continuing influence of US power in the region. It might be expected that given East Asia's – or more specifically, China and Japan's – formidable monetary reserves (Herbert 2000), the chance to develop an effective regional monetary mechanism that allowed both governments to display their regional leadership credentials would prove irresistible. Both the Japanese and

Chinese governments have certainly attempted to use the crisis and its aftermath to bolster their respective positions. China's leaders have made clear that they feel their actions as good international economic citizens in providing stability during the financial crisis were undervalued, while Tokyo continues to try and entrench itself at the heart of the region's production networks and trade relations. However, the principal obstacle to greater regional integration led by either Japan and/or China would not seem to be any bilateral tensions between the two regional giants, nor even Japan's well-known reluctance to do anything that might upset Washington. On the contrary, both China and Japan continue to cede authority for the conduct of regional monetary relations to the IMF – concerned, as they both are, about the implications of underwriting open-ended commitments to their regional neighbours in nascent currency swap arrangements (Ravenhill 2002). In other words, the emphasis of the governments of China and Japan on their national, rather than regional interests, appear to be constraining developments in the one area – monetary cooperation – in which the region seems capable of making substantive progress.

More broadly this situation reflects the limits that the wider global political economy – which the United States has played such a pivotal role in constructing and managing – imposes on the national economic spaces embedded within it. The growing power of financial capital in particular has been at the forefront of the construction of an international economic order that is characterized by a growing disjuncture between economic activities in the 'real' economy of goods and services production and an expanding and increasingly deregulated financial system. In such circumstances, and without a systematic attempt to impose capital controls of a sort championed by Mahathir (see Beeson 2000), even the region's more powerful and independent economies will be constrained by the capacity of 'Wall Street' to translate its narrow sectional interests into global public policy (Beeson 2003). US power, therefore, mediated through key financial institutions such as the IMF, continues to impose limits on the direction of development and regional integration in East Asia. The underlying significance of US foreign policy generally and the IMF's efforts during the Asian financial crisis specifically was to bring an end to the era in which the developmental states of East Asia, such as South Korea and Japan, had flourished.

Neither of the alternative contenders for regional leadership – Japan and China – is well placed to seriously challenge US hegemony. In post-Cold War East Asia a rough balance of power exists in which the

US has the overall advantage and this will continue for some time. In particular, China's nuclear capability and large standing army is offset by the economic significance of Japan, not to mention the large conventional forces on the Korean peninsula, Taiwan, and in Vietnam. Japan has, throughout much of the twentieth century, been a 'subordinate partner' in either a US hegemonic project or an earlier US–British hegemonic alliance (Cumings 1999). Against this backdrop, and at a time when China's political elite is attempting to manage its continued integration into the global capitalist economy via membership of the World Trade Organization, and when Japan's government remains preoccupied with its apparently interminable and unresolvable economic malaise, the prospects for regional cohesion and solidarity do not appear bright. Indeed, it is important to remember that China's rapid economic development is a major threat to the smaller economies of South-east Asia, and suggestions that integration be consolidated through an ASEAN–China free trade agreement might be seen as making the best of a bad job as far as the ASEAN states are concerned (Dwyer 2002). If nothing else, the outbreak of bilateralism across the region is further confirmation of the demise of APEC's multilateral trade liberalization agenda.

Despite these significant obstacles, and despite the fact that the original ASEAN countries will inevitably risk being overshadowed by their larger neighbours, ASEAN+3 remains a continuing source of regional initiatives and diplomacy. Significantly, the region's political elites have been prominent participants in what have become regular summits, and this has been supported by an increasingly substantial array of ministerial and functional meetings. It is not necessary to unambiguously endorse the claim that the nation-states that belong to ASEAN+3 'are definitely relinquishing autonomy in their quest for greater stability and prosperity' (Thomas 2002). But it is necessary to recognize that something significant is happening in the region, something that is intended to give organizational expression to the political and economic ambitions of East Asian elites. At a time when the US economy is not simply looking less robust and more crisis-prone, but is associated with precisely the same sort of 'crony capitalism' that was previously viewed by a number of observers as the key to the Asian crisis, there are grounds for assuming that the ideological or discursive component of US hegemony will be less compelling in Asia (Beeson and Berger 2003). By extension, this may open up a space for alternative Asian economic and political visions, a space that regional elites will use ASEAN+3 to fill if they prove capable of overcoming intra-regional tensions and their historical subordination to US power.

Conclusion: the history and limits of the new regionalism in the Asia-Pacific

This chapter looked at the history of, and limits to, APEC and ASEAN+3 in the context of the changes to and continuities in US power in North-east and South-east Asia. New or revised forms of regionalism in East Asia or the Asia-Pacific, which remain relatively weak in contrast to Western Europe and North America, were examined against the backdrop of the transition from the Cold War to the post-Cold War era. Some observers view the geopolitical and geoeconomic shifts in the 1970s as more important for East Asia than the end of the Cold War in 1989. Nevertheless, the waning of Soviet power at the end of the 1980s altered the dynamics of the United States–China relationship, while the post-Cold War era also saw increased friction in Washington's relationship with Tokyo with regard to Washington's effort to promote the globalization project in the region.

This latter trend came to a head with the Asian crisis in 1997–98. The crisis facilitated US efforts, via the International Monetary Fund, to further wind back state-guided national development as it had emerged in various significant, even paradigmatic, forms in East Asia. The crisis also stimulated or reinvigorated various regional initiatives outside of APEC, as the relative unimportance of APEC and the relative impotence of the Japanese government were both highlighted by the financial crisis. Simultaneously, at the beginning of the 1990s, US–China relations entered a new and more difficult era related, in part, to China's emergence as a major economic force in the region and beyond. This is linked to the Chinese government's enhanced defence spending, military reorientation and upgrading. The events of September 11, however, are powerful indicators of how rapidly new issues can reshape the regional and global order. The reassertion of US military pre-eminence, Washington's insistence that governments declare their support for its war on terrorism and the relative alacrity with which Tokyo and Beijing aligned themselves at least tactically with the US after 9/11 has the potential, at least in the short term, to subordinate virtually all other issues to a global security agenda (Lawrence and Hiebert 2002). In the longer term, however, it is reasonable to assume that other, ostensibly East Asian concerns will reassert themselves. In such circumstances, ASEAN+3, with all its limitations, is likely to provide a far more significant forum for canvassing issues of regional importance than APEC ever did.

Notes

1 An increasingly common convention is to distinguish between private sector-driven processes of economic integration (regionalization) and governmental political cooperation (regionalism). This chapter is primarily concerned with regionalism. See Breslin and Higgott (2000).
2 In the post-Cold War era, East Asia is also increasingly used to refer to both North-east and South-east Asia. The latter usage will be followed in this chapter.
3 For a critical analysis of the idea of a Pacific Century see Berger and Borer (1997).
4 'Open regionalism' is most commonly, and narrowly, defined as a concerted and unilateral process of trade liberalization along MFN – most favoured nation – lines.
5 For a recent and particular sustained critique of the IMF's handling of the Asian financial crisis see Stiglitz (2002).
6 Mitsuzuka subsequently resigned over a corruption scandal at the Ministry of Finance.

5
US Hegemony and Regionalism: The Case of East Asia

Kristen Nordhaug

Introduction

In the 1990s, initiatives for encompassing East Asian regional integration clashed with US-supported trans-Pacific 'open regionalism' and global organizations. In the early 1990s, Malaysia proposed an East Asian Economic Group in competition with the Asia-Pacific Economic Cooperation (APEC). Japan was invited to assume leadership, but the Japanese government declined to respond, probably because it worried about disturbances to its relations with the United States and regional resistance. The outcome was a watered-down compromise where an East Asian Caucus was established as a subgroup within the APEC framework (Higgott and Stubbs 1995).

During the regional financial crisis in 1997 Japan's Ministry of Finance proposed a US$ 100 billion regional Asian Monetary Fund to stabilize regional currencies, with most of the funding from Japan. This scheme was strongly resisted by the United States which supported full control by the IMF. China also opposed Japanese 'yen hegemony'. Japan withdrew its proposal, and the IMF assumed control over the rescue funds.

Thus US dominance, Japanese reluctance to abandon its alliance with the United States and Chinese distrust of Japan impeded East Asian regional organization. Then, in May 2000 a breakthrough occurred. A meeting of regional finance ministers in Chiang Mai, Thailand then agreed on a regional monetary cooperation arrangement which would include the so-called ASEAN+3, that is, the ASEAN countries plus Japan, South Korea and China. Table 5.1 gives an overview of the regionalism initiatives and their outcomes.

Table 5.1   **East Asian economic regionalism since the 1990s**

	East Asian Economic Caucus (EAEC)	Asian Monetary Fund (AMF)	Chiang Mai initiative
Comprehensive East Asian regionalism	Malaysia proposes regional trade negotiations bloc 1990. Established, but watered down to subgroup within APEC.	Japanese initiative September 1997 during regional crisis. Given up in favour of IMF regime.	Proposal 'ASEAN+3' currency swap May 2000. Established.
Rivalling regionalism/ multilateralism	APEC: Trans-Pacific, open regionalism.	IMF	
Position of the US	Against EAEC. Supported APEC as instrument of trade liberalization from 1993.	Strongly against AMF. Strong and successful support of IMF.	Negative about Chiang Mai initiative, but no strong counter-measures.
Position of Japan	Domestic divisions, inaction. Interested in APEC, but not as a strong trade-liberalizing agency.	Initiating AMF proposal. Critical to IMF.	Supporting and probably initiating currency swap proposal.
Position of China	Supportive of the EAEC.	Low-key resistance against Japan-led AMF.	Supportive.

In this chapter I shall try to make sense of these regionalism efforts in the context of East Asian economic integration and US hegemony.[1] My emphasis will be on the efforts at regional monetary integration since 1997. In the next section, I will develop a theoretical framework for this discussion. Thereafter, some historical legacies of the East Asian Cold War state system are outlined and I discuss the reliance of US post-Bretton Woods financial hegemony on Japan, and how the US–Japanese financial and monetary relationship affected East Asian economic transformation in a mainly positive way during 1985–95. In the following section I argue that the US–Japanese–East Asian relationship led to a regional over-investment crisis in 1997. This leads to an investigation of regionalist responses to this situation since 1997. The chapter concludes with a discussion of whether current monetary and financial regionalism in East Asia can be seen as a challenge to US hegemony.

Theoretical perspectives

Various approaches to 'new regionalism' relate ongoing processes of regional organization to a globalized post-Cold War setting. For example, Björn Hettne (1999) contends that the recent wave of new regional organizations and deepening of preexisting regionalism projects should be understood in terms of a post-Cold War order characterized by multipolarity and economic globalization. Multipolarity is more compatible with processes of regional integration than the bipolar Cold War order. Globalized organization of production and financial flows is overwhelming the nation state, and triggers a search for regional solutions. New regionalism is then viewed by Hettne as a Polanyi type 'double movement' societal defence against volatilities caused by economic globalization in a situation where national institutions and actors are unable to provide that protection.

Scholars associated with the Coxian world order approach are more pessimistic about the new regionalism projects. James Mittelman (1999) agrees with Hettne that new regionalism attempts to cope with processes of economic globalization within a multipolar post-Cold War setting. He hopes for a 'transformative regionalism' forwarded by groups that are left out by globalization, but tendencies of transformative regionalism are seen as 'embryonic'. Elite-driven regional responses to economic globalization prevail, including 'autocentric', 'development integration', 'degenerate' and 'neo-liberal' forms of regionalism. These tendencies co-exist in the current regionalization wave, but the neo-liberal variety tends to predominate.

Gamble and Payne (1996) agree. They view ongoing regionalism projects as elite-driven responses to the post-Cold War order of declining US hegemony over the capitalist world economy. New regionalism projects may embody slightly differing balances between free trade and managed trade, yet they share a commitment to open regionalism which is compatible with the globalism of global governance institutions such as the World Bank, the IMF, the WTO and the G7.

There are then two views of 'the new regionalism'. According to Hettne it is a kind of societal protection against economic globalization which goes against the dominant neo-liberal ideologies and policies represented by global governance institutions, while Mittelman and Gamble/Payne view new regionalism as a form of neo-liberal adjustment to processes of economic globalization. Both positions agree that the current world order is characterized by an empowering of global capitalists versus the nation-states through global capital flows and networks of production. Gamble and Payne also arge that the world order is characterized by declining US economic hegemony.

I take a more state-centred view, arguing that the current world order is dominated by a refashioned US hegemony based on a 'mercantilist' alliance between the US government and US-based international financial capital.[2] The US hegemon promotes financialization of the world economy. It has been the main driving force in the process of deregulation of international financial movements since the end of the Bretton Woods system, while its current account deficits have fed these flows. The US hegemon benefits from the ensuing financialization of the world economy due to its seigniorage, that is, the advantages it derives from control of the world economy's reserve currency. In the dollarized world economy of the post-Bretton Woods period the United States has been able to run large current account deficits as most of its imports are paid in dollars, while attracting much of these deficits back in the form of foreign direct investment and portfolio capital.

Huge capital flows in and out of the United States along with a domestic process of financialization of the US economy has enabled Wall Street to regain its position as the financial centre of the world. The recycling of the US current account deficits in the international financial system has been a major cause of the volatilities of 'financial globalization'. International financial flows in conjunction with volatile international exchange and interest rates driven by shifting US policies have fed periodic financial crises, especially in 'emerging economies'.

The Latin American debt crisis in 1982 strengthened the US interest in the IMF and the World Bank. By enforcing macroeconomic structural adjustment and institutional reform these two institutions should promote export-oriented development to make the countries able to repay their debt. The United States had a number of formal and informal means to control the decisions of these institutions when they were deemed important to US national interests.

The United States strives to establish rules of the game that strengthen the position of its financial capitalists. It has a strong interest in promoting free trade in the financial service industry, where US companies have a competitive edge, in ensuring worldwide access of its investors and in liberalizing cross-border financial flows into the US economy.

I shall analyse East Asian regionalism in the 1990s, especially since 1997, as a response to this US financial hegemony. Neo-liberal forms of 'open regionalism' and 'globalism' supported by the United States compete with regionalism oriented to the protection of cultural, social, political and economic orders against US-induced financial globalization. Social protection, however, does not necessarily imply 'transformative regionalism' by the marginalized. The focus here is rather on the protection by local economic and political elites of 'their' social order against US financial hegemony, although they may represent broader societal interests.[3]

US financial hegemony is intertwined with geopolitical hegemony. A major US objective is to maintain a world order where the two other major capitalist core areas in Europe and East Asia rely on the United States for security, supply of strategic raw materials, export markets and (especially in East Asia) the dollar as an international currency. The US ability to ensure this was weakened by the dissolution of the Soviet communist bloc, as indicated by Hettne. Regionalism in Europe and East Asia may further weaken the US position. However, US geopolitical control may be retained through geopolitical rivalry and continuous divisions over foreign policy, security issues and regional currency arrangements within these two areas.

Finally, it should be noted that a region is not a given entity. Rather, it is a contested symbolic construct of territorialized space imbued with a regional identity. Hettne compares the region to Benedict Anderson's notion of the nation as an 'imagined community'. The 'imagined regional communities' will then entail differing and partly overlapping territories and territorial identities. In the East Asian forms of regionalism discussed here the region is imagined as exclusively 'Asian', defined in opposition to the 'West'. In contrast, the type of 'open regionalism' associated with APEC is based on a form of inclusive, 'trans-Pacific' imagery.

The East Asian state system and US Cold War hegemony

The US Cold War strategy in East Asia from the late 1940s was to promote regional economic integration around the defeated Japan, while containing the People's Republic of China. Bilateral security ties were established between the United States and non-communist 'Pacific Rim' countries, with Japan, South Korea, Taiwan, South Vietnam and Thailand, as the main regional allies. They relied on the United States, rather than one another, for security, aid, export markets and oil supplies.

This Cold War order was weakened in the early 1970s with the rapprochement between the United States and China and the US disengagement from Indochina. Market reforms in China and the unified Vietnam allowed for the integration of these socialist countries into the regional trade and investment order in the 1980s. In South-east Asia a process of political integration took place with ASEAN as the key player, bridging previous regional divisions.

In contrast, in North-east Asia, divisions from the Pacific War, the Cold War and regional civil wars continued with hostilities between China and Taiwan and the two Koreas, as well as the stationing of some 80,000 US troops in South Korea and Japan. A deep Chinese distrust against Japan persisted from the Pacific Wars. Japan was reluctant to end its special security relationship with the United States and willingly ceded to US demands for military 'burden sharing'. Thus, North-east Asian divisions and security dependence on the United States were major obstacles to regional political integration.

US seigniorage, Japan and East Asian development

During the 1980s, escalating US current account deficits went along with large federal deficits. The US Treasury Department ('US Treasury') financed the federal debt through the sale of Treasury securities (bills, notes and bonds, or simply 'Treasuries'). Large-scale foreign purchases of long-term treasury-bonds helped to hold down the long-term US interest rate. The realization of these potentials of US monetary seigniorage relied on a symbiotic relationship with Japan. Large proportions of Japan's dollar current account surplus that mainly derived from its trade with the United States were invested in the United States, especially in the purchase of Treasuries. These large-scale Japanese purchases of dollar-denominated assets held down the yen exchange rate, while making 'Reaganomics' become viable (Murphy 1996).

In September 1985 the G5 Plaza Accord initiated an upward pressure on the yen exchange rate relative to the dollar. The initial rise of the yen was reinforced by growing Japanese trade surpluses with the United States, weak dollar policies and large-scale Japanese selling of

US assets in the early 1990s (Murphy 1996:272, 286–7). The exchange rate of the yen more than tripled relative to the US dollar from March 1985 to March/April 1995.

In early 1995 the US Treasury became worried about the problems of Japan's banking sector, and possibly also hints from Japan's Ministry of Finance about a major withdrawal of Japanese investments in US long-term treasury-bonds. The Treasury assumed control over US trade policies and economic relations with Japan. The ministries of finance and central banks of the two sides began to cooperate to strengthen the dollar relative to the yen (Nordhaug 2002b:521–2).

The rise of the yen relative to the dollar had a strong influence on East Asian economic prospects. Major Japanese companies responded to the strong rise of the yen by relocating core manufacturing to East Asia. Soon after the 1985 Plaza Agreement, South Korea and Taiwan also faced US trade policy pressure to appreciate their currencies along with rising domestic wage levels and land prices that undermined their competitiveness. The resulting worsening of the competitive position of North-east Asia coincided with devaluation and policy packages to promote export and foreign investment in South-east Asia and China. Japanese investors in South-east Asia were soon followed by investors from South Korea and Taiwan, contributing to growing economic integration between North-east Asia and South-east Asia and an economic boom in South-east Asia from the late 1980s. Companies from Taiwan and Hong Kong were also investing heavily in Mainland China.

The United States and other Western OECD countries were the main targets of the export of finished goods resulting from this build-up of regional manufacturing capacity through FDI. Investments from Japan and the East Asian newly industrializing countries, South Korea, Taiwan, Singapore and Hong Kong (EANICs) have stimulated increasingly dense intra-regional trade in manufacturing inputs. However, Japanese companies generally declined to move production for Japanese markets abroad, only their production for regional markets and for export to third countries. Export of finished goods from East Asia to Japan was depressed, while the region's imports of key inputs from the Japanese workshop increased. The East Asian countries then had to rely on trade surpluses earned with countries outside the region, especially with the United States, to cover their trade deficits with Japan (Bernard and Ravenhill 1995; Hatch and Yamamura 1996: ch. 10).[4]

Japan's strong position within regional producer networks was not matched by monetary strength. The yen has played a modest role in international transactions. Most of Japan's foreign trade has been paid in dollars, rather than yen, not only in its trade with the United States, but also with third countries, and most of the foreign lending by Japanese financial institutions has been dollar-denominated (Castellano 1999:2–4; CFEOT 1999:appendices I.1–8).

East Asia was a dollar bloc, rather than a yen bloc, where most foreign trade and investment were conducted in dollars. Excepting Japan, most regional currencies were linked to the dollar from the mid-1980s until the 1997 regional currency crisis (including the currencies of China and Vietnam from the early-to-mid 1990s). This also meant that the currencies were loosely tied to one another. These arrangements protected against competitive devaluation and helped the countries to stabilize domestic price levels, while yen appreciation enhanced the region's competitiveness relative to Japan and encouraged the inflow of Japanese investment (Sum 2002:58; McKinnon 2000).

East Asia's export boom 1985–95 was then to a large extent based on successful adjustment to US monetary seigniorage that was underwritten by the use of the dollar in trade and investment relations with third parties, by the linking of regional currencies to the dollar and by the investment of regional dollar reserves in US Treasuries. There was a complementary relationship between US over-consumption and East Asian under-consumption. Much of the dollar surplus earned by the high-saving, high-investing East Asian countries in their trade with the United States was reinvested in US Treasuries and other US securities, thus sustaining the investment rate of the high-consuming, low-saving United States.

The region's adjustment to a dollar standard prevented monetary regionalization, which naturally would have been based on the yen. Dollarization was furthered by the practice of investing regional central bank reserves in US Treasuries. However, the Asian financial crisis demonstrated the financial and monetary vulnerability of regional economies and led to greater interest in effective regional monetary cooperation.

The destabilization of East Asian models of accumulation

Most East Asian countries have had high rates of saving and investment. Excepting Japan, they were competing within export markets with low barriers to entry, while attempting to undertake industrial upgrading to conquer niche markets and move into high-profit yielding export markets. Low profits and fast manufacturing expansion with industrial upgrading required large volumes of investment and credit. The high investment levels increased the risk of over-investment. During the 1990s, high regional rates of corporate investment went along with declining rates of return in most of the countries (Sum 2002:58–9, 61–2).

The regional financial order and monetary regime reinforced tendencies of overproduction and over-investment with lowered investment quality. Financial inflows from Western countries poured into 'emerging economies', while Japan's loose monetary policies from 1992 with low interest rates created surplus liquidity that 'leaked out' to East Asia. Japan dominated foreign direct investment and lending to East Asia, while most of the foreign portfolio investment to the region came from the United States and Europe. Nevertheless much of the funding of these portfolio investments initially came from Japan. International investors engaged in the so-called yen carry trade through borrowing at low interest rates in Japan, exchanging yen into dollars and reinvesting throughout the world, including East Asia (Bevacqua 1998:414–15). Most East Asian governments (with exceptions such as China and Taiwan) liberalized their capital accounts to attract these funds from the early 1990s.

The combination of capital account deregulation, strong growth, monetary stability with de facto dollar pegs, high local interest rates and or/lucrative markets in securities and real estate encouraged large inflows of loans (frequently short-term) and portfolio investment. Hence, the countries became increasingly reliant on maintaining the confidence of foreign investors, and on upholding their dollar peg.

Net private foreign investment in South Korea, Indonesia, Malaysia, Thailand and the Philippines increased from US$ 40.5 billion in 1994 to 93.0 billion in 1996 (Radelet and Sachs 1998: appendix, table 1). These inflows fuelled very high levels of investment. As a result there was a rise in the level of 'bad investment', including investment in financial bubbles, and industrial overcapacity (Bevacqua 1998:416; Wade 2000:102).

East Asian foreign debt soared as a result of the inflow of loans. Large proportions of these loans were short-term (one year maturity or less) which were used to finance long-term investment, and renewed on a regular base. Much of the lending was not hedged against exchange rate changes, and growing foreign debt complicated the option of a 'soft landing' by abandoning the monetary pegs. In Indonesia, Thailand and South Korea – which would all receive 'rescue packages' from the IMF – short-term debt exceeded foreign reserves, and grew at a faster pace than these reserves (Radelet and Sachs 1998: appendix, table 3). Economic stability then relied on the willingness of foreign lenders to renew short-term loans.

The region was adversely affected by the depreciation of the yen following the 1995 'reverse Plaza agreement'. The declining yen affected regional competitiveness within higher-end East Asian manufacturing directly involved in competition with Japanese products, especially in South Korea, and reduced the growth in Japanese foreign investment (Kwan 2001:41–3). The 'rise of China' weakened the competitiveness of ASEAN-four (Thailand, Malaysia, Indonesia and the Philippines) within lower-end manufacturing. Chinese exports were boosted by devaluations in 1990 and 1994, wages were lower than in Thailand and Malaysia, while the skills and level of education of the Chinese labour force frequently were better than in ASEAN-four. Exports from ASEAN-four were increasingly compressed to a narrow range of electronic products leading to enhanced economic vulnerability (Lo 1999; Hughes 2000:238–40, table 4).

Declining export growth and growing current account deficits probably weakened foreign investor confidence in regional assets and currencies. Eventually investors began to sell away South-east Asian currencies during May and June 1997 and a number of major Thai financial institutions failed. By 2 July the Bank of Thailand was forced to float the baht. This was followed by regional contamination in South-east Asia. Foreign lenders refused to renew loans falling due. Large-scale dumping of assets and currencies pushed down their values. There were vicious circles of currency depreciation, increased foreign debt and collapse of domestic financial institutions. The Philippines, Malaysia and Indonesia were forced to abandon their currency pegs in July and August. Taiwan escaped with a moderate depreciation of the NT dollar in October 1997, while the Korean won was floated in late November.

A US\$ 93.0 billion *net inflow* of private capital to South Korea, Thailand, Malaysia, Indonesia and the Philippines in 1996 changed to a US\$ 12.1 billion *net outflow* in 1997 (Radelet and Sachs 1998:appendix, table 1). The IMF signed standby agreements with Thailand (5 August), Indonesia (31 October) and South Korea (4 December), while the Philippines extended a previous IMF agreement. With this regional crisis and the ensuing 'brutal' structural adjustments, there was a growing interest in East Asia in protective monetary regionalism directed against 'Western' intrusion.

East Asian monetary integration efforts: AMF vs IMF

The IMF required the closing of financial institutions, the enforcement of strict regulatory standards and liberalization of the financial system and the capital account in return for emergency funds. At best these policies had little relevance in stemming the crisis. At worst they enhanced investor panic. The IMF was also demanding fiscal contraction and tight monetary policies in a failed attempt to stabilize East Asian currencies. These pro-cyclical policies had a serious effect on regional markets and starved local business of credits. Failure to meet zealous demands for budget surpluses, and expanding domestic debt due to high interest rates weakened foreign investors' confidence. Emergency funds were sliced in tranches to be disbursed over the programme period, pending adjustment performance. These tranches were too small compared to the debt falling due to stem the panic, and disbursement was delayed by drawn-out complicated negotiations (Radelet and Sachs 1998:34–7).

Disillusioned by the IMF's poor performance in Thailand and the unwillingness of the United States to contribute to the bailout fund, the ASEAN countries in August 1997 officially proposed a permanent regional Asian Monetary Fund (AMF) financed by the East Asian countries. The real driving force in this initiative was Japan's Ministry of Finance.[5] The AMF should operate at the regional level to maintain monetary stability. Its total funding would be about US$ 100 billion with Japan as the main contributor. Tokyo had a strong interest in stabilizing regional financial systems. A regional financial collapse would enhance Japan's bad debt problem as Japanese banks had large outstanding loans in the region.

Japan floated the AMF idea during a G7 meeting in Hong Kong in September 1997. The EU countries and the IMF immediately objected to the proposal. During the annual meeting of the IMF and the World Bank in Hong Kong in September/October, US Vice Secretary of the Treasury, Larry Summers also strongly resisted the initiative.[6] The Treasury attempted to accommodate the East Asian countries by assuming a greater responsibility for the emergency funds in return for an abandonment of the AMF plans.

The Western critics argued that two rival monetary funds would create problems of 'moral hazard' by allowing for access to emergency funds without reform. From the Treasury's viewpoint the AMF would reduce American influence on the adjustment processes and impede liberalization of trade and finance. The Clinton administration with the Treasury in the driver's seat had developed a foreign economic policy that targeted a number of 'emerging markets', mainly in East Asia and emphasized US investor interests. The administration supported multilateral agencies such as IMF, OECD, WTO and APEC to promote international financial liberalization. As these policy instruments, alliances and the strategy of targeting East Asia were in place, the administration was in a strong position to use the IMF 'to open Asia' to US investors (Gowan 1999:ch. 5). Concern about East Asian holdings of Treasuries may also have been important. If regional central banks led by the Bank of Japan had sold out from their holdings of Treasuries to finance this costly operation, US long-term interest rates would have soared (Johnson 1998:658).

China was also hostile to the AMF initiative as an effort to impose 'yen hegemony' on East Asia (Rowley 2000a:23). In addition to its support of the US/IMF line, China also contributed to the IMF emergency funds and pledged not to devalue the *renminbi*. The Chinese defence of the reminbi was most important to the stabilization of regional currency exchange rates in 1998. These actions sustained Beijing's regional rivalry with Tokyo. By mid-1998 Beijing criticized the Japanese side for allowing the yen to decline.[7] China's policy was probably also motivated by a strategy of accommodating the United States. In return Beijing hoped for US concessions in the ongoing negotiations on China's entry into the WTO (Bowles 2002:255-7).

Japan withdrew from the AMF proposal and the other East Asian countries gradually followed suit. The AMF initiative was abandoned in November 1997. APEC's meeting in Vancouver 23-4 November backed the IMF's leadership in the financial rescue operation. Shortly afterwards Tokyo announced that its contribution to the regional emergency fund would 'only' be about US$ 20 billion (Rowley 1997).

The new Miyazawa initiative

The Asian crisis was accompanied by growing friction between the United States and Japan over trade policy issues. This appears to have been an important background for new Japanese initiatives for regional monetary integration that first came in the form of a major Japanese aid initiative.

During 1998, US authorities criticized Japan's handling of its banking crisis as well as Japan's declining imports from the region. The United States enlisted support from the G7 and East Asia. Japan came under strong pressure to expand government deficits and imports to promote regional recovery. At APEC's trade ministers' meeting in Kuala

Lumpur in June 1998 an isolated Japan was pressured on 'Early Voluntary Sector Liberalization' within marine and forestry products. Eventually, the Japanese government responded by launching a massive economic stimulus and bank bailout package in October 1998 along with a regional aid initiative that diluted the pressure for trade liberalization (Hughes 2000:232–3).

At a G7 meeting in Washington in October 1998 Japan's Minister of Finance, Kiichi Miyazawa, presented a US$ 30 billion aid plan in soft credits to Indonesia, Malaysia, the Philippines, Thailand and South Korea. Loans made under the plan would be denominated in yen and tied to projects involving Japanese companies. Japan was couching the idea in the context of a broader aid effort involving the G7 countries, the IMF and the World Bank, and thus diluted resistance from the United States and the IMF. Additional Japanese aid commitments followed in December 1998 and during spring 1999 (Vatikiotis with Hiebert 1998/99; Castellano 2000:2). These Japanese funds provided an alternative source of emergency credits without the stringent conditions that accompanied IMF support.

The success of the Japanese initiative is indicated by the fact that East Asian countries in November 1998 declined to force the 'Early Voluntary Sector Liberalization' within marine and forestry products through APEC's agenda. The compromise solution was to defer a decision to the WTO (Hughes 2000:246). But apart from trade policy, Tokyo's regional aid policy was also closely related to its efforts to internationalize the yen.

Regionalization of the yen

For a long time it had been a deliberate strategy on the side of Japan's Ministry of Finance (MOF) to reduce the international use of the yen in order to hold down the yen exchange rate. However, by mid-1998 the MOF began to advocate the internationalization of the yen, focusing on East Asia.

It was argued that the internationalization of the yen would enhance the competitiveness of Japan's financial institutions. Japan's capital market would benefit from yen investments by foreigners and the foreign exchange risks of trade and capital transactions would be reduced (CFEOT 1998, 1999). The pressure to market Japan's government debt may have played an important role in these deliberations. By internationalizing the yen Japan may be able to attract East Asian current account surpluses into its government bond market.

The Euro was launched in 1999. The MOF predicted that it would become a strong competitor to the dollar with 'Euroland', Central and East Europe and Africa as its main area (CFEOT 1999:4). A monetary triadization of the world economy was imminent, but the yen was lagging behind in this process because of its limited use in East Asia. The Asian crisis provided an opportunity for a change of the regional monetary regime as most East Asian countries unlinked their currencies from the dollar. MOF claimed that the pegging of regional currencies to the dollar had been a major cause of the 1997 crisis and recommended that East Asian currencies were tied to a basket consisting of the US dollar, the Euro, and the yen.

In a speech in April 1999, Miyazawa argued that East Asian savings were invested in the West, while the region relied on unstable capital flows from US and European investors. These financial flows should be redirected to go within East Asia. Japan would play a key role at the centre of the regional financial flows, channelling aid and public investment to the region. Internationalization of the yen, financial liberalization, the creation of new financial instruments and tax rebates would attract regional yen holdings into private and public securities.

Regionalization of the yen was also promoted through Japan's foreign aid. Loans made under the New Miyazawa Plan were denominated in yen. In addition, aid loans were used to promote yen-denominated exports from poor East Asian countries to Japan to shield these countries from uncertainties relating to the volatile yen/dollar exchange rate (*Yahoo!* 2000).

Regional currency swaps

The previous discussion has focused on the role of Japanese initiatives. Yet in May 2000 a new regional initiative for monetary cooperation was launched within the ASEAN+3 framework in a meeting of finance ministers in Chiang Mai. A network of bilateral currency swap arrangements should ensure that countries with significant currency reserves would lend foreign currency, mainly dollars, to defend the exchange rates of their neighbours. Japan was a driving force.

The New Miyazawa Plan of autumn 1998 had included bilateral currency swap agreements with South Korea and Malaysia. These arrangements were extended under the Chiang Mai framework while a network of new bilateral swap arrangements have been concluded and signed between countries in the region. The total amount committed in these agreements is US\$ 32.5 billion (AsianInt EIR 2003; Bello 2000; Rowley 2000a, 2000b).

This approach has bypassed the problems of a formal institution that might counter American opposition. Reportedly the US representatives at the Asian Development Bank (ADB) meeting in Chiang Mai were not amused when the currency swap plans were unexpectedly announced. Yet the United States kept a low profile, while IMF's managing director Horst Kohler stated that an Asian Monetary Fund that was complementary to the IMF was acceptable (Liu 2002).

As was previously noted, China's support of the US/IMF line during 1997/98 was partly motivated by its interest in obtaining concessions from the United States in negotiations regarding China's WTO accession. However, these hopes were frustrated. During 1999, relations between the United States and China were rapidly declining following the US bombing of the Chinese embassy in Belgrade in the war with Yugoslavia and the issuing of the 'Cox Report' with a hawkish position on China. By mid-1999 Beijing had abandoned the strategy of accommodating the United States. It now took a greater interest in regional arrangements and supported the process leading up to the May 2000 Chiang Mai proposal (Bowles 2002:257–8). Apparently China and Japan sorted out their differences prior to the meeting and found a formula that smacked less of 'yen hegemony'.

Conclusion

In the first parts of this chapter I outlined a theoretical framework for the study of regionalism as a response to US financial hegemony. In terms of this framework East Asian monetary and financial regionalism since the failed AMF attempt in 1997 can be seen as a form of 'Polanyian' societal protection against US financial hegemony. This Polanyian element was perhaps most clearly seen during the struggle over the AMF in 1997, with Japan and the United States as the main opponents. However, the struggle over the AMF was not solely related to US financial hegemony. Rivalry for regional hegemony between Japan and China also played a role in the defeat of the proposal.

Afterwards Asian monetary and financial regionalism was developed in a more cautious manner, first through Japanese initiatives for aid and internationalization of the yen. The Japanese 'New Miyazawa Initiative' may have served as a regional self-defence against IMF pressure. For instance, Hughes (2000:222) suggests that the competition from the New Miyazawa Plan forced the IMF to take a milder stance towards the East Asian countries. In the next round, a multilateral initiative also emerged with the Chiang Mai currency swap agreement. There has also been extensive discussion within the ASEAN+3 on the pegging of regional currencies to some 'basket' of the dollar, the yen and the Euro, rather than to the dollar, and a project of developing regional bond markets has also been started.

Nevertheless, so far there are few indications of any major change from East Asia's dollar bloc policies and adjustment to US hegemony. Central banks in Japan, China, Hong Kong, Singapore, Taiwan and South Korea have responded to the current 'weak dollar' US monetary policy under the Bush administration with growing purchases of Treasuries to hold down their currency exchange rates and the countries of the region continue their previous dollar quasi-peg policies.[8] East Asia is still a dollar zone. The challenge from ASEAN+3 against US seigniorage has been marginal. As was suggested, the financial hegemony of the United States is strengthened by regional divisions. A major regional challenge is unlikely to occur without reconciliation between Japan and China.

Notes

1   A longer version of my empirical argument is found in Nordhaug (2002a). See also Nordhaug (2002b).
2   The following arguments on US hegemony and 'financial globalization' are based on Helleiner (1995); Gowan (1999, 2003); and Wade (2001, 2003).
3   Similarly in Polanyi's account, landlords and central bankers as well as the labour movement were carriers of social protection.
4   China has broken this pattern and is running trade surpluses with Japan as well as with the United States. Yet it is running a large trade deficit with Taiwan through indirect trade via Hong Kong.
5   Surprisingly, the idea for an AMF financed by Japan probably came from IMF director Michel Camdessus, who feared a shortage of funding for the rescue operations as the United States declined to contribute to the Thai emergency fund. Japan's Vice Finance Minister of International Affairs, Eisuke Sakakibara, took up the idea and presented it as his own. Camdessus later changed his position as the US Treasury, which had not been informed, began to resist the AMF and promised US support to the emergency funds. I thank Robert Wade for this information.
6   During the conference, Sakakibara (see note 5) called a meeting of senior Asian officials to discuss the AMF proposal without informing the US representatives. As Summers learned about this meeting, he entered the room where the Asians were sitting, sat down at the table and said, 'Now, where were we?' See Wade (1999:147, note 46).

7 Beijing's words were not always in accordance with her deeds. The Chinese central bank simultaneously sold off billions of dollars worth from its yen holdings. See Wade and Venoroso (1998b:27, note 36).
8 As this chapter is completed (March 2004) there is much speculation that the falling dollar exchange rate may eventually induce Asian central banks to reduce their share of dollar-denominated holdings of Treasuries in favour of euro bonds. A large sell-out of Treasuries would push up the US long-term interest rate and weaken the US economy.

6
Conflict Management and Constructive Engagement in the Expansion of the Association of South-east Asian Nations

Ramses Amer

Introduction

The main purpose of this chapter is to examine the expansion of membership in the Association of South-east Asian Nations (ASEAN) which took place during the second half of the 1990s and to analyse and assess the relative importance of key factors in this process. Particular attention is devoted to the efforts aimed at implementing the conflict management mechanisms of ASEAN on a wider regional level.

The expansion of membership in ASEAN can be studied from various angles. In the context of this study the focus is on the relative relevance and explanatory value of three factors – economic, political and security – in the process of expanding membership in ASEAN.

The 'conflict management' aspect of this process is studied from two main perspectives. First, expanding the membership of ASEAN is a way to manage conflicts more efficiently between the original and the new member states of the Association. Secondly, through the expansion of the Association the conflict management approach of ASEAN will be spread to a larger part of South-east Asia.[1] In the context of this study the focus is on interstate disputes. Also of importance is the 'constructive engagement'[2] aspect of the process of ASEAN expansion.

The chapter encompasses two main parts. The first part identifies and assesses the conflict management mechanisms for handling interstate disputes within the ASEAN framework. It also examines the negotiation and decision-making processes within ASEAN. The second part is made up of two main sections. The first is devoted to the relations between the ASEAN member states – Brunei Darussalam, Indonesia, Malaysia, the Philippines, Singapore, and Thailand – and the other four South-east Asian states – Cambodia, Laos, Myanmar and Vietnam – leading up to the expansion of membership in the Association. The second section encompasses an analysis and assessment of the relevance and the possible explanatory value of the economic, political and security factors in the expansion of ASEAN. The chapter is concluded by an analysis of the developments relating to conflict management within an expanded ASEAN.

Mechanisms for conflict management within ASEAN[3]

ASEAN's approach to conflict management consists of two main dimensions. The first relates to mechanisms as formulated in different ASEAN declarations and treaties, and the second relates to the way in which the member states of ASEAN negotiate and reach a common understanding on various issues. The following section investigates both these aspects. The mechanisms outlined in this section are those adopted prior to the expansion of membership in the 1990s.

Mechanisms for conflict management

Although ASEAN was created as part of a process aiming at peaceful management of conflicts among its original members, that is, Indonesia, Malaysia, the Philippines, Singapore, and Thailand, the ASEAN Declaration (Bangkok Declaration) (http://www.aseansec. org/3628.htm) adopted on 8 August 1967 did not include specific references as to how this main goal should be reached. More emphasis is put on the promotion of social and economic cooperation among the member states of the Association than on conflict management.

The improvement of relations among the original member states of ASEAN during the period often referred to as the 'formative years', that is, 1967 to 1976, led to the signing of the Declaration of ASEAN Concord and the Treaty of Amity and Cooperation in South-east Asia (TAC) (Bali Treaty) on 24 February 1976, in connection with the First Summit Meeting of ASEAN held in Bali.

The Declaration of ASEAN Concord only relates to the member states of ASEAN whereas the Bali Treaty is also open for accession to non-members. The Declaration of ASEAN Concord contains both general principles relating to the overall goals of the Association and principles relating to the specific goals of managing disputes and expanding cooperation among the member states. One of the stated overall objectives is the establishment of a Zone of Peace, Freedom and Neutrality (ZOPFAN) in South-east Asia.[4] It is also noticeable that the linkage between the internal stability in the member states of ASEAN and the stability in the whole grouping and the achievement of peace and security is made in the section dealing with general objectives and principles. In order to meet this goal all members should strive to eliminate threats posed by 'subversion' to their stability, thus strengthening national and ASEAN resilience. Respect for the principles of 'self-determination, sovereign equality and non-interference in the internal affairs of nations' is emphasized (http://www.asesansec.org/3630.htm).

The Bali Treaty provides more specific guidelines in the field of conflict management. This is particularly the case in relation to the peaceful settlement of disputes (http://www.asesansec.org/1654.htm). According to Article 18 of the Bali Treaty it 'shall be open for accession by other States in Southeast Asia'. The Bali Treaty is divided into a Preamble and five Chapters. Chapters I, III and IV are most relevant in terms of cooperation and settlement of disputes. In Chapter I, dealing with 'Purpose and Principles', Article 2 outlines the fundamental principles that should guide the relations between the signatories to the Treaty. The principles are:

- mutual respect for the independence, sovereignty, equality, territorial integrity and national identity of all nations;
- the right of every State to lead its national existence free from external interference, subversion or coercion;
- non-interference in the internal affairs of one another;
- settlement of differences or disputes by peaceful means;
- renunciation of the threat or use of force;
- effective cooperation among themselves (http://www.asesansec.org/1217.htm).

The principles include three main factors for managing interstate relations: non-interference in the internal affairs of other countries, peaceful settlement of disputes, and, overall cooperation (http://www.asesansec.org/1654.htm).

Chapter III, is concerned with 'Cooperation', and refers to the areas in which mutual cooperation can be established and expanded and also highlights the linkages between cooperation, peaceful relations and non-interference.

In Chapter IV, devoted to 'Pacific Settlement of Disputes', the first Article (13) describes the way in which the signatories should behave in situations in which there is a risk that disputes may arise or have arisen. The Article (http://www.asesansec.org/1217.htm). stipulates that the signatories:

> shall have the determination and good faith to prevent disputes from arising. In case disputes on matters directly affecting them shall refrain from the threat or use of force and shall at all times settle such disputes among themselves through friendly negotiations.

Article 14 is devoted to the creation and envisaged role of a *High Council*. The mediating role of the Council is addressed in Article 15. The Council can assume this role in the event that no solution to a dispute is reached through 'direct' negotiation between the parties to the dispute. The role as mediator can be assumed by recommending to the parties to a dispute appropriate means of settlement. Article 16 displays some limitations to the mediating functions of the Council by stating that the provisions of Articles 14 and 15 shall apply to a dispute only if the parties to the dispute agree to their 'application'. Literally this implies that only the High Council can decide on mediating in a dispute if the parties agree to the 'application' of the provisions, but that the parties to the dispute cannot bring the matter to the High Council (http://www.asesansec.org/1217.htm). However, among some officials and researchers in the South-east Asian region another interpretation is being put forward namely that the High Council can only assume the role of mediator in a dispute if the parties involved agree on bringing the dispute to the Council.[5]

Thus, the Declaration of ASEAN Concord and the Bali Treaty seek to set out the broad goals and aims of the Association, as well as more specific mechanisms and code of conduct necessary to achieve enhanced regional cooperation. The documents aim to provide guidelines for managing interstate relations in general, and the existing and potential disputes in particular. They also show that by the end of the 'formative years' the ASEAN members had achieved a high degree of understanding of how to manage the interstate relations within the grouping.

Conflict management in ASEAN's negotiation and decision-making processes

The ASEAN states have managed to build confidence, familiarity and understanding of each other's positions on different issues through a system of informal and formal meetings between the leaders, ministers and senior officials of the member states. Achieving a high level of interaction, cooperation and understanding between the original member states of ASEAN was a gradual process during the formative years leading up to the First Summit Meeting in 1976. ASEAN is also known for its decision-making process that requires that all decisions be reached by consensus. Particular emphasis has been put on promoting and achieving regional resilience based on the internal resilience of each of the member states through economic development, which would result in greater political support for the governments and lead to enhanced political stability.

With regard to conflict management, ASEAN's approach has been geared towards preventing the emergence of new disputes and conflicts, while simultaneously preventing existing disputes and conflicts from disrupting interstate relations. In the context of ASEAN's conflict management approach, a central element is the consultation process called *musyawarah* which is informal in character and aims at settling differences by preventing them from arising. The practice has evolved from the practices applied in villages in Indonesia, Malaysia and the Philippines. The aim of the process of *musyawarah* is also to achieve unanimous decisions; that is, consensus, known as *mufakat*. This has become a crucial part of decisions-making processes within ASEAN. These principles of *musyawarah* and *mufakat* are important mechanisms in the conflict management process since it aims at preserving peaceful relations between the member states of ASEAN by such measures as avoiding, defusing and containing issues which could lead to open interstate conflicts (Askandar 1994:63–5; Caballero-Anthony 1998:51–62).

What is the importance of conflict management in ASEAN?

The ASEAN approach to conflict management through the negotiation and decision-making processes as well as the mechanisms and provisions provided by the Declaration of ASEAN Concord and the Bali Treaty tertify to the importance placed by the member states of ASEAN on the need to manage interstate disputes through peaceful means. Resolving such disputes is undoubtedly one of ASEAN's highest priorities. Achieving formal resolution of interstate disputes within ASEAN should not be carried out in such a way as to disrupt the relations between the parties to the disputes. Therefore it can be said that conflict resolution is both desirable and a goal for the ASEAN members, but not when it is at the expense of maintaining stable interstate relations within the Association.

The expansion of ASEAN in the 1990s[6]

This expansion of membership in ASEAN was the culmination of a process of gradual rapprochement between the member states of ASEAN members (ASEAN-six)[7] and Cambodia, Laos, Myanmar and Vietnam, respectively. The gradual rapprochement with Laos and Vietnam went hand in hand with the regional initiatives to resolve the Cambodian conflict in the latter half of the 1980s, with the major breakthrough in improved relations following the formal resolution of the Cambodian conflict through the Paris Agreements on Cambodia of October 1991.[8]

The rapprochement between ASEAN and Vietnam was illustrated by the establishment of full diplomatic relations between Vietnam and Singapore and between Vietnam and Brunei Darussalam, thus bringing about normal relations between Vietnam and all ASEAN members. Vietnam acceded to the Bali Treaty in 1992, became an ASEAN Observer the same year and was granted full membership in ASEAN in 1995.[9] In the case of Laos, accession to the Bali Treaty also took place in 1992, and in the same year its became an ASEAN Observer. Finally, Laos was granted full membership in the Association in 1997. Following the United Nations peacekeeping operation and the formation of a new coalition government after general elections in May 1993, Cambodia's relations with ASEAN were normalized and expanded. Cambodia acceded to the Bali Treaty in 1994 and became an ASEAN Observer in 1995. Finally, Myanmar was brought closer to ASEAN through a process which was officially termed 'constructive engagement' by ASEAN (Ajibewa 1998:31–2; Malik 1997:60–1). Myanmar acceded to the Bali Treaty in 1995, became an ASEAN Observer in 1996 and was granted full membership in ASEAN in 1997. This overall process led to the expansion of membership in ASEAN from six to nine members by 1997.[10]

Cambodia was supposed to have joined ASEAN in July 1997, alongside Laos and Myanmar, but Cambodia's membership was put on hold due to the internal political problems in the country, that is, the militarized fighting in July 1997, which led to the ouster of the then First Prime Minister Prince Norodom Ranariddh by Second Prime Minister Hun Sen.[11] Eventually, Cambodia was admitted as ASEAN's tenth member through a decision taken at the Sixth ASEAN Summit in Hanoi on 16 December 1998.[12] The 'special ceremonies of admission' were organized in Hanoi on 30 April 1999 (http://www.asesansec.org/328.htm).

Expanding ASEAN membership as constructive engagement and conflict management

The process of rapprochement and gradual expansion of ASEAN brought to an end the animosity and mutual suspicion that had characterized ASEAN's relationships with the Indo-Chinese countries – Cambodia, Laos, and Vietnam – from 1975 when the Second Indo-China War ended with communist forces gaining power in all three countries. The Vietnamese military intervention in Cambodia in late 1978, which resulted in the overthrow of the existing government and the establishment of the People's Republic of Kampuchea, led to open animosity and confrontation between ASEAN and the Indo-Chinese countries. A deadlocked diplomatic situation prevailed for the first half of the 1980s until early Indonesian–Vietnamese contacts and dialogue brought about a wider dialogue process and the Jakarta Informal Meetings on the Cambodian situation from 1988. This rapprochement continued during the process leading up to the resolution of the Cambodian conflict and also after the signing of the Paris Agreements of 1991 (Saravanamuttu 1996:37–62; Amer 1996b:63–117).

Relations between ASEAN and Burma/Myanmar was not characterized by any similar animosity or confrontation. Burma/Myanmar did conduct a foreign policy characterized by isolationist tendencies and this implied that interaction with ASEAN was limited but not bad per se. Burma/Myanmar supported ASEAN's stand on the developments in Cambodia (Amer 1994). Thus, the process of expanding relations and the gradual incorporation of Myanmar in the ASEAN framework for regional cooperation grew out of a different kind of relationship from those between ASEAN and the three Indo-Chinese countries.

It can therefore be argued that the process involving ASEAN and Myanmar was different in nature from the processes involving the ASEAN and the three Indo-Chinese countries. This situation has to be taken into consideration when analysing and assessing the expansion of ASEAN membership since 1995. It is also highly relevant when looking at the degree of 'constructive engagement' that has been involved in ASEAN's policies towards the other four South-east Asian countries in the processes of expanding relations and integrating new members into the Association.

In regard to 'conflict management' the major development has been the expanded acceptance of the Bali Treaty as a framework for handling interstate disputes by peaceful means and as a code of conduct to be observed in interstate relations among the countries of South-east

Asia. This process of expanded acceptance took place from 1992 onwards.

Bringing countries which were earlier perceived as potential or real threats and even as outright enemies into the framework of regional cooperation, as has been developed by the ASEAN members, and eventually accepting these countries into the Association as full members can be seen as an exercise in conflict management by ASEAN. This process can also be seen as an attempt aiming to expand the ASEAN framework and approach for conflict management within the Southeast Asian region for the sake of regional peace, security and stability. In fact expanding membership in ASEAN and expanding the acceptance of the ASEAN framework for conflict management within the region can be viewed as a process of conflict management brought about by various means which form part of a broader policy of constructive engagement towards the Indo-Chinese countries and Myanmar.

The 'constructive engagement' policy towards Myanmar did not serve the purpose of engaging a potentially threatening and assertive neighbour, as has been the case in regards to ASEAN's policy towards China. The policy of constructive engagement towards Myanmar seems rather to be characterized by a desire to influence domestic development in Myanmar in a positive direction through increased economic and political interaction as well as through the integration of the country in the mainstream of regional cooperation in South-east Asia. If there is a security dimension it is rather to balance off the Chinese influence in Myanmar by bringing the country closer to the other South-east Asian countries within the ASEAN framework (Ajibewa 1998; Malik 1997).

The notion of threat is relative and the situation can of course differ from one ASEAN member state to another. In the case of Thailand the so-called 'China-threat' has been less prevalent than in the cases of Indonesia and Malaysia, to name two examples. In the case of Thailand, developments in Myanmar have caused security concerns. Thailand has been facing a large-scale refugee problem emanating from Myanmar, as well as a spillover of fighting between the armed forces of Myanmar and opposition forces into Thai territory (Ganesan 1999).

Factors in the expansion of ASEAN[13]

In the context of the following analysis and assessment it is important to recall that from the outset the expressed goal of ASEAN was to promote social and economic cooperation among its members. However, several observers favour the assessment that more has been achieved in terms of cooperation in the political and security fields as compared to the economic field (Chin 1997). This points to a development of a security community among the ASEAN member states.

The relative importance of three factors will be discussed and assessed in this section namely the economic, political and security factors. Approaching the analysis of the relevance of these factors, one must take into consideration that there was an ASEAN perspective and motivation, as well as the perspectives and motivations of the individual member states within the Association influencing its decisions on rapprochement with the neighbouring countries and on expanding membership. Furthermore, Cambodia, Laos, Myanmar and Vietnam also had their respective perspectives as well as motives and goals for seeking better relations with ASEAN, for integrating into the regional framework for regional cooperation, and for seeking membership in ASEAN.

Another pertinent aspect to take into consideration is the interconnection between the three factors. This can be shown by looking in turn at conflict management and constructive engagement. Successful conflict management creates conducive conditions for both economic and political cooperation and it contributes to the enhancement of the security of the countries in South-east Asia. Constructive engagement aims at creating better relations and to mitigate potentially threatening countries, that is, increase security, through expanded political and economic cooperation. The connection between the three factors is also illustrated by the growth triangles and sub-regional economic zone schemes that have been initiated or are at the planning stage. Such schemes show that they are not only spurred by purely economic considerations but they also serve as vehicles to enhance political cooperation and thus contribute to enhanced security through expanded overall cooperation between the involved countries (Acharya 1995; Weatherbee 1995).

The economic factor

The economic factor encompasses trade and investment and broader economic cooperation within the region to promote economic growth and overall development. Given the disparity in the level of economic developments among the ASEAN-six and between them and the other four countries – Cambodia, Laos, Myanmar and Vietnam – the priority given to the different factors varies considerably.

As seen from the ASEAN-six perspective the economic rationale for expanding membership in the Association in South-east Asia can be identified as follows – creating a larger market for intra-ASEAN trade within an expanded ASEAN Free Trade Agreement (AFTA) encompassing the whole of South-east Asia, facilitating and creating conducive conditions for overall economic cooperation with the South-east Asian region.

As seen from the perspectives of Cambodia, Laos, Myanmar and Vietnam, the economic benefits of closer cooperation and eventually membership in ASEAN was to increase investment by the ASEAN-six, to increase export opportunities to these countries and to get more assistance in development efforts from the ASEAN members.

The pattern of economic interaction between the ASEAN-six and Cambodia, Laos, Myanmar and Vietnam, respectively, shows that prior to the Asian Financial Crisis (AFC) there had been an increase in ASEAN-six investment in the other four countries in the 1990s. ASEAN-six investment was an important contribution to overall foreign investment in the other countries. Individual ASEAN members were leading trading partners of the other four countries. Thus, as seen from the perspectives of Cambodia, Laos, Myanmar and Vietnam, the ASEAN-six taken together or as individual members were of major importance both through investments and as trading partners.

The picture is different when assessed from the ASEAN-six perspective for two main reasons: first, trade with the other four South-east Asian countries was a limited part of the overall trade of the ASEAN-six, and second, the investment by the ASEAN-six in the other four countries was limited in comparison with the amount of foreign direct investment (FDI) in the ASEAN-six themselves. However, the amount invested in Cambodia, Laos, Myanmar and Vietnam constituted a fairly important share of the foreign investments made by investors from the ASEAN-six.

The AFC had major impacts on both investment and trading patterns, in particular investment levels dropped considerably.[14] However, this did not impact on the expansion of membership as the decision in principle to accept new members had been taken before the AFC.

The political factor

As seen from the perspective of the ASEAN-six, expansion of membership was a process aiming to achieve the fulfilment of the overall aim and goal set out in 1967 to bring about or create an Association encompassing all ten countries in the South-east Asian region, that is,

fulfilling the notion of 'One South-east Asia' (Chin 1997). This fundamental vision and goal is the major underlying political motivation
and rationale for initiating the process aiming to achieve an expansion
of membership in ASEAN. Without this political motivation an expansion of ASEAN would not have been envisaged and not initiated from
the outset.

The rapprochement between ASEAN and Cambodia, Laos, Myanmar
and Vietnam, respectively, can be viewed as politically motivated or
initiated because a political interest existed in improving relations. The
willingness and interest among all the South-east Asian countries to
first improve and then strive to expand relations with each other indicate that there was a basic region-wide political willingness to do so.
This willingness was brought about by changes at the domestic,
regional, and global levels which made it possible to rethink earlier
foreign policy priorities and reshape interstate relations within South-
east Asia. Some of the major changes were: the initiation of reform and
renovation in the three Indo-Chinese countries, the process leading up
to the resolution of the Cambodian conflict through the Paris
Agreements of October 1991, and the end of major power confrontation and normalization between China and the Soviet Union and
between the Soviet Union and the United States, that is, the end of the
Cold War.

The political willingness is displayed by the fact that ASEAN actively
sought to build better relations with the other four South-east Asian
countries by gradually integrating them into the ASEAN framework for
regional cooperation and eventually granting them full membership in
the Association. The other four South-east Asian countries actively
sought to improve relations with the ASEAN member states through
expanding political and economic interaction.

In addressing the political factor it is important to highlight the fact
that changing the political systems of the new member states was not a
prerequisite to be accepted as member states of ASEAN. In other words
ASEAN did not place political conditions on the new members when
they were accepted into the Association, nor did ASEAN try to impose a
particular political system on the new members. For example Vietnam
and Laos joined ASEAN although the two countries were and still are
governed by Communist parties. The fact that Myanmar was under
military rule did not prevent it from being accepted as a member in
ASEAN.

The case of Cambodia is interesting in this context since Cambodia's
membership was put on hold owing to the internal political problems

in the country, that is, the militarized fighting in July 1997 which led to the ouster of the then First Prime Minister Prince Norodom Ranariddh by Second Prime Minister Hun Sen. Cambodia was admitted following general elections in 1998 which resulted in a new coalition government with Hun Sen as sole Prime Minister. ASEAN did not oppose Hun Sen assuming that ministerial post. Instead it was the context and also timing of the takeover in 1997 just ahead of the formal admission of Cambodia into ASEAN that influenced ASEAN's decisions. In the case of the other three new members, no dramatic political changes occurred in the run-up to admission. The ASEAN stand did relate to the internal developments in Cambodia and this at a time when Cambodia had acceded to the Bali Treaty. The ASEAN policy also has to be understood in the context of the ASEAN policies on Cambodia during the Cambodian conflict 1979–91 (Saravanamuttu 1996). This created a precedent of ASEAN 'involvement' which did not exist in relation to any of the other South-east Asian countries.[15]

The security factor

The security factor should be seen as an ambition to create a more stable regional environment for the individual countries to concentrate on development efforts as well as enhancing the possibility of inter-state cooperation by creating better relations between the various countries. Seen from this perspective there are at least two dimensions of security: one relating to the internal development in the various countries and assuring that other countries in the region do not under-mine efforts aiming at enhancing internal security and stability, and the other at the interstate level aiming at bringing about a more secure regional environment through the establishment of better relations among states and through the management of potential disputes between neighbouring countries.

The threat perceptions and animosity that existed in the region between ASEAN and the Indo-Chinese countries during the Cambodian conflict in particular up to the mid-1980s are relevant when discussing security. There was also tension and confrontation in bilateral relations between Thailand and each of the Indo-Chinese countries mainly due to the conflict in Cambodia and the Vietnamese military presence there for a decade up to 1989, as well as the disputes between Thailand and Laos over border issues and the cross-border activities of Laotian refugees based in Thailand. Rapprochement, nor-malization of relations, expanding cooperation and the integration of the Indo-Chinese countries in the ASEAN framework for managing interstate relations within South-east Asia have all been initiatives which have been motivated by a desire to secure a more stable security environment within the region. This meant establishing regional order based on shared perceptions about the necessity for enhanced regional cooperation and respect for agreed rules and norms for interstate behaviour.

One specific security concern relates to China's military links with Myanmar and how this has been perceived by a number of ASEAN members. The speed with which Myanmar was integrated into the ASEAN framework for regional cooperation can partly be attributed to the aim of achieving the goal of ASEAN-ten by the thirtieth anniversary of the Association in 1997. However, the security dimension with the ambition of balancing China's influence in Myanmar with an integration of Myanmar into ASEAN and into the ASEAN framework for regional cooperation certainly contributed to the swiftness of the process (Ajibewa 1998; Malik 1997).

As noted earlier, admitting Myanmar as a member was part of a policy of 'constructive engagement' rather than a direct security concern about that country from ASEAN as a whole. However, in the case of Thailand, with disputed borders, large-scale refugee problems and spillover of fighting from Myanmar into the country, there were security concerns before admission and also in the period following admission (Amer 2001/02; Amer 2000; Ganesan 1999).

The relative importance of the three factors

The political factor seems to have been crucial in creating the necessary basic conditions for an expansion of membership in ASEAN the first place, that is, the ASEAN-six had from the outset formulated the vision and goal of 'One South-east Asia' with all ten South-east Asian countries as members of the Association. As noted earlier this was a necessary condition for an expansion to take place at all. There was also a political interest among the other four South-east Asian countries to improve relations with the ASEAN countries and to gradually integrate into the regional framework for regional cooperation.

The security factor is relevant given the history of internal conflicts as well as interstate conflicts in the region. Expanding the acceptance of the Bali Treaty as a code of conduct for interstate relations and expanding ASEAN membership within the South-east Asian region are processes aiming at enhancing the overall security in the region by promoting regional cooperation.

The economic factor does not seem to be such a crucial factor in explaining the urge to expand ASEAN membership within South-east Asia as seen from the ASEAN-six perspective but is of considerable importance for Cambodia, Laos, Myanmar and Vietnam, as other ASEAN members are major foreign investors and trading partners of the four countries. It has to be pointed out that the assessment of the economic factor is not influenced by the impact of the AFC. The relative relevance and explanatory value of the economic factor is assessed on the basis of the situation and conditions prevailing during the period leading up to the expansion of membership in ASEAN.

Conflict management in an expanded ASEAN[16]

If the achievement in conflict management among the ASEAN states is examined from the perspective of the prevention of military conflicts, the track record of ASEAN is impressive since no dispute has led to a militarized interstate conflict between the original member states since 1967. In fact, earlier research suggests a high degree of success in managing conflicts between the original member states of ASEAN.[17] However, this does not imply that all the disputes have been resolved or that disputes in general do not occur. Some disputes have been resolved while others remain unresolved. The unresolved disputes have been contained and defused through various conflict management mechanisms.

On a less positive note, in the midst of the AFC, disputes among some of the ASEAN members re-emerged (Ganesan 1999). One example is the increased tension between Malaysia and Singapore in 1998 which centred over three main issues – namely, water, Malaysian workers' savings, and railway land – most of which have been in evidence for years without causing such a level of tension (Ganesan 1998). It seems likely that this heightened tension had its roots in national mobilization in the face of the economic crisis on both sides rather than the issues as such. Although relations have stabilized, the disputed issues are high on the agenda between the two countries and are often highlighted on both sides of the causeway (Nathan 2002).

The expansion of ASEAN membership in the 1990s brought additional disputes into the Association, thus further complicating the task of managing them. Among the disputes involving the new member-states, some have been settled while others remain unsettled. The level of tension relating to the unsettled border disputes varies considerably.

In terms of conflict management strategy the member states of ASEAN have displayed a preference for bilateral talks and dialogue on the disputes with other members of the Association.[18] However, in recent years Indonesia and Malaysia have agreed to refer the sovereignty disputes over Pulau Sipadan and Pulau Ligitan to the International Court of Justice (ICJ) and Malaysia and Singapore have done likewise with regard to the sovereignty dispute over Pedra Branca/Pulau Batu Puteh (Amer 1998; Amer, 2000; Amer 2001/02). This displays a willingness among some ASEAN members to seek international arbitration when bilateral efforts to resolve disputes are not sufficient to bring about solutions.

The bilateral efforts to manage and settle disputes can be facilitated and/or supported by the mechanisms for conflict management created by ASEAN and by enhancing the effectiveness of these mechanisms. This relates to ASEAN's role as facilitator rather then as an active third-party mediator in the disputes. However, it does not preclude the role of ASEAN itself being enhanced as long as it is within the limits set by the ASEAN framework for conflict management.

In this context it is important to assess the possible role that the ASEAN framework for conflict management can play in the context of the disputes among the member states of the Association. The question is how to make the framework even more suited to meet the challenge of existing and future disputes. The first step in such a process would be to establish the High Council. This has proven to be a difficult task as it took 25 years after the adoption of the Bali Treaty before ASEAN adopted the 'Rules of Procedure of the High Council of the Treaty of Amity and Cooperation in South-east Asia' on 23 July 2001 (http://www.asesansec.org/3639.htm).

The long period needed in order to reach an agreement on such rules indicates that the informal and formal political cooperation among the ASEAN members could be enhanced in order to remove the lingering feelings of suspicion about the intentions of fellow member states. Another factor that has to be taken into consideration is that a High Council created on the basis of the provisions of the Bali Treaty could have considerable power through decisions it could make relating to disputes. Making the High Council a decision-making body would increase the degree of institutionalization within ASEAN and this would be a step away from the more informal approach preferred within the Association. An additional dimension would be concerns about the possible multilateralization of bilateral disputes.

With reference to the adoption of the rules of procedure for the High Council, it can be said that the agreement on such rules indicate that the ASEAN member states are committed to the establishment of the Council and to strengthening the regional conflict management mechanisms. Furthermore, by agreeing on the rules of procedure the member states display an enhanced level of trust towards each other or at least a diminishing level of mistrust. The adoption indicates that the ASEAN member states have mitigated the earlier fears among some of them with regard to the potentially considerable powers of the High Council, and about the possible negative impact of the multilaterization disputes. The rules of procedure ensure that the Council cannot be used against a member state. This was most probably a necessary condition in order to secure the adoption of the rules.

Through the adoption of these rules of procedure, ASEAN has brought about conducive conditions for the establishment and activation of the High Council – a Council to which the member states could turn for assistance in resolving border disputes if negotiations between the parties to the disputes fail. Whether or not the High Council will be activated and be allowed to assume such a role will depend on the willingness and readiness of the member states of ASEAN to bring disputed issues to such a regional body.

In this context it is necessary to clarify that ASEAN is not intended to formally act as a third-party mediator in the disputes involving its member states unless it is ascribed or asked to do so by the member states. Instead the Association is intended to serve as a vehicle to promote better relations among its member states. This is done by creating conducive conditions for increased interaction through the overall cooperation carried out under the ASEAN umbrella. Another role that ASEAN can play is through the formulation and adoption of mechanisms, which can be utilized by the member states to manage their disputes. ASEAN can also establish principles for how its member states should behave towards each other.

This implies that in order to achieve peace and stability in South-east Asia the member states of ASEAN must act in such a way as to peacefully manage the existing and potential interstate disputes among them. Consequently, failure to do so can be attributed to the member states involved in the disputes and not to the Association as such. Furthermore, ASEAN can urge its member states to seek peaceful solutions to such disputes, but it cannot force them nor directly intervene to try and halt a dispute unless the parties to the dispute ask ASEAN to intervene in such a manner.

Notes

1   In the context of this study the region of South-east Asia is defined in the traditional sense, i.e. as encompassing ten countries: Brunei Darussalam, Cambodia, Indonesia, Laos, Malaysia, Myanmar, the Philippines, Singapore, Thailand, and Vietnam. Following the independence of East Timor, there is the potential to expand this notion of the region of South-east Asia to include eleven countries. However, this is not the case in the context of this study.

2   The basic idea behind constructive engagement is that by engaging a state which is perceived as threatening or aggressive into a framework of dialogue and other confidence building measures (CBMs), it brings about improved relations and thus make the threatening states less inclined to engage in aggressive behaviour. The CBMs can range from diplomatic initiatives and expanded political contacts to upgrading economic cooperation through expanded trade and increased investments.

3   For a discussion of the developments in the 1960s and the factors shaping the creation of ASEAN in 1967 with particular emphasis on the conflict situations, as well as more extensive analysis of key ASEAN declaration and treaties see Amer (1997, 1998).

4   The ASEAN member states had adopted *Kuala Lumpur Declaration* on 27 November 1971 which called for the creation of a ZOPFAN in South-east Asia. The full text of the 'Zone of Peace, Freedom and Neutrality Declaration. Kuala Lumpur Declaration' can be found at http://www.asesansec.org/3629.htm.

5   This can be exemplified by the fact that this interpretation was prevalent in the author's discussions with officials and researchers in Malaysia in August 1998.

6   For an interesting analysis of this expansion process and its initial impact on ASEAN see Chapter Four in Acharya (2001).

7   Brunei Darussalam joined ASEAN as the Association's sixth member on 1 January 1984.

8   For details on the improvement of relations between ASEAN and Vietnam see Amer (1996a). On different aspects of the process leading to resolution of the Cambodian conflict and the role of different actors, see among others Alagappa (1990); Amer, Saravanamuttu and Wallensteen (1996); and Frost (1991).

9   For details on Vietnam–ASEAN relations during the first half of the 1990s see Amer (1996a); Hoang (1994); and Nguyen (1993). For a recent study on this relationship in the post-Cold War era see Nguyen (2002).

10   For different aspects of the growing regionalism and security cooperation in South-east Asia during the 1990s see among others Acharya (1993); Chin (1997); Kurus (1993); Paribatra (1994); and Snitwongse (1995).

11   For the official ASEAN position see Paragraph 15 in *The Joint Communiqué, The Thirtieth ASEAN Ministerial Meeting, Subang Jaya, 24–25 July 1997* (The text of the Communiqué can be found at http://www.asesansec.org/4010.htm.

12   In the Ha Noi Declaration of 1998 adopted on 16 December 1998 in connection with the Sixth ASEAN Summit, it is stated in Paragraph 2 that: 'We

have decided to admit Cambodia as the tenth member of ASEAN and instructed the Foreign Ministers to organize special ceremonies of admission in Hanoi.' The text of the Declaration can be found at http://www.asesansec.org/875.htm.

13 The approach used in this section is derived from the one used in Amer (1999). The analysis has been expanded while statistical details relating to the economic factor have been reduced. For details relating to trade and foreign direct investment see Amer (1999).

14 For a detailed analysis of the implication of the AFC on regional cooperationin South-east Asia see Amer and Hughes (1999). This study examines the impact on the whole region whereas many other studies neglect the impact on the four new ASEAN member states. For example Shaun Narine only devotes half a page to the impact on those four countries compared to the two chapters on the impact and response of the ASEAN-six (Narine 2002).

15 The ASEAN policy towards Cambodia during this period has been analysed by Acharya (2001).

16 This section draws on the approach applied in Amer (2003).

17 For a more detailed argumentation along this line see Amer (1998).

18 This is most clearly displayed in relation to the way in which border disputes among the member states are managed. For studies on this issue see Amer (1998, 2000, 2001/02).

7
Informal Regionalism in the Gulf

Ane Roald Mannsåker

Introduction

Most scholars consider the Iraqi attack on Iran in 1980 as an attempt to gain regional dominance. Stress is put on varying factors to arrive at this conclusion. Three main arguments are advanced: First, many focus on *geopolitics* and the long-standing border disputes (see among others Chubin and Tripp 1988). They point to the disagreement over the Shatt al-'Arab waterway, which was also the official *casus belli*. A second explanation is the many *cultural and ideological controversies* between the two countries: see for instance Marr (1985), Khadduri (1988), Cordesman and Wagner (1990), Helms (1984) and Hiro (1991). And thirdly, on a more specific level, Hiro (1991) and also Heradstveit (1987) propose that it was *fear of the Iranian Islamist revolution* and its effect on the Iraqi Shi'i majority that prompted the decision.

A strong emphasis on the international level alone, often prescribed by realist theories within political science, could lead scholars to dismiss the national scene as insignificant. However, domestic politics in Iraq have been characterized by a multitude of groups actively taking measures on the regional scene as well to strengthen their own leverage vis-à-vis the regime. In this light, it seems peculiar to underline only external factors. Newer regionalism theories open up space for a multitude of informal, regionalizing actors on a sub-state level (see for instance Bøås 2003; Gamble and Payne 1996; Hettne 2003), and could therefore help us understand the role of the political opposition inside Iraq and how they also influenced the regional level.

In contrast, this chapter seeks to take the domestic scene in Iraq explicitly into account. Through a case study of the process leading to the Iran–Iraq war (1980-88) it explores the relationship between the

Iraqi opposition and Saddam Hussein's foreign policies. On a more theoretical level it provides us with an interesting example of how formal and informal regional dynamics may evolve in different directions, through discussion of how the Iraqi regime and the Iraqi opposition developed divergent, inverse relations with Iran. It should be noted, however, that by focusing solely on the internal causes of war, one leaves out many interesting aspects on the international level.

Informal regionalism

Barry Buzan's *People, States and Fear* (1991) constitutes the theoretical starting point for this chapter, providing an approach to how states interact in regions. Central to his work is the concept of 'security complexes'. These are groups of states characterized by an inward orientation because threats are perceived more acutely over short distances. Patterns of amity and enmity constitute durable features of the relationship between the states within such a complex.

Even though minority groups are mentioned, Buzan does not accord them any independent, active role in regional dynamics. Non-state actors can also influence patterns of amity and enmity within a region. In order to account for this, works of authors like Bøås, Marchand and Shaw (2003), Söderbaum (2002), Swyngedouw (1997) and Jessop (2003) are included in my framework. This allows me to acknowledge that the Iraqi opposition, which relies heavily on forming alliances within the region, should also be regarded as a regionalizing actor. Through relations with the neighbouring states an informal regionalism of several scales emerges, which cannot be accounted for through the framework of Buzan alone.

Buzan and the Iraqi state

The state is another important notion in Buzan's work. He presents three aspects of it: the idea of the state, which is the most important aspect, its territorial basis and its institutional basis (Buzan 1991). Any state needs to be defined with regards to these three basic aspects, but different groups within a society could have conflicting views on how this should be done. In the case of Iraq, the Ba'thist regime met fierce opposition from both the Kurdish and the Shi'i opposition regarding all three aspects of the state.

As a socialist party, the Ba'thist regime envisaged a secular ideational basis of the state. It was therefore attacked by the Shi'i opposition who saw it as imperative to build the state on Islamic values. In principle, the regime also talked about the Iraqi state as one where ethnic affiliation should play no major role.[1] This idea clashed with that of the Kurds, who agitated for autonomy based on ethnicity. The Kurdish claims for autonomy also challenged the regime's view on the territorial basis of Iraq. Finally, both the aspirations for an Islamic state nurtured by factions of the Shi'i opposition, and the Kurdish aspirations for autonomy challenged the power and scope of the political and administrative institutions as they were set up by the Ba'thists.

Again, it is difficult to account for the active role of the opposition in challenging the Iraqi state by using more traditional regionalism theories only. The informal regionalism literature allows us to explain how the Iraqi opposition made use of the regional scale to gain leverage and strength in its conflict with the regime.

The Iraqi opposition under Saddam

After the fall of Saddam Hussein's regime it has become evident that the Iraqi political scene is one of numerous factions and convictions. Many of these same groups existed under Ba'thist rule (1968–2003), when they often had clandestine or exile organizations. In political orientation, they varied from the secularly oriented Iraqi communist party, the national liberalist al-Wifaq al-Watani (the National Accord); the Kurdish parties like the KDP (the Kurdish Democratic Party) and the PUK (the Patriotic Union of Kurdistan); and the religiously (Shi'i) oriented ones like Hizb al-Da'wa al-Islamiyya (the Islamic call party) and the SCIRI (The Supreme Council for Islamic Revolution in Iraq).

Among these not all should be expected to have had the same influence on the regional game; those who had the largest potential for this were the Kurdish and the Shi'i parties. In the case of the former, this was because of the latent secessionist threat from Kurdish society combined with the uneven distribution of oil reserves in Iraq. In the latter case, their leverage was a result of the Shi'i majority in the Iraqi population and their relations with the Shi'i population and religious groups of Iran. We will therefore concentrate on the Kurdish and Shi'i parties.

Iraq's relationship with Iran

Before we start analysing the activities of the Iraqi opposition, a brief overview of the relations between Iran and Iraq at a state level are warranted. This provides us with the necessary background to assess and compare the formal interstate processes between Iraq and Iran, and the informal or transnational processes between Iran and the Iraqi opposition.

Patterns of amity

Patterns of amity between Iraq and Iran do not present themselves in obvious ways to the observer. Nevertheless there have been periods of non-conflict when the countries, although not altogether inclined towards one another, have also had a relationship that was not characterized by intense conflict or severe rhetoric.

In some instances there have even been attempts at striking agreements and building alliances, for instance concerning the Shatt al-'Arab (see Map 7.1). This is a waterway where the Persian Gulf eats its way into the land and meets the Tigris and has been a source of conflict between Iran and Iraq for many decades. It is of vital importance to the latter since it is the sole outlet to international waters from the two Iraqi cities Basra and Faw. The only other Iraqi port of impor-

Map 7.1   The Shatt al-'Arab waterway, Warba and Bubiyan

tance, Umm Qasr, is also awkwardly situated in the backwaters of the two Kuwaiti islands of Warba and Bubiyan. In 1937, however, a frontier treaty was signed, establishing the thalweg line (the deepest point) in the Shatt al-'Arab waterway as the dividing line for four miles in the area of the Iranian port of Abadan (Khadduri 1988:40). The same goodwill seems to have played a role when Iraq took the initiative to form first the Saadabad Pact, allying Iran, Iraq, Turkey and Afghanistan, and later, in 1955, the Baghdad Pact, allying Turkey, Iran and Pakistan (Khadduri 1988:39–40).

These pacts never came to have any real bearings on the regional patterns of amity and enmity. Shortly after the coup of 1958, Iraq's new president 'Abd al-Karim Qasim, decided to withdraw from the agreement altogether, and thereafter new disputes on the Shatt al-'Arab waterway erupted (Tripp 2000:140, 163–4).

All in all, one could question the strength of such a pattern of amity between the two. The agreements and treaties seem to have lacked the political power required to produce real changes in regional patterns of amity and enmity. The pattern of amity appears marginal or fragile next to the more established or dominant pattern of enmity, which we will concentrate on in the following section. Yet, the pattern of amity, however weak it may seem, might offer an explanation as to why war between Iran and Iraq did not break out before 1980.

Patterns of enmity

The relationship between the rulers of former Mesopotamia and Persia was a troubled one for centuries. Underlying factors, like ethnic and sectarian divisions, were part of the controversies. They had their roots in the sixteenth century, when the Persian Empire re-emerged and sought to expand its authority to the areas where the Shi'i shrines were, that is, in modern Iraq (Khadduri 1988). The main bone of contention, however, was the border separating the empires where, in particular, the Shatt al-'Arab waterway caused disagreement.

When the borders between the Ottoman Empire and Persia were decided upon, the line was drawn a few kilometres east of the Shatt al-'Arab waterway. Later, it was moved to the eastern riverbank of the Tigris, where it remained until 1969. The Shah then abrogated the old agreements, claiming that the thalweg should be the ruling principle (Farouk-Sluglett and Sluglett 1987; Khadduri 1988; Marr 1985; Tripp 2000).

In 1974 fighting broke out between the Kurdistan Democratic Party (KDP) and the Iraqi army over the implementation of the Manifesto of

11 March 1970, an agreement governing the status of the Kurdish areas. Iran intervened on the side of the Kurds, and this almost led to the outbreak of war between Iran and Iraq. In 1975 an agreement was made in Algiers that secured mutual non-interference in domestic affairs from both Iranian and Iraqi sides, and settled the long-standing dispute over the Shatt al-'Arab waterway (Farouk-Sluglett and Sluglett 1987:131–2, 165–72; Tripp 2000:200–1, 212–13).

Khuzestan is another area that has contributed to the pattern of enmity between the two states. A small area in the west of Iran, it was originally called 'Arabistan', and was a semi-independent state under the Ottomans. The inhabitants were Arabic speakers, but the area was later given to Iran, and the population was slowly rendered Persian. From the late 1930s, several regimes made claims to reintegrate 'Arabistan', as it was systematically called on the Iraqi side of the border, into Iraq.

In the early 1960s, the Iranian government was worried that Iraq would extend the border dispute along the Shatt al-'Arab waterway to include Khuzestan. This prompted the first establishment of relations between Teheran and the KDP. Soon both military equipment and other goods crossed the border into Iraqi Kurdistan, although in relatively modest quantities (Tripp 2000:165).

These issues and events made up the patterns of amity and enmity between Iran and Iraq, constituting the context in which the Iraqi opposition manoeuvred. No actor operates in a void, and the Kurdish and the Shi'i opposition groups skilfully took advantage of the pattern governing the relation between Iran and Iraq in order to further their own interests. On the other hand, Iran has also benefited from the Iraqi opposition by developing a relationship with Iraq in ways beneficial to itself.

Activities of the opposition

Having established the context in which the Iraqi opposition operated, I will now turn to an analysis of its activities. In 1968, a *coup d'état* inaugurated the era of the Ba'th Party in power in Iraq. But very soon it met opposition from the Shi'i opposition parties that threatened the ideational and the institutional basis of the state.

The Shi'i opposition is stirred into action

In the first period after the takeover, the president at the time, Ahmad Hassan al-Bakr, made efforts to appear to be a pious man. Nonetheless,

Map 7.2   Khuzestan

the politics of the Ba'th Party was essentially secular, and the Shi'i were grossly underrepresented in the administrative and political institutions. The Shi'i clergy soon began voicing protests against these features of the regime's policies. The Ba'thists reacted by prohibiting religious teaching in schools and expelling people whose ancestors had come from Iran several centuries ago, under the pretext that they were 'Iranian' (Tripp 2000:202–4).

The agitation intensified, and in 1977 various Islamist factions, among them al-Da'wa, turned an annual religious march from Najaf to Karbala into a prolonged political demonstration with 30,000 participants.[2] When the government tried to halt the march, rioting broke out in both cities (Tripp 2000:215–17).

These demonstrations and revolts did not contest the institutional basis of Iraq per se; they did not agitate for the establishment of special Shi'i institutions. Rather, the protests were oriented towards the Sunni community and its monopolization of political institutions. Yet one might claim that they threatened an informal political institution that defined representation in political and administrative offices as preferably or predominantly Sunni Arab.

However, the agitation seems to have been perceived as a threat to the ideational base of the state to the extent that prominent members of al-Da'wa called for the establishment of an Islamic state. An Islamic government would have meant turning the organization of society upside down, and would moreover imply that the whole population was to be subject to Shari'a and the Shi'i interpretation of Muslim practice. This would be far from the secular idea of the Iraqi state as conceived and promoted by the regime. Moreover, demands for such a reorganization of the Iraqi society implied a direct threat to the Iraqi institutions, since the occupation of many offices would then be reserved Shi'i clerics instead of secular-oriented Sunnis, which was the norm in Iraq. The revolts eventually led to the arrest of 2,000 persons, and eight religious leaders were sentenced to death. Shi'i study circles were closed down and a number of *ulama* left the country.

The Iranian revolution

The Iranian revolution and the Shi'i

With the revolution in Iran in 1979, the Iraqi Shi'i intensified and radicalized their struggle.[3] The Iraqi regime feared that the Islamic revolution would spread into southern Iraq by means of the Islamic opposition parties.[4] This was reflected in the fact that the Iranian revolution was barely mentioned in the regime newspaper *al-Thawra*. On 7 and 14 February, for instance, its main headlines were the former president Bakr complaining that 'To give the Nobel Peace Price to Begin and Sadat is an offence to the rights of the world's peoples', and 'Yemen salutes the holy and noble efforts of Syria and Iraq to engage in a union' (author's translation). The events in Iran were summarily presented in a few lines at the bottom of the page.

The idea of the Iraqi state was being challenged in more dramatic ways than before. The regime chose to meet the steadily increasing popular protests with yet another round of mass arrests, executions and the expulsion of Shi'i *ulama* (Tripp 2000:220–1). Several Shi'i groups, among them al-Da'wa, then agreed on the need for militant action against the regime. This had the approval of the Shi'i *ulama*, to which the regime reacted promptly with mass arrests and executions. Membership of al-Da'wa was made illegal with retroactive effect.[5] When the Islamic Task Organization carried out an assassination attempt on Tariq Aziz, the deputy prime minister, the regime answered by executing Ayatollah Muhammad Baqir al-Sadr, one of the leaders of al-Da'wa. This was the first time a senior member of the Shi'i clergy had been executed. There were also mass deportations of Iraqi Shi'a of Iranian descent (Farouk-Sluglett and Sluglett 1987:200; Nakash 1994:137–8; Tripp 2000:228–30).[6]

Compared to earlier protests, radicalization seems to have taken place on two levels. On the one hand, parts of the Shi'i community appeared inspired by the newly established clerical rule in Iran and now claimed the need to establish an Islamic state, thereby threatening the secular state as an idea.[7] Moreover, the notion that violent action was needed suggested that persons holding high positions in state institutions could be threatened, as happened in the assassination attempt on Tariq Aziz. In Iraq, with such a high level of conflict revolving around all three aspects of the state, the attempted killing of the deputy prime minister seemed like a serious attack on the whole regime. Judging from the harsh retaliations, it was also perceived that way by the government.[8]

The revolution and the Kurds

There is a discrepancy between my own interviews and the literature regarding the effect of the Iranian revolution on Kurdish activities. Simons (1994:270) claims that the instalment of the new regime in Teheran had no positive effect on the Kurds since the former had 'little interest in minority rights'. By contrast, Fu'ad Mahsoum states that the Iranian revolution marked the beginning of a somewhat closer attachment between Iran and the Kurdish organizations:[9]

Iran under the Shah cooperated with Saddam's regime. After the Iranian revolution we were revitalised, the borders opened, and we went in and out as we pleased. A delegation, among them myself, met with Khomaini in Paris twice and we agreed on some common steps. We profited from the general situation of chaos at the time of the revolution ... The operations were done continuously, especially from the beginning of the Iranian revolution until the beginning of the Iran–Iraq war.

Mahsoum appears to be trustworthy as he actually participated in the negotiations and meetings mentioned above. His claims also seem plausible since Khomaini possibly did not feel obliged to honour international treaties, such as the Algiers Agreement, made by his predecessor. On the other hand, what felt like a revitalization for the members of the PUK may have seemed less substantial when watched from the outside.

Close ties between the Kurdish movement and Iran probably felt less threatening to the Ba'thist regime than that of the Shi'a's, in the sense that the latter constitute a majority in the Iraqi society, and that an Islamic revolution by force would imply an overthrow of the sitting regime. On the other hand, a rapprochement between the Kurds and Iran did have the potential of threatening both the territorial and the ideational basis of Iraq, as it might provide the Kurds with the reinforcements needed to succeed either in their claims for regional autonomy within the Iraqi state, or in their claims to establish an autonomous state of Kurdistan.

The Kurdish fight for rights

The Kurdish fight for rights, however, started long before the Iranian revolution, threatening the ideational, territorial and institutional bases of the Iraqi state.

The Manifesto of 11 March 1970

In 1968 fighting erupted between the newly installed Ba'thist regime and the KDP, the latter receiving military equipment from Iran. The Iraqi regime finally engaged in negotiations with the KDP, realizing it would be practically impossible to control the Iranian-backed Kurdish forces. Another fear was that a prolonged war could lead to a takeover of non-Ba'thists in the army, where the Ba'th Party had yet to consolidate its power base. So in 1970 the Kurds obtained the most far-reaching concessions they had ever been conceded. The Manifesto of 11 March 1970 included recognition of Iraqi Kurdistan as a distinct region, with its own political institutions and wide-ranging cultural rights (Farouk-Sluglett and Sluglett 1987:129–31; Khadduri 1988:53–54; Marr 1985:222–3; Tripp 2000:199–201).

This Manifesto was probably perceived as a threat to the Iraqi state on several levels. First, the ideational base of the Iraqi state as defined by the regime was one where ethnicity should play no role within the state borders. Kurdish demands for recognition of cultural rights were therefore in conspicuous contradiction to the Ba'thist ideal. Secondly, the demand for local, Kurdish institutions constituted a threat to the institutional basis of the Iraqi state since the latter might lose influence, scope and power. Finally, the Manifesto may have been regarded as an initial threat to the territorial basis of the Iraqi state.

When the Manifesto came to be implemented, however, an arabization process was initiated in the areas around Kirkuk, which also happens to be where some of the richest oilfields are located (Farouk-Sluglett and Sluglett 1987:129–32). These subversive actions might be an indication that the government perceived the Manifesto as a threat to the Iraqi state, but they also led Barzani, the leader of the KDP, to mobilize for war again in 1971. It received assistance from Iran and from the US as allies of the Shah, support that encouraged the KDP to oppose Baghdad's efforts to introduce Kurdish autonomy on their own terms (Marr 1985:235; Simons 1994:268–9; Tripp 2000:211–12).

Al-Da'wa and Iran: close links?

In 1964 Khomaini fled to the city of Najaf, where he stayed until 1978. The leading Iraqi Shi'i clerics – al-Sadr and al-Kho'I – were already based there and the thinking was close to that of Khomaini's (Farouk-Sluglett and Sluglett 1987:195–6; Tripp 2000:204, 220).

Whereas one of my interviewees[10] claims that personal bonds were established, Farouk-Sluglett and Sluglett (1987:196) are of the opinion that the contact between Khomaini and these Iraqi clerics was fairly limited. Both could be right. The contact may have been limited, but nonetheless sufficient to establish personal relations, reinforced by the likeness of their thinking (Farouk-Sluglett and Sluglett 1987:196).

Ibrahim al-Ja'fari of al-Da'wa, however, downplayed their links to Iran, stating that they were not as close as those to, for instance, the SCIRI.[11] This might be correct even though one should also be aware of the context in which the statement was made. In August 2002, the Iraqi opposition was preparing itself for the possibilities of the United States going to war against Saddam. Although wary of American interference, al-Da'wa might have wanted to downsize its ties with Iran in

an attempt to further their chances to participate in a US-led reconstruction of the country.

The actual strength of the ties, however, is not so important. What
matters is the Iraqi regime's understanding of the situation. If it interpreted the events as an expression of close rapport between the Iraqi
Islamist opposition and the Iranian regime, this would lead to a
strengthening of the pattern of enmity between the two countries,
regardless of the real situation.

The regime's sanctions towards al-Da'wa seem to indicate that the
threat was perceived to be serious. The possibility of Islamist parties
growing stronger unleashed successive waves of repression aimed at
political activists that could be linked to al-Da'wa and others like it.
This is illustrated in a whole range of documents from the Iraqi intelligence which report on persons being arrested, families of the party
members being denied work, or, simply, close monitoring of their
political gatherings.[12]

Khuzestan

The Iranian engagement (real or imagined) in the affairs of both the
Kurdish and the Shi'i opposition reinforced the pattern of bilateral
enmity. The Iraqi regime retaliated by permitting a small group of Arab
separatists from Khuzestan to operate from Iraqi soil in the 1970s.
However, they were less threatening to the Iranian state than the KDP,
with Iranian support, was to the state of Iraq (Tripp 2000:201).

Fierce rhetoric

In February 1980 Saddam Hussein revived the issue of Khuzestan. The
word 'Arabistan' figured frequently in the regime newspaper *al-Thawra*
in the months before the Iran–Iraq war, and the rhetoric was biting.
On 11 October 1979 the main headline announced that 'The Iranian
regime sends its repressive attacks against the Arabs and the Kurds', the
article reporting that 'Among the works of repression and terror that
the government forces pursue against the compatriot Arabs, the radio
of Teheran informed that the government forces arrested 30 Arab com-
patriots in the city of al-Muhammara in Arabistan.'[13]

The repeated appearance of articles reporting from Khuzestan and
the level of animosity expressed through the language could be an
indicator of the salience of the subject for the Ba'thist regime.
Considering the nearly non-existent Iraqi coastline, a possible inclusion of Khuzestan in Iraq would have reduced the country's vulnerabil-

ity regarding access to international waters and increased stability in its oil exports. These prospects probably increased Saddam Hussein's interest in the province.

However, none of my interviewees were willing to portray Khuzestan as an issue of extreme importance as a factor in the upcoming war with Iran: 'They constitute small groups that really have no essential importance at all ... The effect is virtually zero.'[14] Khuzestan is also very seldom mentioned in the literature as an issue that prompted the war.

Nevertheless, the use of language in *al-Thawra* does give us an instrument to gauge the pattern of enmity between Iran and Iraq. The epithets 'repressive', 'terrorist', 'despotic' and 'racist' are repeatedly used to describe the regime of Khomaini in the last six months of 1979 and throughout 1980.[15] This could be a measure of Iraqi animosity towards Iran, hence indicating how relations had severely deteriorated compared to the situation immediately after the ousting of the Shah.

War in Kurdistan

The most important instance of Iranian meddling in the domestic affairs of Iraq came in 1974–75. Through their intervention on the side of the Kurds, the latter were able to pose serious threats to both the ideational and the territorial base of the state.

As already noted, Barzani's rejection of the implementation plan for the Manifesto of 11 March 1970 led to yet another war between the KDP and Baghdad in 1974 (Tripp 2000:211). The Iraqi army succeeded in cutting KDP's supply lines from Iran, and the latter responded by contributing with heavy military equipment (Marr 1985:233; Tripp 2000), and also entering Iraqi soil with two regiments (Simons 1994:269).[16] By March 1975 there were 60,000 casualties on the Iraqi side (Hiro 1991:17). The war had lasted for almost a year when Iraq entered into negotiations with Iran.

The Algiers Agreement

At this stage (mid-1970s) neither Iraq nor Iran wanted open war (Tripp 2000:212), and both wished to see an end to the Kurdish issue: Saddam Hussein in order to secure his political survival, and Iran to prevent the Kurdish revolt spreading to the Iranian parts of Kurdistan (Farouk-Sluglett and Sluglett 1987:170; Marr 1985:233). With the agreement reached in 1975 in Algiers, Iran withdrew its support to the KDP (and all other Iraqi opposition movements) in return for Iraqi recognition of the thalweg as the demarcation line in the Shatt al-'Arab waterway (Simons 1994:269, Tripp 2000:212).[17]

The Kurdish resistance soon withered. About 70 per cent of the Peshmergas, the Kurdish militias, turned themselves in to the government forces (Marr 1985:234), and many others fled the country (Simons 1994:270). The agreement was perceived as a betrayal by the KDP. As Mahmoud Uthman put it:

> The Iranians weren't really interested in helping the Kurds, they were only helping their own interests, so they eventually went and made this agreement (i.e. the Algiers Agreement). So there were setbacks for the Kurdish movement from two sides, both from the Iranians and from the regime.[18]

Who was jumping which scale?

What was new in 1974 was the degree to which a foreign state was drawn into the conflict. The Kurdish decision to make an alliance with Iran could be seen as an attempt to jump scales. They may have realized that they would not be able to obtain their political goals on their own terms while operating on the national scale only. In order to put greater pressure on the Iraqi government, they moved the issue one level up: to the regional scale.

However, one might also put it the other way round. Maybe it was Iran that decided to move down to the local Iraqi level in order to obtain the recognition of the thalweg and to prevent a further escalation of the conflict. Instead of aiding the Kurds to obtain a wider range of rights, Iranian involvement led to a bargain, which the two states used to settle old scores between them.

The opposition and the process leading to war

This overview of the activities of the Iraqi opposition provides us with the background to assess their influence on the process leading to the Iran–Iraq war. What seems clear from the above analysis is that any role the opposition might have played has been indirect. There was no incident or development neither within the Kurdish nor within the Shi'i movement that in itself could explain the Iraqi decision to go to war with Iran.

If the Iran–Iraq war actually was caused by the controversy over the Shatt al-'Arab waterway, the Kurds apparently played an indirect role. Their own war against the Iraqi army in 1974–75 precipitated the

Algiers Agreement, in which Iraq ceded the exclusive rights to the waterway in return for the non-intervention of Iran in its domestic affairs. When asked, my interviewees gave the territorial dispute as the cause of this war, while downplaying their own role in it. Only after probing would they admit a possible indirect influence through the Algiers Agreement.

However, doubts have been raised as to whether this was the real rationale behind the invasion. As Farouk-Sluglett and Sluglett (1987:256) note, the division of the waterway along the thalweg line was already established, apparently providing enough room for both states to navigate the river. The issue hardly seems important enough to go to war over.

The opposition and regional patterns of amity and enmity

It might be easier to understand how the activities of the opposition influenced regional patterns of amity and enmity. Changes in these would lead to an altered power balance in the region, thus preparing the ground for war.

By finding a common cause in the wish to weaken the Iraqi regime, both the Iraqi opposition and Iran took advantage of the other in order to further their own interests. The Kurds benefited from this mutual exploitation by receiving support in the form of military equipment and other goods. Iran benefited from the subversive activities of the Kurds to soften the Ba'thist regime and thereafter force through their interests in negotiations.

The reciprocity of the relationship is also evident in the case of the Iraqi Shi'i. After the revolution, Iran benefited from its contacts with the Shi'i in Iraq by inspiring them to oppose the regime. Some of the Shi'i political groups in Iraq received support from the Iranian state through their ties with high-ranking Iranian clerics. These ties were to grow stronger in the years to come, and were not yet fully developed in the 1970s.

The relation between Iran and the Iraqi opposition represented an inverse version of the pattern of amity and enmity at the state level. Where the bilateral interstate pattern between Iran and Iraq was one of enmity and distrust, the pattern between Iran and the Iraqi opposition was characterized by amity and cooperation, although the Algiers Agreement shows that the Iranian commitment was guided by pragmatism.

This mutually beneficial relationship strengthened the pattern of enmity in the region. Iran and Iraq had tried to improve their relations in the past, but these efforts seemed weak when compared to later developments. At the same time as Iran had supported Iraqi groups, Iraq had also made use of the same tactics against Iran. This led to a serious deterioration in the bilateral relationship.

Looking at the years from 1968 to 1980 as a whole, Iraq was exposed to more serious threats from Iran than vice versa. The latter supported several of the chief opposition groups in the former, and through them threatened the Iraqi state in its ideational, territorial and institutional bases. Iraq in turn also supported the Iranian opposition, but the groups it assisted were less significant in Iran. Such support was on a smaller scale than in the military operations, carried out by the Iranian army on Iraqi territory.

By the end of the 1970s, the power balance between the two states had changed, with the Iraqi opposition being the actor that influenced this situation. From 1974–75 with the Algiers Agreement and the war that preceded it, Iraq was weakened in its bilateral relationship with Iran. Iraq's inferior position was confirmed through Iran's demonstration of strength. Teheran had won on the issue of the Shatt al-'Arab waterway, and had settled its other border disputes with Iraq. The latter was thus the party that had most reason to feel dissatisfied with the status quo.

With the Islamic revolution causing general havoc in Iran, Saddam Hussein may have seen a possibility to regain some of his former power. He had managed to get a somewhat firmer grip on the domestic opposition. The regime of the Shah on its side had fallen and the new regime still seemed unconsolidated and fragile. However, the prolonged bilateral war that followed is an indication that the power balance had not changed much since the revolution.

It is in this respect that one can claim that the Iraqi opposition influenced the decision to invade Iran in 1980. There was no single incident or opposition group that precipitated the regime's resolution. Yet, their activities as a whole over several years contributed to a strengthening of the pattern of enmity between Iran and Iraq, and an altered power balance.

Where the Buzanian road meets its end

The analysis in this chapter has to a large extent built on the work of Buzan (1991) in terms of the main analytical categories. However, it seems clear that many aspects of what has been described cannot be catered for by his framework. The supplement of newer theories on regionalism can help us understand the processes that took place between the opposition and Iran.

Formal versus informal processes

One of the main problems or limitations concerning Buzan's framework is his sole focus on the formal processes of regional security. This means that there is room only for initiatives made by states. Hence, actions of other actors, both at the sub-state level like the Iraqi opposition, and on a supra-state level, are excluded from analysis.

Among those who have looked into regionalization processes while including a broader range of processes and actors are Bøås, Marchand and Shaw (2003). They seek to focus on the previously neglected issue of 'regional interactions which mostly emanate from non-state actors and which are not covered by any formal agreement' (Ibid:198). One of their main arguments is that such informal processes are important because they do not necessarily follow the same directions as the formal ones at the state level.

This perspective harmonizes well with my analysis of the years preceding the Iraqi invasion of Iran. One cannot deny that state-to-state relations have had an important part in forming relationships within the security complex. However, what escapes attention when looking through the lens of Buzan's framework alone is the independent agency of the Iraqi opposition.

Yet, Buzan does make reference to minority groups in his work by stating that one state 'taking interest' in another state's minority groups would influence the regional patterns of amity and enmity (Buzan 1991:189–90). Could the Iranian government be taking advantage of the Iraqi Kurds for their own ends be understood as an example of this? Or does Buzan instead make reference to situations where a state wishes to incorporate a group that is perceived ethnically to belong on its side of the border? The distinction between an earnest wish to bring all members of a group within the borders of one state and more complicated politics is not evident. In most cases other considerations like control over natural resources, political power or wealth will be part of the picture, as it is in the case of the Iraqi Kurds or the Arabs of Khuzestan. The Iranian government surely did not involve itself with the Iraqi opposition because it was endeavouring to improve the conditions of the Kurds as a people; its repression of the Kurds within its own borders confirms this.

What is unaccounted for in the Buzanian framework, however, is the active role the Iraqi Kurds and Shi'i themselves assumed in order to increase their leverage on the Iraqi regime. This was done by consciously seeking to strike alliances where regional patterns were dominated by enmity, jumping scales from the local to the regional in order to further their own goals. This is seen most clearly in the rapprochements between various groups in the Iraqi opposition and Iran. The fact that such alliances were made despite changing regimes in Teheran bears witness to this being not just the result of matching ideological sympathies, but rather of pragmatism inspired by a common adversary.

Informal or semi-formal relations?

The bonds established between Iran and the Iraqi opposition groups cannot thus be accounted for in the strictly state-centric framework offered by Buzan. Rather, they can be viewed as an example of the informal regionalisms that are formed outside the scope of the state. This is what Bøås, Marchand and Shaw (2003:198) refer to as interactions 'which mostly emanate from non-state actors and which are not covered by any formal agreement'.

For instance, the relationship between al-Da'wa and Khomaini seems to have been one where the Iraqi opposition was influenced by the latter, and where they sympathized with many of his views on the relationship between religion and politics. Even though closer relations were later formed between the SCIRI and the Iranian regime, the initial phase seems to have been characterized more by informal contact and much less by signed agreements on paper.

Yet, one should perhaps discuss whether one should qualify all relations between the Iraqi opposition and states in the region as informal ones. Clearly at least one of the parties would be a non-state actor at least nominally. However, when the Kurdish parties sent a delegation to negotiate with Khomaini in the mid-1980s, one could maybe argue that it was an example of a semi-formal relationship rather than a purely informal one. The political leadership of the Kurds negotiated with the political leadership of Iran, and the agreement was subsequently duly agreed.

Inverse regionalisms

A central contention in reflectivist approaches to regionalism is that informal structures often will differ from formal ones. This seems to apply also to the Iraqi opposition and its initiatives within the regional security complex. As a corollary to their fierce conflict with the Iraqi regime, they have displayed inverse patterns of amity and enmity compared to those of the state. In the case of Iran, where the pattern has been dominated by enmity for several decades, the Iraqi opposition secured good relations with several Iranian regimes in its efforts to revolt against the regimes of Saddam Hussein and his predecessors. Where Iraq had good relations, as they were for a long time with Kuwait, the relations of the opposition have ranged from enmity to indifference (Roald 2004). As soon as the Iraqi–Kuwaiti relationship developed in a more antagonist direction, as it did in the period after 1990, the Iraqi opposition initiated cooperation on both formal and informal levels.

Conclusion

The case of the Iraqi opposition and the role it played in the process leading to the Iraqi invasion of Iran in 1980 provides us with an example of how regional dynamics may develop in different, even divergent directions at the formal and informal levels. The various parties in the Iraqi opposition were informal sub-state actors operating on the regional scene. Through their work, actively seeking alliances on the regional level in order to increase their own leverage, they affected the regional dynamics between states.

When looking at the 1970s and 1980s we see that the tension between the Iraqi regime and the Iraqi opposition has resulted in their having inverse relations with Iran. The relationship between the opposition and Iran cannot be analysed or explained by relying only on realist approaches to regionalism, of which Buzan may be said to be a representative. Since the Iraqi opposition actually did have an indirect influence on regional dynamics, confining oneself to an analysis of only state-level interactions means that one misses out on important, sometimes crucial, aspects of the processes at hand.

Although much has been written on integration in the Middle East, most contributions have centred around pan-Arabism and state-led projects, or attempts at economic integration (see, for instance, Hudson 1999). Much less has been produced with a specific focus on informal processes and the workings of actors in the region other than the states themselves. It is therefore both useful and necessary to add more reflectivist theoretical approaches that can take such non-state, more informal, actors and relationships into account.

Notes

1 The Ba'th Party has been very ambiguous on this point. For a thorough introduction to the Iraqi Ba'th Party and its ideology, see for instance Batatu (1978) or al-Khalil (1989).
2 Interview with Hussein Sha'ban in his home in London 24.08.2002.
3 Interview with Hussein Sha'ban in his home in London 24.08.2002.
4 Interviews with: Ibrahim al-Ja'fari in the offices of al-Da'wa in London 29.08.2002, Wafiq al-Samarra'i in his home in London 30.08.2002, Hussein Sha'ban in his home in London 24.08.2002 and Fu'ad Mahsoum in London 30.08.2002.
5 Interview with Ibrahim al-Ja'fari in the offices of al-Da'wa in London 29.08.2003.
6 [IRDP-NIDS-713192] in BOX0011, [IRDP-NIDS-713267] in BOX0011 (the Iraq Research and Documentation Project – IRDP – is a database of Iraqi intelligence documents captured during the Gulf War in 1991, located at Harvard University).
7 Interview with Hussein Sha'ban in his home in London 24.08.2002; see also [IRDP-NIDS-886843] in BOX0061, a complete presentation of the ideology of al-Da'wa which states that 'The establishment of an Islamic state in one or more of the Muslim countries' (my translation) is among their goals.
8 See for instance [IRDP-NIDS-713210] in BOX0011, which is a handwritten decree signed by Saddam Hussein ordering al-Da'wa members and persons associated with them to be regarded as traitors and punished accordingly.
9 Interview with Fu'ad Mahsoum in London 30.08.2002; see also [IRDP-NIDS-826740] in BOX0045 for instance, which discusses Iranian support of the KDP.
10 Interview with Hussein Sha'ban in his home in London 24.08.2002.
11 Interview with Ibrahim al-Ja'fari in the offices of al-Da'wa in London 29.08.2002.
12 See for instance [IRDP-NIDS-713210] in BOX0011, [IRDP-NIDS-321561] in BOX2171, [IRDP-NIDS-321562] in BOX2171, and [IRDP-NIDS-330953] in BOX2177.
13 *Al-Thawra* Thursday 11 October 1979, front page, author's translation.
14 Interview with Wafiq al-Samarra'i in his home in London 30.08.2002.
15 See for instance *al-Thawra* 5 July 1979, 11 July 1979, 20 August 1979, 11 October 1979, 2 December 1979, 4 January 1980, 25 January 1980, 4 May 1980, 8 May 1980, 21 May 1980, 1 September 1980, 2 and 15 September 1980.
16 Interviews with Fu'ad Mahsoum in London 30.08.2002 and Mahmoud Uthman in his home in London 28.08.2002.
17 Interview with Hussein Sha'ban in his home in London 24.08.2002.

18 Interviews with Mahmoud Uthman in his home in London 28.08.2002 and Hussein Sha'ban in his home in London 24.08.2002.

8
Discordant Discourses: South(ern) African Narratives on Zimbabwe's Crisis

Sandra J. MacLean

The current crisis in Zimbabwe has important implications for neighbouring countries and for the Southern African region as a whole. This chapter questions why, then, have regional leaders and especially South African President, Thabo Mbeki, been reluctant to condemn the Mugabe regime for its human rights abuses or to exert pressure more forcefully for resolution of the situation. I argue that African leaders – Mbeki in particular – are entangled discursively in portraying to different audiences competing options of African development. The tacit (and occasionally overt) support for the Mugabe regime by Mbeki and other African leaders is consistent with their periodic use of contentious identity markers such as colonialism, race, land and pan-Africanism as strategies to foster support domestically, especially in rural communities. Such discourses do not cohere well, however, with the language of African renewal, 'renaissance' and modernization within the embrace of global neo-liberalism – imagery that invariably is invoked by the same leaders when addressing external donor and business communities (Barrell 2000).

The chapter draws on the 'new regionalisms' literature to demonstrate how various representations of Africa and of South(ern) Africa converge and compete as the ideas and forces that propel political action on Zimbabwe by different sets of actors. Given that it is concerned with 'the multitude of strategies and ideas about a particular region, which merge, mingle and clash' (Söderbaum 2002:4), the new regionalism approach (NRA) helps to expose various discursive disjunctures – state/civil society, elite/poor, black/white and North/South – that both impede progress on the resolution of the Zimbabwean crisis and encumber development in the region. The first section traces the regional dynamics that shaped the development and recent decline of

Zimbabwe. The second explores the implications of the crisis for the region and the responses of regional actors, particularly President Mbeki. The final section attempts to draw conclusions regarding the regional dynamics involved in eventual prospects for peace and prosperity in Zimbabwe.

Regional dimensions of Zimbabwe's political economy

The Southern African region has played an important role in the development of Zimbabwe (previously Rhodesia), but throughout history the use and enjoyment of the regional space has varied significantly for different groups of Rhodesians/Zimbabweans: colonisers compared with colonised, black compared with white, female with male, and the majority Shona with the minority Ndebele ethnic group. Each of these groups has interacted within, and identified with, the region in different ways. As a result, the defining features of politics, economics and social life in the region have been taken up and reproduced in strikingly different narratives. An analysis of Zimbabwe shows that the divergence among narratives has increased since independence in 1980. Whereas a discursive consensus on race, land, sovereignty, and development appeared to be emerging in the nation-building period of the early 1980s, these issues became increasingly contentious after economic decline began later in the decade. At least some of the fractiousness was fueled by Robert Mugabe, leader of the ruling Zimbabwea African National Union-Patriotic Front Party (ZANU-PF); he has frequently evoked anti-colonial, anti-white imagery, especially during elections, as a tactic for regime maintenance. Yet, the fact that his popularity, especially in the rural areas, remained intact until recently suggests that his invective resonated with many Zimbabweans.

Blaming colonialist actors and structures for conditions of inequality and deprivation serves to deflect attention from the government's inability or unwillingness to redistribute assets (Mbiba 2001). Therefore, other government leaders often use it, not unlike Mugabe has done, to score political points, especially with poor constituents. However, alternative narratives that support neo-liberalism and global partnership have become increasingly powerful within the business communities of the region, and they underscore current relations between Southern African government leaders and the external donor and business communities. As a result, regional leaders, Mbeki in particular, walk a precarious line in balancing these incompatible discourses, a situation that has been highlighted by the crisis in Zimbabwe.

Zimbabwe in the region

Pre-independence

Zimbabwe's political economy has been integrated with the greater region at least since the early nineteenth century when the Shona people who occupied the territory of present-day Zimbabwe were joined by the Ndebele who were fleeing from the Zulu war in the south of the continent. Meanwhile, the Afrikaners, Dutch settlers who had arrived in the Cape area of South Africa in the 1600s, were being pushed into the territory by a wave of more recently arrived British settlers. The discovery of gold in the Transvaal in the 1800s brought the British inland also, and unleashed a fierce competition among the British, Afrikaners, Germans and Portuguese for control over Africa's vast mineral reserves.

The British assumed control in the area that is now Zimbabwe, largely through the efforts of the mining entrepreneur, Cecil Rhodes, who 'organized a "pioneer column" of European colonists to settle what is now Zimbabwe', then set up the British South Africa Company (BSAC), for which he received a Royal Charter to administer the region of Southern Rhodesia (present day Zimbabwe) (Carmody 2001:74). A period of 'state-building' followed throughout the region as the territory was carved up among the various European powers. It was during this period that the modern geophysical identity of the region was constructed (Söderbaum 2002:62):

> The minerals offered enormous opportunities and the colonialists tried to create the conditions for mineral exploration. This necessitated and gradually led to the formation of a truly regional space. The BSAC territories, the Protectorates as well as Mozambique quickly became part of an integrated regional system, which centred on the mines in South Africa and to a lesser extent in Southern and Northern Rhodesia.

This was largely an imposed regional identity, constructed by external agents. Nevertheless, the indigenous people were drawn into this 'imagined' community, especially as migrant labourers moved throughout the region in search of work in mines or on plantations. The workers' experience of the region was much different from that of their colonial overseers', however, and hence alternative discourses of regional development began to form. While the colonialist discourse of Southern Africa was of profit, wealth and rapid development, the workers' discourse centreed on the misery of human exploitation (Davidson 1994:17).

The dual nature of the development discourse was amplified by the establishment of a 'settler colony' in Southern Rhodesia and the enactment of various laws to secure the superior position of the white settlers. One of the more important pieces of legislation was the Land Apportionment Act of 1930, which divided the land for settlement by race, with the minority Europeans receiving most of the best arable land (Carmody 2001:75). Although this system of land tenure resulted in a profitable agricultural sector, it was extremely inequitable and it spawned considerable resentment among the black population – to the extent that, by the 1960s, Britain was prepared to introduce majority rule. The white settlers' response, however, was to elect in 1962 the reactionary Rhodesian Front (RF) Party, headed by Ian Smith. Three years after being elected, Smith issued a unilateral declaration of independence (UDI) from Britain, a gesture that was quickly countered by the imposition of United Nations sanctions on Rhodesia. The trade sanctions forced a new level of regional cooperation and, at least in the early years, the changes – especially import-substitution industrialization (ISI) and closer relations with South Africa – boosted the Rhodesian economy (Carmody 2001:76). However, the strengthening economy did little to reduce the growing militancy in the black population, and violence provoked by the severe inequality of the colonial structure escalated into a liberation war that lasted for seven years.

During the war, the quality of regionness and the sense of regional identity were further strengthened by the links that were developed between various actors in neighbouring states and the two ethnically divided, black movements (the Shona-based Zimbabwe African National Union and the Ndebele's Zimbabwe African People's Union). For example, the ZAPU guerrilla movement used Zambia as its base of operations, while Mugabe, as leader of the ZANU movement, received support and shelter in exile from President Samora Machel of Mozambique (Chan 2003:5). By the end of the 1970s, therefore, when the Rhodesian war was coming to an end, regional dynamics – by this time, rather fraught and certainly complex – were an important ingredient in the conditions that brought British colonialism to an end in Rhodesia and paved the way for the independence of Zimbabwe. Indeed, it was leaders from the region – the internationally respected statesman and first President of Tanzania, Julius Nyerere, along with Zambian President Kenneth Kaunda, and Mozambique's President, Machel – who were instrumental in getting Mugabe and the ZAPU leader, Joshua Nkomo, to the negotiating table, despite the 'bad blood' which existed between the two (ibid.:11). These negotiations, presided over by Britain's Lord Carrington, culminated in the 1979 Lancaster House Agreements that ended the war, set the stage for multi-party elections and majority rule the following year, and set conditions for resettlement of peasants on white-owned farmlands.

Post-independence

Robert Mugabe and the ZANU Party won the elections and gained immediate support at home and abroad with calls for reconciliation, especially between the races, and a policy of Growth and Redistribution that soon resulted in significantly improved social conditions. However, after a brief positive surge in the economy, decline set in and debt began to grow.

Also, old tensions between the Shona/ZANU and Ndebele/ZAPU forces were reignited in Matabeleland in the early 1980s. The violence in Matabeleland stemmed from long-standing ethnic rivalries, fueled by 'a growing perception in Matabeleland that the government was not responsive to the region's needs' (Alexander 1991:584), but an important subtext was land redistribution. Throughout the country, peasants were reacting to the government's lack of action on resettlement promises by squatting and 'poachgrazing'. In most areas, the government responded by arresting squatters and bulldozing dwellings, but according to Chitoyo (2000:12):

> in Matebeleland, this exercise was carried out with an exceptional degree of violence. Crops were burnt; villagers were openly murdered or simply disappeared. Atrocities were performed by the Fifth Brigade in the 'dissident' war that took place between 1981 and 1987 ... The genuine land grievance of Matabeleland peasants were subsumed by a wider and brutal struggle against a local insurgency of ex-ZIPRA [the ZAPU army] combatants.

In retrospect, there have been analyses suggesting that the government's vicious response to the Matabeleland uprisings was a harbinger of the ruthlessness that the Mugabe government was shown to be capable of a decade and a half later. However, it is interesting that, at the time, the brutality did not engender much outrage outside of Zimbabwe, and the Mugabe government continued to operate without sanction or censure from the international community.

To some extent, attention was diverted from Zimbabwe to South Africa, where new regional political tensions were emerging around the cracks appearing in the apartheid system. South Africa's ruling National Party was alarmed by the loss of its white 'buffer zone' to the north, as black governments that were either socialist or sympathetic to Marxism assumed power in Angola and Mozambique in the 1970s and Zimbabwe in 1980 (Jenkins 2002:19). The National Party's response was an attempt to destabilize the neighbouring states. 'Total Strategy', as the policy was named, created havoc throughout the entire region, but the landlocked state of Zimbabwe was particularly affected by South African bombing of the Beira Corridor through Mozambique that was Zimbabwe's main trade route to the coast. Zimbabwe deployed troops to the area in attempts to open the corridor and also to resist the South African backed rebel RENAMO forces that had engaged the government of Mozambique in civil war (Chan 2003:35). This was yet another step in strengthening the sense of region (albeit through contestation over the preferred developmental trajectory) and increasing institutionalization of regional identity, followed with the organization of the group of anti-apartheid states surrounding South Africa – the 'Front-Line States' – and the creation of the Western-backed Southern African Development Coordination Conference (SADCC) to foster trade among themselves, thereby decreasing the dependency on South Africa, the Preferential Trade Area for Eastern and Southern African States (PTA) and the continental-wide Organization of African Unity (OAU) (ibid.).

Post-apartheid

If the apartheid years contributed significantly to the quality of regionness, the dismantling of the apartheid regime in the early 1990s established a common developmental project for the region. However, the post-apartheid years have brought another set of troubles, and Zimbabwe has been one of the most negatively affected countries in Southern Africa. One immediate problem for Zimbabwe was its trade relation with the 'new' South Africa. Soon after the African National Congress (ANC) government was installed in 1994, South Africa became a member of SADC (the Southern African Development Community, which replaced SADCC), and agreements were made with other countries in the region to renegotiate the Southern African Customs Union (SACU). South Africa's entry into the regional trading community was met, for the most part, with guarded optimism by the other members; there was speculation that the hegemon could be an engine of growth for the entire region, but also the worry that it might engulf its weaker neighbours. A briefing paper produced in 1997 by Rob Davies, a leading South African economist, suggested that the more negative projections were proving to be the more accurate: although there had been a marked increase in trade within the region, South Africa's ratio of exports to imports had increased from 5:1 in 1993 to nearly 7:1 in 1996 and, overall, there had been a significant widening of the imbalance in visible trade.

In Zimbabwe's case, the most severe blow came in the early 1990s when South Africa imposed punitive duties on its textile, clothing and footwear imports after a bilateral trade agreement that had existed between the two countries ended.[1] Although the industry was initially able to weather this shock, it could not withstand the pressures of trade liberalization in the 1990s (Carmody 2001:109). Furthermore, the collapse of this industry was part of a broader pattern of deindustrialization and decline. There is a continuing debate about the reasons for the dramatic downturn in the Zimbabwean economy in the 1990s; some emphasize the salience of national policy choice (Jenkins 2002), while others hold structural adjustment primarily responsible for the country's economic collapse (Carmody 2001). More likely, the decline was due to a combination of factors – regional as well as international and domestic. In particular, there were significant new pressures to the economy in the region from the opening up of South Africa; for instance, as well as the new tariffs, there was an almost immediate increase in the inflow of informal/illegal goods when apartheid ended as well as a loss of professionals and trained workers to the larger and richer market. At the same time, however, even the World Bank acknowledged that their imposed policies of trade liberalization would likely produce 'significant deindustrialization' in fragile African economies (Biggs et al. quoted in ibid.: 120). And, certainly, there were serious lapses in government policy. Two of the most significant of these, in terms of the political signals they sent as well as the burden they put on the already battered economy were: first, the decision in 1997 to remit huge reparation payments to veterans of the independence war; and second, the decision in 1998 to send troops to the war in the Democratic Republic of the Congo (DRC) (MacLean 2002).

These two events signalled a major turning point in the evolution of Zimbabwe's policy direction, but also in the constitution of its national identity, both within and outside the country. Until then, Zimbabwe had been viewed as a state in serious decline, but which, for the most part, was still playing by generally accepted rules of legitimacy and accountability, even if not always successfully meeting the highest standards. However, the two extremely costly decisions, taken without public consultation when the country's economy was in extremis, were unmistakable indications that Zimbabwe was slipping into serious crisis (MacLean 2002). Myriad reports out of Zimbabwe over the past two years have been of increasing economic decline, intense civilian suffering, and the Mugabe regime's ever-intensifying oppression and disregard for the law.

South(ern) African responses: discordant discourses

As appalled observers watched, seemingly helplessly, escalating violence and threats of violence tarnished the elections of 2001 (national) and 2002 (presidential). In 2002, external election observers, including the Commonwealth election team, declared that Mugabe had won the presidential election by unfair means (Raftopoulos 2002). The United States, Britain and the EU governments were quick to condemn the illegality of the elections. Soon thereafter the Commonwealth suspended Zimbabwe for one year, and the EU imposed diplomatic sanctions and travel bans on Mugabe, his family and several top-ranking government officials. Other national governments imposed diplomatic sanctions and the government of Britain and the European Council froze assets of Zimbabwean government members (Bank of England 2002).

Meanwhile, however, while the G8 New Partnership of African Development (NEPAD) partners condemned Mugabe, his African neighbours were rallying in his support. Nigerian, South African and Namibian election observers gave their endorsement to the elections and the Organization of African Unity (OAU) team announced that 'in general the elections were transparent, credible, free and fair' (BBC News, 14 March 2002, 'Head to Head ... '). Immediately after the election, 'the presidents of Kenya, Zambia and Tanzania fully backed Mr. Mugabe' (BBC News, 14 March 2002, 'Africa Backs ... '). SADC's Council of Ministers, declared the election 'substantially free and fair' (Ibid.). The only censorial African voice was SADC's Independent Parliamentary Reform that stated that the election 'did not conform with norms and standards' (ibid.).

The African and Western differences that emerged around the 2001/2 elections have persisted. Although few Western powers and organizations have been actively engaged in the Zimbabwean crisis, and some (Belgium and France) have relented on travel sanctions, most have remained publicly critical of the Mugabe regime. Most African leaders, on the other hand, continue either to refrain from criticizing or even actually to support Mugabe and the ZANU-PF leadership (Grubel 2003). These divisions between African leaders and other involved international players came to a head at the end of 2003. After the initial measures in 2002, the Commonwealth had later extended its sanctions until the Heads of State meeting in December 2003.

When the meeting was held, the decision was made to extend the sanctions once again with the stated hope that this measure would encourage dialogue between ZANU-PF and the opposition Movement for Democratic Change (MDC) (Ashby and Esipisu 2003). The six member group that decided on the issue had mixed views – Canada and Australia were in favour of extended sanctions, Jamaica and India were neutral going into deliberations, and South Africa and Mozambique were strongly opposed – and the final decision was extremely contentious. The two African countries represented the prevailing African view, hence the decision severely tested any appearance of unity within the Commonwealth and highlighted the divisions between the Africans and Western members of the organization. Subsequently, when Mugabe responded to the Commonwealth decision by pulling Zimbabwe out of the organization, the rift widened further (White 2003).

For many observers, the stance taken by most African leaders has been puzzling and disappointing. As the situation has steadily and rapidly deteriorated over the past three years, expectations had grown among interested international actors that regional leaders and particularly President Mbeki would lead diplomatic efforts, initially to protest the abuses of the ZANU-PF regime, and later, as that objective proved fruitless, to negotiate Mubage's departure from office. These seemed to be prudent actions given the potential costs of Zimbabwe's problems for South Africa and the Southern African region generally. During the present crisis, the Zimbabwean government has not been 'pulling its weight' in the region; for example, it has not met payments to neighbours for 'items such as port and rail services' (SAMP 7 October 2002).

Also, the economic decline has direct negative implications: 'the government's exchange rate policy has fueled the smuggling of goods' (Ibid.) and the migration of Zimbabweans has created considerable problems for neighboring states, from the logistics of dealing with increased movements of people to the xenophobic responses of the home population to the migrants (SAMP 2, 13 and 18 October 2002).

While some sectors are not necessarily adversely affected by conflict and certain sectors in some neighbouring countries may even benefit from Zimbabwe's conflict, there has been speculation that, overall, the impact on investment in the region is likely to have been negative. At least one observer, for instance, attributed the drop in value of the rand in 2001 to 'negative publicity surrounding events in Zimbabwe' (Schwab 2001:121). The same author argued also that declines in tourism in Botswana, Malawi and South Africa in 2000/2001 were due, at least in part, to the situation in neighbouring Zimbabwe (ibid.: 122). The value of the rand has improved since and tourism, at least in South Africa, rebounded in 2002, but it is difficult to know whether these economic improvements would have been greater or would have happened sooner if Zimbabwe had been stable.

At the very least, the apparent diffidence of Mbeki and other African leaders in the face of the appalling lapses in governance in Zimbabwe threatens the goodwill they so carefully cultivated with external NEPAD 'partners'. Many of the latter see the reaction to the Zimbabwean crisis as a clear indication that the leaders are not seriously committed to the democracy and human rights objectives they outlined in NEPAD and there is concern that their reluctance to deal forcefully with Mugabe puts the fledgling peer review mechanism[2] in serious jeopardy. As Ian Taylor (2003:348) argues:

> Unfortunately, Zimbabwe was in many ways the test case for evaluating the credibility of NEPAD and a clear opportunity for African leaders to signal that they had changed their ways. It is quite clear that this has not happened and that NEPAD's trustworthiness lies in tatters.

The discrepancy between African leaders' reaction to the Zimbabwean crisis and the strategy for development that was outlined in NEPAD is striking. Yet, it should not, perhaps, be surprising as it reflects the dichotomous development discourses that operate in the region generally and especially in South Africa. Mugabe is not the only African leader to use anti-colonial, anti-white rhetoric on selected occasions to gain domestic support and to use a very different text at other times, especially when speaking to white business or external donors. The texts on governance used by many African leaders in describing the Zimbabwean situation are often dramatically different from those that are associated with NEPAD, largely because they are directed at different audiences. As is indicated by one of the main criticisms leveled at it, the NEPAD discourse was not directed at the domestic grassroots, at least not initially, but instead, was intended for external donors. For this purpose, it was introduced using the 'up-beat' language of African renaissance – optimism, renewal and growth to occur through cooperation and partnership with dominant international players and by embracing neo-liberalism. The Zimbabwean crisis, by contrast, is portrayed to concerned actors in the West as an African problem and a 'national' issue to be resolved internally by the 'Zimbabwean people' themselves.

To African audiences, meanwhile, the Zimbabwean crisis is frequently described in terms of African deprivation, racial discrimination and victimization by (neo)colonial oppressors. Dual images of exclusion/independence and inclusion/acquiescence apply thoughout Africa, but they are playing out prominently in the domestic arena in South Africa. David Coetzee (2001), editor of *South Scan* outlines these in relation to the New African Initiative (the prototype for NEPAD):

> the NAI can be seen as a regional development of the ideas inherent in South Africa's own macro-economic GEAR (Growth, Employment and Redistribution) plan – another liberal economic scheme. Criticism has been mounting because it [GEAR] has yielded no growth, no jobs, and a growing gap between rich and poor. It mirrors structural adjustment plans to the north and its perspectives are built into the NAI plan.

According to Coetzee, not only is there widespread opposition to embracing neo-liberalism as the development strategy for South Africa and for the Southern African region, but the overly statist analysis that informs the official New African Initiative (NAI, and thus NEPAD) discourse is problematic. Aside from largely ignoring the democratic concerns and objections of civil society groups, it presents a very skewed and inaccurate picture of the African economy by neglecting the extensive, informal, largely illegal sector. Moreover, by presenting African governments as equal leaders of equivalent states, it conceals the 'massive diversity' – in terms of accountability, capacity, legitimacy and so on – that exists in economy and governance. Finally, liberal assumptions about the possibility of unilateral progression toward democratic institutionalization and culturalization tend to ignore the social upheavals – and hence possibility for different political trajectories – that attend economic restructuring.

As a broad generalization, reactions to the NAI/NEPAD (and GEAR) agendas fall along class and/or ideological lines, with support from those who favour neo-liberalism – business, the government and international donors/institutions – and opposition from labour, the poor and many civil society organizations. However, such generalizations do not adequately capture the complexity of the debate on neo-liberalism in South(ern) Africa. For instance, broad issues of ideology and/or social choice are played out within South Africa's foreign policy strategy of adaptation to a complex post-Cold War environment (Schraeder 2001). As Schraeder (ibid.:239) observes, 'President Mbeki has made the African renaissance and South Africa's unique place at the intersection of the African continent and the northern industrialized democracies the cornerstone of South African foreign policy.' The various identities associated with this unique place – newly democratic country, 'rainbow nation', regional superpower, African leader, international good citizen – require that the country's foreign policy serves multiple objectives.

Domestically, both the restoration of the military's institutional credibility and efficiency and the establishment of civilian control over the military are required for the consolidation of the new democracy. Internationally, the 'principle of universality' (that is, establishing diplomatic relations with all countries) as well as membership and leadership in international organizations signal an intention to play a key leadership role in promoting the norms and values of humane internationalism. With the notion of renaissance, Mbeki hopes to create positive attitude and momentum at home and to restore South Africa's credibility, after years as a pariah state, by signifying the country's willingness and its ability to assume leadership in the region, in Africa and in the world (ibid.).

The imagery of 'renaissance' is compelling and the term itself is ideologically neutral so as to appeal to the broadest constituency. However, it has proven to be very difficult to serve the mixed motives that underscore the renaissance and NEPAD discourses in South Africa. Debates and struggles on the issues have created divisions within the government, especially at the parliamentary committee level, as well as within the ruling African National Congress (ANC) party which has fractionalized into the minority groups who either support a liberal internationalist position or continue to adhere to the party's traditional socialist (and self-consciously Africanist) values, and the majority who have adopted a pragmatic, 'geo-economics' position (ibid.:238). Outside the government, divisions centred on the renaissance/NEPAD discourse have been even more evident. Large sections of civil society, and labour in particular, have been particularly resistant for the past several years to the government's support for neo-liberal norms and strategies, in large part because the economy has not grown sufficiently or quickly enough to meet domestic demands for social reforms. COSATU (Congress of South African Trade Unions) has 'read' the government's language of renaissance as a neo-liberal text and recently scornfully dismissed NEPAD as 'domestic liberalism exported to the continent' (*Africa Confidential* 2002:3).

The different reactions to the South African government's text on renaissance/NEPAD spill over into the Southern African region. Most directly, regional integration through organizations such as the Southern African Development Community (SADC) is featured as an important vehicle for meeting NEPAD's objectives. Given that, the ideological debates and class divisions that exist with South Africa apply also at the regional level. COSATU, for instance, has received support in its struggles against the institutionalization of neo-liberalism from labour in neighbouring countries. However, there are further nuances in the debates at the regional level due to South Africa's unique position in the region and in Africa, both historically and in the contemporary period. For example, as Simon (2001:385) points out, expressions of interest by South African business to expand beyond national borders have aroused significant negative reaction from local businesses in neighbouring countries. The reasons for the objections vary, according to Simon (2001:385) but tend to involve 'old grievances' stemming from the apartheid years, fear of heightened economic competition and/or the perception that cultural and racial insensitivities exist (or may exist) on the part of (especially white) South African businessmen.

These reactions reflect ambivalent views within the region on South Africa's relations with its neighbours, and therefore different readings of the renaissance/NEPAD texts and its subtexts. One of the latter involves the image of South Africa as an emerging global player and hence the logical choice to lead the region into full integration in the global political economy. According to Simon (2001:388–9), this representation of a global future for Africa has been used frequently by South African businesses attempting to broaden their operations in Africa. It is consistent with the optimistic projections put forward in the mid-1990s based on the assumptions that the newly integrated South Africa would become the 'engine of growth' for the region. However, this also contrasted directly with a view based on fears that

South Africa's economic ambitions would have negative consequences for neighbouring countries. Simon's research confirms that such concerns are still held by businessmen who 'have leveled accusations of neo-colonialism, exploitation, "trying to gobble up Africa" and the like' (ibid.:385).

Internationally, Mbeki has attempted to maintain the international good citizen profile that South Africa was awarded during, and in the aftermath of, the transition to democracy. He is also attempting to generate support for NEPAD among international donors. Yet, he must also be mindful of the resentment that still exists in indigenous populations because of colonialism. It is therefore not politically expedient to be seen by his poor, black citizenry as kowtowing to rich, white interests. This is particularly pertinent for the issue of land ownership: other countries in the region besides Zimbabwe – notably South Africa and Namibia – are under pressure to honour their promises for land redistribution. Indeed, Namibia has recently announced that it would begin a process of land expropriation, albeit on a 'willing buyer/willing seller' basis (Vries 2004). When governments are slow to move on resettlement or other redistribution measures[3] or when they are compelled to make unpopular choices (for example, support for neo-liberal policies), recalling long-standing cleavages and wounds can be a powerful political tool for shifting responsibility and securing political support.

A complicating and related factor involves the norm of sovereignty. African leaders have been strident defenders of the principle of sovereignty. The state sovereignty discourse in Africa has served multiple purposes. More positively, post-independence, state leaders have defended the sovereignty rights of states as a protective edifice for self-determination within which colonialist dependencies would be thrown off and national identity could be constructed. However, jealous guarding of sovereign rights and privileges has also been identified as one of the obstacles to good governance and to cooperative regional arrangements in Africa. Analyses presenting this view argue that sovereignty 'rights' have provided a protected venue for governing elites of some African states to construct networks of extraction for their own personalistic and regime interests (Clapham 2001). In such states, frequently referred to as 'failed' states in the literature, the ruling regimes have maintained power and privilege through collusion with networks of violence, conflict (Duffield 2001) and warlordism (Reno 1998). Zimbabwe has not yet degenerated to the degree of the most severely affected of these countries – that is, civil war has not yet broken out and rebel groups and/or warlords have not yet been identified. Yet, the conditions in Zimbabwe (personalistic rule, rent-seeking behaviours of government elites, egregious abuse of human rights and so on) closely resemble those of countries identified as sites of serious human insecurity crises (MacLean 2002).

Such situations have given rise to a re-examination of the norm of sovereignty. A compelling case is now being made by some that *de jure* sovereignty, in which government leaders have legitimacy conferred on them mainly by the fact that their country is a legal entity in international law, is insufficient and may in certain circumstances contribute to human insecurity. As was argued by the 2001 report of the International Commission on Intervention and State Sovereignty (ICISS 2001:xi), 'state sovereignty implies responsibility, and the primary responsibility for the protection of its people lies with the state itself'. When states are unable or unwilling to meet that responsibility, outsiders have not only a right, but also a responsibility to act. In the words of the ICISS Report, 'where a population is suffering serious harm, as a result of internal war, insurgency, repression or state failure, and the state in question is unwilling or unable to halt or avert it, the principle of non-intervention yields to the international responsibility to protect' (ibid.).

The Zimbabwean government has repeatedly insisted upon the 'right' of Zimbabweans to make their own choices for governance and other Southern African leaders have supported that principle on several occasions. Yet, the vast majority of reports coming out of Zimbabwe suggest that ordinary citizens have little opportunity to exercise free choice, but instead, are being increasingly victimized by their government. The Zimbabwean government has clearly demonstrated its inability to protect its people, and its willingness to use them, often in excessively brutal ways, to maintain the regime's power. It seems very clear that in the interests of human security, and to prevent wide-scale bloodshed, the international community, including (and perhaps especially) neighbouring states have a responsibility to attempt to protect Zimbabwe's citizens.

Conclusions

The Zimbabwean crisis is one of the most recent examples of an African state degenerating under the weight of various internal and external pressures. It also exposes the need for, and yet the unwillingness or inability of, leaders in the region to respond to these requirements. If left to fester, the situation can have serious destabilizing effects on the Southern African region. Direct negative effects are likely to continue as Zimbabwean problems spill over borders in a variety of forms: refugees, crime, trade disruptions, aid requirements, and so on. Also, investors in several sectors are likely to shy away not only from Zimbabwe in its economic and political free-fall, but from neighbouring countries whose leaders appear to outsiders to be making insufficient effort to restrain the Mugabe regime in its egregious abuse of power.

However, just as the combination of domestic, regional, international and transnational pressures has made it impossible for Mugabe to continue to employ contradictory texts as a strategy for regime maintenance, it is proving to be extremely difficult for Mbeki and other leaders to take a consistent position on Zimbabwe. They are faced with the challenge of attempting to lead their countries into full membership in the global political economy and urged, as the price of membership, to 'take the high road' by publicly working for democracy and human rights (with Zimbabwe as the first major test of their commitment to these ideals). Yet, histories of oppression, apartheid, structural adjustment, and inadequate investment and response by the West to emergencies such as Rwanda or HIV/AIDS have kept alive the discourses of anti-colonialism. Such discourses can be used conveniently by leaders to explain away policy failure or contradictory pressures, especially when, in the minds of many Africans, neo-liberal policies are associated more with social deprivation and the political economy of violence than with the restoration of flagging economies (Moyo 2001). Therefore, while the politics and discourse of NEPAD have been useful in exposing the contradictory texts of many African government leaders and international sanctions and while it may have some positive impacts in promoting and strengthening norms of human rights and democratic governance, the inability of the international community to change the actions of African leaders has been clearly illustrated by the Zimbabwean crisis.

The Zimbabwean crisis has illustrated that crises of state collapse are beyond 'national' and/or 'state' emergencies. The reaction by Mbeki (and other regional leaders) to Mugabe's leadership, and indeed, the development of the Zimbabwean crisis itself supports Söderbaum's (2002) observation that: '[d]uring the last few decades, a new political economy has emerged as a consequence of economic globalization and the retreat or "unbundling" of the state. Regionalism is taking place in a context heavily influenced by economic and political (neo)liberalism and economic globalization. These at least partly new characteristics have deep implications on the power relations in society. Often it leads to a new mix and balance between state, market and society actors within the individual countries, with implications for the way regionalism is played out in practice.'

Söderbaum's comment suggests the need for moving beyond the state, in terms of both analysis and governance practices. Yet, most proposed strategies for improving the Zimbabwean crisis, or of collapsing or collapsed states in Africa, generally involve some means of 'improving' the state: by changing the regime in power, imposing conditionalities on the government, building capacity in the bureaucracy and so on. It is not that such initiatives are inappropriate, but they are insufficient. The degeneration of the state in Zimbabwe is the result of events occurring at the nexus of domestic, international, regional and transnational politics. The process of state-building that is occurring presently in Zimbabwe – the new social hierarchies that are being established, changes in land ownership and other forms of wealth, and the struggles to capture political office – that are becoming increasingly manifest need to be analysed within the context of regional social dynamics and broader levels and aspects of political economy.

To conduct such an analysis involves understanding the importance of the regional space in African political economy, but also looking beyond state and interstate actions to take seriously the activities and discourses within civil and 'uncivil' societies. This means giving credence to second-tier diplomacies by non-state as well as state actors, and supporting the activities of NGOs and churches that are working in areas of human rights, constitutional and legal reform, conflict resolution and reconciliation and so on. It also means exposing the malignant, arcane networks associated with the political economy of conflict that link governmental behaviour in Zimbabwe with war and resource extraction in the DRC, for example (see next chapter).

To promote economic growth and construct an effective regional security community requires moving beyond state-only strategies, and looking to novel governance arrangements that take heed of the social structures, power hierarchies, economic associations and discourse that actually exist 'on the ground' in Africa, as well as the regional dimensions of these relationships. Such rethinking is emerging in various practices as well as in several new analytical approaches to global governance, the political economy of violence, warlord politics and new regionalisms. Indeed, by ignoring or overlooking the regional and transnational dimensions of the crisis in Zimbabwe, we miss an opportunity to expose the full range of factors that led to the situation and those that will bring peace and reconciliation to the country and region.

Notes

1 Carmody (2001:109) reports that tariffs of 70 per cent to 100 per cent were imposed in 1992, while Dashwood (2000:155) reports that a 45 per cent duty imposed in 1995 was raised to 40–85 per cent in 1997.
2 For a good discussion of the Peer Review Mechanism, see Cilliers (2002).
3 In Zimbabwe, the government support for the emergence of a black bourgeoisie beginning in the mid-1980s was at the expense of the redistribution strategies promised by the ZANU government at independence and set out soon thereafter in the *Growth with Redistribution* policy (Dashwood 1996). Several scholars have pointed to a similar process occurring in South Africa. I discuss this in MacLean (2001).

9

The Logic of Disorder: 'Malignant Regionalization' in Central Africa

Ian Taylor

The Great Lakes region of Africa is currently characterized by conflict and disorder, with concomitant social, political, not to mention ecological, dislocation and displacement. The war(s) in the Democratic Republic of Congo (DRC) and its borderlands are a catastrophe in the heart of Africa. At the formal level, the Southern African Development Community (SADC) is riven by tension and rivalries that profoundly calls into question the 'official' region-building project. Yet, at the same time, and in contrast to the fissures within SADC generated by the conflicts, another type of regional networking has been assiduously crafted. This networking, very often clandestine and illegal, has helped craft a form of regionalization that may not be recognizable at first glance, but is surely there and is as 'real' – if not more so – in the DRC than any *formal* regionalism.

Indeed, the war in the DRC has made well-placed individuals and groups considerably richer and has created a milieu whereby a wide variety of networking involving states, mafias, private armies, 'businessmen' and assorted state elites has developed, as recent reports by the United Nations (2001) and the International Crisis Group (2000a) have shown.[1] This 'new' form of regionalization, based essentially on a form of kleptocratic political economy, may be termed 'malignant regionalization' in the sense that it undermines coherent developmental projects and the prospects for peace and stability. It is a form of novel regionalization that Timothy M Shaw (2000) refers to as 'war economy' as one of his five typologies of regionalization currently remaking Africa.

In this discussion, I would like to expand on how this amounts to a type of regionalization that we need to take on board if we are to attempt (or at least start) to comprehend the processes currently

147

reconfiguring Central Africa. In order to try and understand this, the insights provided by the New Regionalism Approach (NRA) combined with the theoretical concepts provided by Patrick Chabal and Jean-Pascal Daloz are deployed.

The new regionalism approach and Africa

In contrast to formal orthodox approaches to regionalism, the New Regionalism Approach pioneered by Björn Hettne has been more sensitive to 'bottom-up' processes that are not considered by more orthodox approaches (see Hettne, Inotai and Sunkel 1999). This is particularly important in the study of the political economy of contemporary Africa as state and institutional-based analyses (which derive much of their insights from the study of formal processes in the developed world) simply do not give us much conceptual purchase – they are talking of a different world, as it were. Obviously, we should not discard the role of the state in Africa and the activities of institutions *are* important, but at the same time, the effectiveness of such bodies is limited and, it must be said, restricted to a select number of African spaces, mostly located in the southern cone of the continent. If we are to try and understand the multifaceted processes that mark out Africa's political economy, the political, private, social, ecological, and informal/illegal aspects of regionalizing impulses, *alongside* the formal institutional and economic aspects, need to be analysed and understood.[2] In this sense, the NRA asserts that 'regionalism' comes in a wide variety of forms and guises, some not immediately recognizable, and that as a consequence 'theorizing ... has to be a rather pluralistic exercise' (Hettne and Söderbaum 1998:14).

If we are to talk specifically of Africa, the Western bias of much of the previous literature on regional processes must be challenged and the study of regionalizing tendencies of whatever guise – both formal and informal – in the developing world clearly needs greater examination if we are to construct a more global overview of contemporary regionalism (Payne 1998). Fredrik Söderbaum (1998:91) captures this view when he states that the NRA is based on 'the recognition that the Eurocentric and unrealistic assumptions of orthodox theory do not apply in the industrialized world and certainly do not apply in the developing world'.

According to the NRA, there are two regionalizing processes that may be identified. 'Regionalism' refers to the often formal projects with particular plans and strategies and that often lead to institutional arrangements. 'Regionalization' on the other hand refers to the actual processes that result in forms of cooperation, integration, connectivity and convergence within a particular cross-national territorial area. Orthodox approaches to regionalizing have invariably neglected this latter, often more informal, though no less tangible, set of processes (Hettne and Söderbaum 2000:458).

By focusing on the 'real' regions, the NRA has granted a useful set of analytical tools by which the diverse sets of regionalizing processes may be better understood. In the context of this particular study, the recognition that regionalisms in Africa are multi-layered and can and do involve transnational networks that may or may not be legal, or that reflect Jean-François Bayart's 'criminalization of the state' in Africa is fundamental (see Bayart, Ellis and Hibou 1999). Such regionalisms involve the participation of a multitude of actors, both 'state' (whatever that may actually mean) and non-state players. This is essential, particularly in Africa, as much of the social and economic interconnectedness remain at the nexus of formal/informal, legal/illegal, national/global and so on, constituting what has been called the 'three economies of Africa' (Freeman 2000). In such a milieu, formal activities, quantifiable through orthodox analyses, only tell one part of the story: there is a conceptual gap that does not allow us to analyse the informality of trading networks that are typical of much of Africa's political economy, for instance.[3] The NRA approach, focusing as it does on both formal and non-formal, gives us scope to investigate precisely the type of malignant regionalization that currently typifies central Africa. As Shaw (2000:401) writes on the NRA:

> [Its] inclusion of non-state and non-formal interactions between the national and global levels enables it to treat the interconnections between more and less statist relations, as well as to transcend the official by recognizing how the latter relates to the unofficial in a myriad of ways: the multiple conceptions of 'regions', as well as diversity of issue areas, from ecologies and ethnicities to civil societies and private armies.

The complexities and heterogeneous nature of regionalisms in Africa clearly provide a study in how regionalizing tendencies take on a variety of forms that play out at a diverse set of levels, not all of which are recognizably legitimate or constructive. Yet they are still forms of regionalisms.

The instrumentalization of war in Central Africa

When Laurent Kabila took over the seat of government (if not power) after Mobutu's inglorious evacuation in early 1997, excited observers hastily proclaimed that Kabila was 'different' and that a formal regional project could use this difference constructively – hence the newly-named entity known as the Democratic Republic of the Congo being admitted post haste into SADC. Such optimism over the character (as well as the scope for manoeuvre) of Kabila was rudely disappointed as almost immediately, Kabila entered into deals with mining companies, such as American Mineral Fields and Anglo-American, and Belgian investors such as Texaf, George Forrest International, Petrofina and Union Minière. These Belgian companies in particular, had benefited substantially under the old Mobutu regime (see Baracyetse 1999). The reasons for such continuity in the country's political economy lie in a combination of Kabila's predisposition to continue 'business as usual' and the historical milieu within which he found himself upon taking power, as well as the various motives for struggling to overthrow Mobutu, not all them centred on noble aspirations for a better Congo. As one Congolese official put it (Wrong 2000:291):

> You know, in the fight against Mobutu, not everyone shared the same objectives ... Some people wanted to change society. Some just wanted to replace him. It's the principle of '*Ôte-toi de là, que je m'y mette*' (Get out of the way, so I can take your place).

Indeed, the state of region-wide disorder and the opportunities this offered, as well as the already extant networks of power and patronage, afforded a logical modus operandi for a variety of actors operating within areas where the formal state was in a process of eclipse.[4] These circumstances have in turn increased the likelihood of what William Reno referred to as 'warlord capitalism' and the 'shadow state' (see Reno 1998).

This point needs expanding since I think that the exploitation of war and the process of state collapse by warlords and other opportunists follows its own logic which not only provides a powerful disincentive to ending conflict, but can also be evidence of a 'new' (if perverse and wholly undesirable) type of regionalization. This coincides with what Timothy Shaw (2000:406) refers to as a 'quite distinctive form of new regionalism in Africa ... the emergence of the minerals and mafias syndrome in which scarce resources are exchanged for protection, as well as regime enrichment and aggrandisement'. Patrick Chabal and Jean-Pascal Daloz's (1999:xviii–xix) analysis relating to the 'political instrumentalization of disorder' is very useful in this regard.[5]

> This refers to the process by which political actors in Africa seek to maximize their returns on the state of confusion, uncertainty and sometimes even chaos, which characterizes most African polities ... [W]hat all African states share is a generalized system of patrimonialism and an acute degree of apparent disorder ... and a universal resort to personal(ized) and vertical solutions to societal problems.

From this perspective, disorder – and often a state of outright war – is not necessarily considered to be a state of dereliction or failure by certain African elites, but is rather a malignant condition offering significant opportunities to those in positions to exploit such situations. Indeed, wars may be motivated from the start by economic motives and objectives (Berdal and Malone 2000). Such circumstances generate their own instrumental logic of accumulation and can serve to attract 'businessmen' and other 'entrepreneurs' wishing to construct commercial linkages with power-holders in situations where instability persists, but where the ability to operate effectively in an environment virtually free from legal/ethical constraints can bring major rewards. According to the weekly South African business periodical *Financial Mail* (15 January 1999)

> If the risks are high in Angola or the Democratic Republic of Congo (DRC) where President Laurent Kabila's troops are battling rebel forces, the business rewards can be dazzling. These and other warring African countries, like Sierra Leone and the Republic of the Congo (Congo-Brazzaville) are rich in mineral deposits with scant, if any, regulatory restrictions – a glittering lure for foreign companies.

Indeed, conflict-ridden spaces offer a form of malignant competitiveness for both patron and client that can prove highly profitable. Ironically, particularly given the involvement of South African business interests in such conflicts, the constituency that is most enthusiastic about the economic aspect of Thabo Mbeki's 'African Renaissance' concept – South African capital – is also willing to exploit circumstances like those in the DRC that directly contradict the President's vision.

The dynamics of instrumentalized disorder thus serve to limit the ability for reform and development in two ways according to Chabal and Daloz (1999:162):

> The first is that, where disorder has become a resource, there is no incentive to work for a more institutionalized ordering of society. The second is that in the absence of any other viable way of obtaining the means needed to sustain neo-patrimonialism, there is inevitably a tendency to link politics to realms of increased disorder, be it war or crime.

From the instrumentalization of disorder perspective, far from being a humanitarian and developmental disaster which sabotages ambitions for the African Century, for well-placed elites and businessman, the wars in the Great Lakes region stimulate and intensify conditions of dependence and uncertainty that offer potentially substantial resources for those able to take advantage. This explains much of the foreign intervention in the DRC: it is not only about preserving national security and defeating enemies, it is also about securing access to resource-rich areas and establishing privatized accumulation networks on a region-wide basis that can emerge and prosper under conditions of war and anarchy. In this sense, war assumes the characteristics of a business venture, the beneficiaries of which are unlikely to give up the venture easily. As Akiiki Mujaju (1999:7) writes, the DRC 'does not invite intervention only by being incoherent and divided. Its wealth such as gold and diamonds are an attraction to fortune seekers. Therefore ending the war is not in line with the special interests of many actors.'

In the Great Lakes region today, privatized armies whose chains of command are uncertain, and who may or may not be connected to the state, demarcate 'their' territory and struggle over resources, constructing a form of regionalization with similar like-minded entrepreneurs based on clandestine networking and smuggling. Naturally, many of these actors often make some claim to politics – usually based on a spurious reformist platform – but the economic motive in the context of a hollow state appears naked and wholly brazen.

In this sense we can say that the regionalization being staked out in conflict areas of the DRC may be, in a perverse way, socially constructed by actors sharing particular interests and agendas and who carve out territories based on the instrumentalization of disorder but in partnership with others in a 'togetherness of criminality'. This is most apparent with regards to the big men involved in this malignant regionalization who share an inter-subjective understanding of their own positions of power and prestige and concur on the logic that the state of which they have at least nominal control is 'theirs' to do with as they please. In sharing such identities, the defence of one is the defence of all. Arguably, the socially constructed regionness advanced by Mugabe, Kabila senior, Dos Santos and Nujoma, in tandem with their business partners and political allies, was no less 'real' than other forms of regional identities and connections. That the citizens of such territories may not share (literally and figuratively) in this brotherhood of debasement and disorder reinforces the notion that regionalizations are multifaceted and operate at a host of levels, often in contradiction with one another: 'we should be wary of simply assuming that there is a single voice and a single actor operating from within territorial boundaries' (Breslin and Higgott 2000:348).

Accepting this, the main cause of the fighting in the DRC is now economic gain. In many respects, therefore, the war in the DRC can be understood as part of what Jeremy Weinstein referred to as 'Africa's scramble for Africa'. 'Since the fall of the colonial powers', Weinstein (2000:17) argues:

> Resource extraction has been largely the province of post-independence leaders – many of whom followed the lead of their former colonial masters to create vast personal fortunes. The current war in the Congo is surprising to the extent to which participating states have blatantly advertised the economic motivations underlying their participation. Intervening states have sought a direct share in Congo's revenues from the extraction of mineral and other resources.

Such activity has built up a series of interlinking regional connections that have constructed what may be seen as a form of malignant regionalization centred in Kinshasa and extending outwardly via mineral concessions and other economic centres to Harare, Luanda and Windhoek (and of course, onwards to Geneva, Brussels, Lisbon, Paris and so on). This form of regionalization shadows the type of transnational networking and linkages that already exist 'from below' *vis-à-vis* the trading interactions between Central Africa and Europe so excellently covered by Janet MacGaffey and Remy Bazenguissa-Ganga (2000). In regionalization literature, the 'hubs and spokes' of connectivities are often discussed. Is such malignant regionalization in central Africa anything less than a form of hubs and spokes?

The development of a malignant form of regionalization was particularly blatant in Laurent Kabila's case, with the DRC big man assiduously constructing patronage networks to serve as resources through which clients might be rewarded for their support and which stretched beyond Kinshasa to link up with a variety of region-wide and indeed global players. For instance, in September 1998 Kabila decreed that all purchases of gold and diamonds must be in Congolese francs (brought in on 30 June) and go through a newly established state purchasing company. This allowed him to bring the country's revenue under his direct control and thereby offer the incentive of cash rewards to his supporters throughout the DRC (*The Economist* 24 October 1998:88). Kabila also seized all the assets of the Canadian gold concession, Banro Resources Corporation, a company with which he had formed a contract before becoming Congo's president. This provoked Arnold Kondrat of Banro to remark to a Congolese employee that: 'Your President is a crook and this country is going to suffer a lot in a very short time. You Congolese must know that this country and all its minerals are not yours but ours'.[6] Such blatant disregard for the rights of ordinary Congolese supports William Reno's (1998:219) argument that

> The problem for the Congolese is not necessarily the weakness of their organizations or their demands but that their rulers have been able to dominate the country's abundant natural resources and to call on a wide array of outsiders to help them do so.

It is therefore not surprising that the anti-Kabila Movement for the Liberation of Congo (led by Jean-Pierre Bemba, a 'businessman' with extensive regional contacts and who prospered under Mobutu), quickly announced that this nationalization was annulled. Thus, if Banro wishes to retain its assets, it must negotiate either with an unstable regime, or a rebel movement with no identifiable political or social programme, other than the Kabila regime, no doubt to install an equally rapacious and unstable administration in its place.

Turning to another spoke in this malignant regionalization, Robert Mugabe and his ministers, generals, relatives and close associates have accrued substantial personal benefits from the pillaging of the Congo (Rotberg 2000). Mugabe is anxious to ensure that the clique surrounding Kabila (the son, this time) remains in power not only because he is underwriting Zimbabwe's military costs, but also so that he can pay his debts to the government-owned Zimbabwe Defence Industries (some US$250 million). The spoke in this particular case extended both ways as the Kabila regime tolerated the exploitation of the conflict for personal profit by a number of Zimbabwe's ruling elite in return for renting out the Zimbabwean army. According to one source 'Zimbabwean generals, politicians and the ruling ZANU-PF party have invested an estimated $47 million in timber, mining and retail deals'.[7] In addition, of the $50 million worth of supplies contracted by Zimbabwe to supply Kabila's army and the Zimbabwean army in the Congo, a major private beneficiary was General Vitalis Zvinavashe, commander of the Zimbabwean Defence Force, whose trucking company was subcontracted through a subsidiary.[8] Zvinavashe's brother was also awarded a lucrative deal to export products to Kinshasa.[9]

The regional connectivity feeding off the conflict is exemplified by the Zimbabwean company Osleg, which was formed in late 1998 specifically to buy diamonds and gold from the DRC. To date, it remains in contractual partnership with Comiex, a company owned by the military commanders of Kabila's army. Osleg has contracted a deal to trade gemstones worth around US$5 million per month, supposedly to offset the costs of Zimbabwe's deployment in the Congo. However, Osleg is owned by General Zvinavashe and Job Whabira, Permanent Secretary in the Defence Ministry, as well as the chiefs of two mineral parastatals (Stiff 2000:253–65).

For its part, the Angolan government intervened in response to reports from its intelligence sources that linked UNITA with Congolese rebels, thus threatening the Dos Santos regime's own corrupt patronage networks built around Angola's lucrative oil industry. Put simply, Dos Santos's primary objective appears to be the prevention of an UNITA-friendly regime in Kinshasa. However, invading the southwest of the DRC also gave easier access to Cabinda (an Angolan enclave separated from the rest of the country by a sliver of DRC territory) in order to attack Cabinda separatists. Luanda's political elite also secured profitable networks through Angola's national petrol company, Sonangol, which was granted concessions and marketing rights by Kabila. It is also well known that Isabelle, the daughter of Dos Santos, runs various diamond-buying operations in the DRC in collusion with other senior Angolan. Namibia's US$25 million trade deal with Kabila, which stands to benefit key players associated with the Nujoma regime similarly played a role in Windhoek's decision to enter and remain involved in the war.[10]

Mugabe and his associates are not the only parties guilty of exploiting the commercial opportunities available in the DRC and in the eastern part of the DRC, there is a form of regionalization, much of it constructed around ethnic networks and connections, that profits elites in both Rwanda and Uganda. It is no surprise that within this other malignant regionalization – a Tutsi-based network of military and economic power – both Kigali- and Kampala-located elites have concentrated their interventions around the DRC's key mineral deposits.[11] The NRA asserts that 'the regional frontier may very well cut through a particular state's territory, positioning some parts of the state within the emerging region and others outside' (Hettne and Söderbaum 2000:462). This is certainly true of the malignant regionalization going on at the geographic nexus of North and South Kivu province in the DRC with western parts of Uganda, Rwanda and Burundi, extending possibly over into Tanzania and based on clandestine smuggling networks operating alongside both formal and informal trading links, raising questions about the very nature of borders and what territoriality and sovereignty mean today in Central Africa (see Mbembe 1999). The ethnic and social history of this region, both pre- and post-colonial in nature, helps give a sense of identity, if not regionness, with Banyamulenga operators collaborating with Tutsi soldier-entrepreneurs in the business of extraction and accumulation.

On the illegal side to these 'spokes', this has itself helped build a regionalization based on smuggling and plunder. As soon as the Rwandan/Ugandan-backed *Rassemblement Congolais pour la Démocratie* (RCD) established itself at Kisangani under the Ugandan People's Defence Forces' (UPDF) protection, Ugandan commanders were accused of getting involved in 'business deals', 'car robberies' and of 'losing [the] war objectives' (ICG 2000b). One of these commanders was Museveni's half-brother, Salim Saleh, indicating the meshing of state-derived authority with local private business connections. Saleh has been involved in gold deals, in tandem with Lieutenant-Colonel Jet Mwebaze, a leading Ugandan general in the Congo, with dealers from Israel.[12] Saleh is also linked with Uganda's force commander in the Congo, Brigadier Kazini, Jet Mwebaze's brother and a cousin of Museveni's wife.[13] Salim Saleh, with his business and military networks linked to the state and the army, typifies much of the ongoing instrumentalization of conflict for personal profit that marks out the new regionalization in Central Africa:

> General Saleh deployed gold diggers. When the war broke out in Congo, they saw it as a windfall, literally a gold mine. You don't need to look far for evidence of this shameful degeneration on the

part of the UPDF. All you need to do is look at the line up of UPDF commanders who have been deployed to conduct the war in Congo. It is a group of men rotten to the core.[14]

In April 1999, a newspaper based in Goma attacked the Ugandans saying 'people who came as liberators are now massively looting and smuggling from Congo'. This came at a time when the Uganda Revenue Authority and Civil Aviation Authority were complaining to the Ministry of Defence over various deals between Ugandan generals and Congolese military personnel and businessmen. Reports say items smuggled out of Congo are mostly coffee, timber and minerals – gold and diamonds – while petroleum products and sap from rubber trees are illegally brought to Uganda, mostly being brought in on military vehicles that are never checked.[15] This malignant regionalization was described by one source as thus:

At the border areas like Ariwara and Paidha, hordes of Congolese cross daily to Uganda to sell their products like coffee, cotton and timber. And in a blatant abuse of the two country's authorities, untaxed petroleum products imported using Congolese documents enter Congo for a few moments and re-enter Uganda to be sold at about 300 per cent profit, with a litre of petrol in Arua costing between Sh800 and Sh900, rendering the normal petrol stations useless ... The rate at which Ugandans are logging in forests inside Congo is alarming; the virgin forests there are being depleted at a fast and uncontrolled rate. A less harmful side of the smuggling operates in the reverse direction, with several private-owned and army chartered planes reportedly used for airlifting consumer goods to Kisangani, Bunia and Goma.[16]

Ironically, Paul Kagame of Rwanda and Yoweri Museveni of Uganda were touted as belonging to a new generation of African leaders who would advance the African Renaissance (Ottaway 1998). They are now 'on the verge of becoming the godfathers of the illegal exploitation of natural resources and the continuation of the conflict in the Congo'.[17] The turmoil in the DRC has illustrated how quickly these so-called 'new leaders' have lost a good deal of their credibility, raising questions 'about the capacity of any autocratic strongman to contribute in the long-term to an African renaissance. Despite the fact that all of these leaders had replaced brutal and corrupt regimes, and despite all the talk of solidarity, their interests clearly diverged, in some cases into open conflict between former colleagues-in-arms'.[18]

Just as regionalization can be constructed upon joint interests and concerns, so too can it be *deconstructed*. This occurred in late 1999 when four days of fighting between Ugandan and Rwandan troops around Kisangani was blamed on money and egos, with both sides competing to support the RCD. The RCD split, with Wamba dia Wamba aligned to Uganda and based in Kisangani, whilst Emile Ilunga sided with the Rwandans and kept the majority of the RCD in Goma.[19] Reports have subsequently alleged that the fighting 'stemmed mainly from competition over access to Congo's valuable natural resources'.[20]

All these examples support David Shearer's (1997) argument that 'wealth can be a powerful disincentive to resolve a conflict'. If there is money to be made out of conflict, then the prospects for building an African Renaissance along the lines advanced by Mbeki are bleak. Whilst Mbeki aims to build a region and a continent based on good governance and other familiar ingredients, the 'real' regional processes, particularly in the Great Lakes area may sabotage such pretensions. Indeed, the political economy of conflict militates against such ambitions. Angola's recent war was driven by access – either legal or illicit – to its vast natural wealth. Liberia's civil war ended only after the main protagonist, Charles Taylor, won an election based on the distinctly undemocratic precept that a 'no' vote would mean war. Taylor had financed his own insurgency from illicitly granting timber, rubber and diamond concessions to various 'investors' (Atkinson 1997; Reno 1998). This itself was based on a malignant form of regionalization encompassing not only Liberia, but also Sierra Leone, Burkina Faso, Guinea, as well as Libya (Aning 1997). Similarly, Sierra Leone's brutal civil war engendered a system of covert regional networks that openly fought over control of the country's diamond fields (Smillie, Gberie and Hazleton 2000; Reno 2000b). The conflict in the DRC and the form of regionalization engendered display similar if not more pronounced characteristics.

Certainly, the continued fighting in the DRC has inextricably linked political and economic developments in both the wider Great Lakes and Southern African regions, and the rebellion in South Sudan, creating regionalizations within a broader 'regionalization of African wars' stretching from Khartoum to Luanda and cutting the continent in half. At its peak, the conflict witnessed the military involvement of eight outside states (Angola, Chad, Namibia, Sudan and Zimbabwe broadly in support of the Kabila clique, with Burundi, Rwanda and Uganda against). In many respects the DRC represents the geographical arena in which a number of the national disputes of its neighbours are being resolved through the use of military force while clandestine economic networking goes on. This is partly because the DRC's geography, limited infrastructure and anarchic interior offer sanctuary to a number of dissident groups, but also because the region offers rich pickings to those willing to stake out their claims.[21]

What is clear is that the fighting within the DRC will not cease until its troubled neighbours also resolve their problems. This is something that the region's leaders have been aware of for some time and although this fact may complicate any potential peace process, it does mean that opportunities exist for dealing with a number of conflicts at once through a series of trade-offs and linked agreements.[22] On the negative side, however, since the Lusaka agreement (10 July 1999) focused purely upon the DRC and did not even include all the belligerents to the conflict, even if it could be successfully implemented – which is doubtful – it is unlikely to provide a sound basis on which to achieve a durable end to the hostilities or to build up a new and less corrupting form of regional solidarities and connections.

Yet, with the type of regionalization in Central Africa based on corrupted abilities to lay claim to the mantle of state, it is doubtful whether many of the current elites in the formal region (or even the wider international community, for that matter) can bring themselves to confront the reality of malignant regionalization even if it stares them in the face. The use and abuse of the 'organized hypocrisy' of sovereignty has clearly allowed an assortment of actors to successfully construct a number of commercial and military alliances involving state leaders and their courtiers as well as private corporations (Krasner 1999). In short, a number of state elites in the Great Lakes and Southern African regions use the mantle of sovereignty not to promote the collective good, but instead use it to help bolster their own patronage networks and weaken those of potential challengers (Reno 2000c). In such circumstances, relying upon the very same state elites to end the conflict will be inherently problematic.

In relation to the idea of an African Renaissance, a proto-pan-African regionalist project as it were, several points are relevant. First, given international society's reluctance to intervene over the war in the DRC, the conflict does present an opportunity for Africans to find their own solutions to this problem. While this seems unlikely, given the pervasive logic of malignant regionalization among the region's power-holders, it may well be the least worst option, given international society's impotence on this issue. Clearly, it is axiomatic that there is only so much outsiders can do to resolve conflicts like that in the DRC. It is also obvious that a regionalism based on shared developmental goals would require African elites to share a set of political aspirations that place the interests of the continent's poor at the centre of their political agendas. It is impossible to do this if elite belligerents do not want it or view such ambitions as threats to their positions. That is why the form of malignant regionalization that marks out Central Africa is so destructive, despite possessing a corrupt logic all of its own.

Another side-effect of the malignant form of regionalism that we have witnessed in Central Africa is the unhealthy willingness to support fellow elites with military force regardless of their domestic record. This situation has serious – and negative – repercussions for attempts to defend human rights, democracy and accountability. It also sabotages the wider aim of ridding the continent of the corrupt Big Men who have done such a disservice to Africa. As Human Rights Watch Africa argued, such a scenario 'could rule out, at least in the short term, the forging of inclusive political and security alliances in the region that could benefit all Africa's peoples.[23] Clearly, where leading protagonists are engaged in corruption, resource exploitation and shady deals, and war assumes the characteristics of a business venture, how can 'one develop a clear conception of peace and reconstruction in this process?' (Campbell (1999). Such conclusions are undoubtedly pessimistic but *do* simply reflect the situation on the ground. According to Campbell (1999) the unpalatable reality of the new regionalization in Central Africa is that

> Those who profit from war as a business will agree to peace accords while making mobilizations and troop movements for war. The battles in Kisangani exposed the reality that there were and are elements that do not want an end to the war. Was the battle in Kisangani a ruse to undermine the Lusaka accord? War is more profitable for these elements than peace.

It is therefore necessary to rethink how, or indeed *if*, long-term peace and a more development-minded regionalism can be advanced given the political economy of the Great Lakes' crisis and the type of regionalization being established in the heart of the continent. Certainly, malignant regionalization 'cultivates precisely the societal disorganization and weakness of government agencies that development experts identify as key causes of Africa's economic crisis' and which goes directly against the notion of an African Renaissance (Reno 2000c).

This analysis links together regional studies with peacemaking and conflict resolution. In the past it was received wisdom that parties would only resort to violence when channels for debate and dialogue were closed. But in environments where war has become a business and disorder is being deployed for political purposes, the inadequacies of our present conceptual tools for resolving conflicts are glaringly obvious. These circumstances have led some analysts to conclude that the use of force against the worst offenders is not only justified but the only viable route to long-term peace. David Shearer (1997:858) has argued that 'in many cases, support for one warring side against another is a valid response that can hasten the end of conflict and restrict the loss of life'. The important questions for such analysts are which side, when and how? On the other hand, some analysts have suggested that would-be peacemakers should avoid getting embroiled in other people's wars.[24] This problem is likely to puzzle policy-makers for some time to come.

Globalization and malignant regionalization

So how does this malignant regionalization tie in with global processes? Globalization is obviously asymmetrical and variegated and its impact upon different spatial entities varies. As such it takes advantage of, indeed exacerbates differences as much as, if not more than it produces a uniform new world. In doing so, counter-reactions and contradictions are generated. Certainly, the new regionalizations in Africa are connected to processes associated both with globalization and with the specific historical experiences of a particular space. Local and global processes are interlinked, 'since any particular process of regionalization in any part of the world has systemic repercussions on other regions, thus shaping the way in which the new world order is being organized' (Hettne 1996). Within this context, globalizing impulses push for a reconfiguration along the lines of (Western-derived) ideal types of socio-economic governance. Ironically, the neo-liberal principles governing the global economy and that have been foisted onto the continent in the form of Structural Adjustment Programmes and other conditionalities, have provided the structural context that has helped cultivate the forms of regionalization that mark out Central Africa.

Indeed, global liberalization has stimulated a variety of regional linkages and cross-border networks, with transcontinental spokes linking such activities to the outside world. In this we can see a remarkable similarity between such regionalizations and the type of relations and forms of social, political and economic organization that mark out the war economies, particularly in Central Africa. Thus instead of bringing about stability and (legitimate) growth, impulses generated by globalization have contributed to the development of malignant regionalizations and decidedly quasi-feudal forms of political economy (Duffield 1999).

As William Reno (1998) has persuasively argued, two paradoxes are particularly evident in the neo-liberal approach to reform and development in Africa. First, rulers of weak states who face severe threats from strongmen, and the most intense pressures from outsiders, are the most consistent and thorough in destroying any remaining formal institutions of state. Secondly, outside creditors, foreign firms, and even some officials from stronger states participate in or support hard-pressed rulers' attempts to deal with political events in this unexpected fashion. This type of regional solidarity amongst corrupt big men is an apt description of what has occurred in Central Africa as the likes of Mbeki and Dos Santos rushed in to aid Kabila, thereby setting in motion the construction of a novel form of regionalization.

No longer is the state leader necessarily interested or dedicated to a project that is devoted to establishing control over a specific recognized territory, with all the bureaucratic encumbrances and requirements to maintain some form of consensual balance (Duffield 1998). Now, with their position threatened by the various tendencies associated with the penetration of globalizing impulses, the informalization of economic and political activity seeks to counterbalance the erosion of state capacity and power. By expanding internal *and external* clientistic networks in a form of malignant regionalization, elites within conflict-ridden spaces pursue what Mark Duffield refers to as 'adaptive patrimonialism' (Ibid.) This regionalization of course is not at all the type expected when the DRC was granted membership of SADC, although this malignant regionalization is certainly a lot more relevant when discussing the DRC's role in SADC.

The type of neo-liberal solutions advanced by the dominant agents of globalization actually deprive rulers of weak states the means to maintain their patronage networks and thus erode the base upon which the neo-patrimonial state is predicated. In Ankie Hoogvelt's (1997:175–6) words, this 'manner of reining in the rent-seeking state and its officials dissolves the patrimonial glue that holds the society together. It brings about fragmentation as erstwhile clients are now forced to seek their own benefits independent from the central author-ity'. This of course is not to romanticize the neo-patrimonial state in Africa as its development and existence has been largely negative and predatory (see Chabal 1994). Having said that, its decline may strip away the last vestiges of stability (however achieved) and lead to some-thing worse. Morris Szeftel (2000:303) argues that

> Liberalization created new opportunities for private appropriation of public resources ... More importantly, by reducing the role of the state, the donors both reduced its resources and the opportunities for access to those resources. At the same time the crisis [of develop-ment] did not reduce dependence on state resources for private accumulation. Corruption has tended ... to go well beyond the appropriation of surpluses and extend to the looting of the very fabric of the state itself.

In this sense, instead of representing the antithesis of what formal regional projects should look like, the type of alliances and regionaliza-tion currently reconfiguring the DRC may well offer a prophetic vision of what over-hasty liberalization may have in store for vulnerable and peripheral areas of the world, particularly those with elites who are willing to indulge in such practices and in situations where the mainte-nance of patronage is the bedrock upon which politics is grounded.

One-size-fits-all rolling back of the state has probably increased the likelihood of warlord capitalism and the instrumentalization of disor-der. In his discussion of another area of Africa ravaged by malignant regionalization, Paul Richards (1996:36) asserts that under SAPs and post-Cold War scarcity in the continent, the African state 'shrinks – both physically ... and sociologically (in terms of the groups it can afford to patronize). The regime's priority attention has to be given to maintaining loyalty among the security services'. This elevates the role and power of those with weapons and prioritizes their needs over the wider needs of society, cultivating an air of warlordism either in service to the incumbent who wears the (thin) mantle of sovereignty, or to challengers.

Indeed, in an ironic twist, liberalization may actually coincide with and/or facilitate a further slide away from formal regionalism. This is because those engaged in warlord capitalism will seek to reduce the provision of public goods as a means to abet a clientist culture of dependency in order to consummate business. This is typically centred around personalized networks and access to well-connected elites, rather than through 'normal' public service channels, which have been looted of any resources anyway (Reno 2000a:442–3). Thus both the capacity to administer and advance regional integration projects at the formal and institutional level *and the rationale* are undermined, to be replaced in many cases by the informal and illegal. From the perspective of the warlords and big men, pursuing some form of formal regionalism does not make sense as they are not interested in some regional public good or advancement. Furthermore, committing themselves to a formal regional pact may actually lead to inhibiting factors (norms, sanctions, even military interference from fellow member states upset by their behaviour) that could threaten the continuation of their destructive activities. The neo-liberal ingredients of globalization may well then actually legitimize the peeling away of the state while at the same time helping to lay the foundations for decay and clandestinity.

From this perspective, it is necessary to strongly reject those who somehow celebrate the informalization of Africa's political economy as some sort of 'alternative modus operandi' for Africa's development.[25] Surely, 'if the critical problems of mass poverty and deprivation in the Third World are to be dealt with, concerted action by the state will be needed. Local people do not have the resources to solve these problems through their own efforts alone ... Participation is highly desirable but the poor cannot survive on rhetoric and idealism' (Midgley 1986).

Obviously, our analysis must focus on the here and now, on the rise of informal economies and other scenarios, in (ever-increasing) parts of the continent. Having said that, malignant regionalization as advanced by the big men, and even the survival strategies as crafted by the ordinary person, are not ways by which the continent can advance. As Colin Leys (1994:36) rightfully remarks:

> Contrary to the wishful thinking of some observers [the increase in the informal] is part of the pathology of Africa's collapse, not a seedbed of renewal. Anyone who believes that, for example, carrying sacks of cocoa beans on bicycles along devious forest tracks to sell them illegally across the frontier is more promising for the economy than taking them directly to the port by truck, is not to be taken seriously. People resort to the second economy for survival, to escape the predations of the corrupt and parasitic state machinery, that is all: they bribe the police to look the other way, they pay no tax, and the roads still get worse.

Unless this sort of environment is addressed, and rapidly, malignant regionalizations may come to characterize the norm on the continent, to the detriment of the majority of Africa's peoples.

Notes

1 It should be noted that the UN report is seriously flawed by its concentration on the activities of the 'uninvited' combatants in the DRC (Rwanda and Uganda) while not interrogating sufficiently the role of the 'invited' participants such as Angola and Zimbabwe.

2 Regarding such multifaceted processes associated with contemporary regional projects in Africa, perhaps three books stand out thus far: Daniel Bach's collection from 1999; Real Lavergne's collection on West Africa from 1997 and Michael Niemann's book published in 2000. Lavergne's book stresses the importance of a sense of community identity in constructing regional projects, an approach that resonates somewhat with aspects of the NRA.

3 For an excellent study of one such facet of this, see Janet MacGaffey (1991) on the real economy of Zaire.

4 This scenario had been long developing within the Congo, where regionalization tendencies based on tribalism and ethnic polarization, stoked by ambitious local big men and tacitly tolerated by the centre in Kinshasa as a means of providing a skeletal form of 'governance' and control, had long been a feature of post-colonial Congo, accelerated under Mobutu – see Kalele-ka-Bila 'Regionalist Ideologies' and Longandjo Okitakekumba 'State Power under MPR Control: An Interpretative Essay', both in Kakwarha Mbaya (1993).

5 This shares a similar point of departure from William Reno's work on instrumentalized corruption in 'shadow states'. See in particular the developed analysis in William Reno (2000a).

6 Quoted in 'Corporate Pirates and Other Scoundrels in the Congo War', http://www.africa2000.com/UGANDA/introdgeopolitique.html.

7 'Kabila Mining Deal Seen as 'Payment' for Mugabe Forces', *Sunday Independent* (Johannesburg) 8 November 1998.

8 'Private Firm to Aid Kabila's War', *Business Day* (Johannesburg) 27 September 1999.

9 'ZDF Chief in DRC Mining Ventures', *Africa News Service* 26 September 1999.

10 According to reports, President Nujoma owns a 25-square kilometre opencast diamond mine at Maji Munene, 45 kilometres from Tshikapa in the DRC. This was apparently handed over to Namibian army officials in August 1999 by Kabila – *Windhoek Observer* (Windhoek) 3 June 2000. Currently, Sacky Shanghala, Special Assistant to Prime Minister Hage Geingob; the Permanent Secretary in the Ministry of Defence, Erastus Negonga; T. Lamek; Andrew Ndishishi, Permanent Secretary in the Ministry of Trade and Industry; Major General Martin Shalli, the Namibian army chief; Deputy Police Inspector General Fritz Nghiishililwa; and retired Police Inspector General Raonga Andima are directors of the organization –

August 26 Company – that runs the mine on a day-to-day basis – *The Namibian* (Windhoek) 23 February 2001.

11   (Weinstein 2000:17). I am of course aware that this nascent 'Tutsi empire' is based on myths related to ethnicity and a particular historic reading of a constructed region. See Lemarchand (1999).

12   'Uganda's Congolese Treasure Trove', *New African* (London) May 1999.

13   'Congo Wealth Lures Africa's Power-players', *The Independent* (London), 31 October, 1998.

14   *New Times* (Kampala) 12–18 October 1998, cited in ICG (2000b).

15   *New Vision* (Kampala) 18 April 1999.

16   Ibid.

17   *Business Day* (Johannesburg) 18 April 2001.

18   Human Rights Watch Africa (1999) 'Between a Dream and a Nightmare', http://www.hrw.org/hrw/worldreport99/africa/index.html.

19   See 'Carve-up in the Congo', *Le Monde Diplomatique* (English edition), (Paris) October 1999.

20   'Uganda Explains Clash with Rwanda', *Associated Press* (Kampala) 25 August 1999.

21   UN (1996) *Report of the International Commission of Inquiry* (UN document S/1996/195 of 16 March 1996) New York: United Nations, 1996.

22   See 'Quiet African Push for Peace', *Mail and Guardian* (Johannesburg) 2 October 1998.

23   Human Rights Watch Africa (1999) 'Between a Dream and a Nightmare', http://www.hrw.org/hrw/worldreport99/africa/index.html.

24   See for example, Christopher Clapham's comments in *The Guardian* (London) 20 May 2000.

25   Although of course I understand why it is that many ordinary Africans feel they have no alternative. On this, see Mwanasali (2000).

10
Conclusion: Possible Projections for the Political Economy of Regions and Regionalisms

Morten Bøås, Marianne H. Marchand and Timothy M. Shaw

This final reflective chapter constitutes an extension of the critical revisionist perspective proposed in our introduction. It also seeks to place the ongoing debates about regions and regionalisms, new and old, in the perspective of contemporary analyses and discourses in related fields of social science, particularly privileging the four 'silences' or oversights identified in the first chapter.

More states/more regions?

As political geographers suggest, the globe's geographies have changed fundamentally in the last two decades or so. We are now experiencing multiple or overlapping sovereignties, sometimes referred to as the 'New Mediaevalism' (Kobrin 1999). One important consequence of these changes is that regions have become central features of the world by 2005 and are likely to continue to be so no matter how they are defined or ranked. We would suggest that this is so for at least five interrelated reasons.

First, *the end of bipolarity led to an unanticipated proliferation of states*, some two hundred by the turn of the century. Although it is often thought that new states are particularly jealous of their recently gained sovereignty, it appears that the exigencies of the global political economy also force the same states into concerted responses and policy initiatives at the regional level. Clearly, together more states can generate more regions. This is especially likely if many of these new regimes are rather problematic or tenuous. Most of the post-1990 states, especially in Central Europe and Central Asia, are poor, small and weak:

'fragile' indeed (DFID 2005). Such regimes face competition from and corruption or corrosion by increasingly powerful mafias and militias (see *The Economist* 2005 on LICUS from the World Bank and 'fragile states' from DFID), with profound implications for global security and stability as well as human/national development/security. So regionalist responses may in part be an attempt to augment tenuous state sovereignty and security?

Furthermore, the burgeoning development policy literature and debates on fragile states, low-income countries under stress, and difficult environments (DFID 2005, IBRD 2002) indicate that many of the issues confronting these states include a regional dimension. (See *The Economist* 2005 on regional dimensions of conflicts in Liberia and Sierra Leone). The point is that regions not only represent a level of analysis, but also provide a context for addressing development problems, building security complexes and related policy initiatives.

Second, *the myriad forces that are present in 'globalization'* generate uneven impacts and opportunities, both within and between states. One reaction to such unevenness is to advance regionalism to both contain and exploit globalization (Mittelman 2000: 109–61; see also, for instance contributions in the present volume by Beeson and Berger, Bull and Sanchez Bajo). And, as examined in the sections below, some of the new technologies and relationships associated with the globalization 'nexus' or 'syndrome' (Mittelman 2000, 2004) facilitate regional as well a global development.

Third, as a corollary of a growing number of regions, *inter-regional relationships*, mainly cooperative but sometimes competitive, have also been increasing: that is, links between, say, ASEAN and EU (Robles 2004), EU and NAFTA or the EU and Mercosur (Sanchez Bajo in this volume). One of the implications is that region-building, leading to such inter-regional relationships, is creating its own dynamic of more region-building. In short, regions seem to at least be competing with states as one of the main ordering principles of global geo-economics and politics.

Fourth, *progress in regional negotiations and institutions* is not inevitable; regressions/dilution/divisions are also possible. So the expanded and redefined SADC is not as resilient as its predecessor, SADCC. Likewise the EU may be in danger of over-expanding, from 15 to 25 and then even more associate/accession candidates. Yet advocates of regions' expansion seem to be unaware of this danger. In short, there will be continuing shifts in emphasis among levels – macro, meso and micro – and between more formal and informal regionalisms over time.

And finally, *regionalism may be under threat* from shifting policy priorities displayed by the US government. On the one hand, the Bush administration has been advocating and advancing a set of bilateral free trade treaties with its preferred partners rather than pursuing multilateralism. On the other hand, when possible, and fitting its overall trade and investment agenda, the US government has pursued distinctive regional (e.g. FTAA) or global (e.g. WTO) multilateralism. In other words, changing policy priorities of the hegemon may affect the potential for regionalism, not just in the Western hemisphere, but also in other regions of the Global Political Economy (GPE).

Studies within the 'new regionalism' genre assume that regionalism is both formal and informal involving a heterogeneous and fluid set of state and non-state actors and interests. Furthermore, it is not limited to interstate relations in a few formal sectors such as the economy, environment, society and polity. Advocacy of regional development may be articulated by a myriad of actors as a form of 'regional diplomacy'. Implementation of regional strategies in turn can be considered a variety of 'regional governance'. Curiously, regionalisms have increased at century's turn despite the absence of a global agency to advance regions other than the UN's several regional Economic Commissions; but these are largely confined to economics and development. In short, like coalitions or networks around the Ottawa and Kimberley Processes, regional diplomacy and regional governance seem to be rather 'organic' processes involving a variety of heterogeneous actors. As suggested in the next section, studies of regionalisms may now be at a crossroads.

Contributions to/from literatures on regions and regionalisms

A set of overlapping theoretical perspectives and empirical studies contributes to, as well as benefits from, the growing analysis of regions and regionalisms. The mutual connection with established social science disciplines like economics and political science (including international relations and foreign policy) is well-known and-recognized. Here we proceed to go beyond these familiar regionalist contributions to genres like development (Payne 2004) and more recent global/globalization studies. We would also venture that business, criminal, island, migration and 'new security' studies might also generate insights into new regionalisms.

Even today, most analyses of regions focus on the formal economy and polity, compatible with orthodox social science. Fortunately, some recent studies venture beyond these state and economy centred analyses. For instance, Payne's new comparative regional compilation (2004) seeks to analyse and understand 'development' within a 'region', which is necessarily interdisciplinary and problematic. Certainly, regionalism is an increasingly established strand (focus?) in the interdisciplinary study and policy of development.

Given the ubiquity of global studies and globalization, and their implications for regions and regionalism, they can generate insights into the intermediary level of diplomacy and governance. As Payne (2004: 9–12) notes, there are important and intense debates within the burgeoning globalization literature from 'sceptics' to 'hyperglobalizers' with the 'transformationalists' preferring the middle ground. Regions and regionalism bring the added dimension of territoriality to the study of globalization.

And 'global studies' may come to succeed international studies/relations if Martin Shaw's (2003: 40–1) critique of the latter is sustained:

> the discipline of international relations, much more than the core social sciences, was a Cold War product; it represented the bifurcation of superpowers and blocs rather than the burgeoning global relations that underlay them ... the transformation of international relations is ... very problematic. The international and the global are not two ways of expressing more or less the same idea ... global transformations involve the reconstitution rather than the simple undermining or overcoming of state forms and interstate relations.

This could imply that the study of regionalism, regionalization and regions will become even more prominent in the near future. Not only does it provide an entry into processes of global economic, political and social restructuring, thus undercutting Martin Shaw's critique of international relations, but it also still values territories and territoriality and thus avoids many of the problems of 'vagueness' associated with globalization and global studies.

In addition to overlapping, interdisciplinary studies of development and globalization, we suggest that at least five other themes may hold relevance for new regionalisms.

First, while globalization is inseparable from the market, it is increasingly recognized that not all *regional capitalisms* are the same. The established Anglo-American variety may be hegemonic as well as global but it can also be contrasted with the more corporatist variant in continental Europe, including Scandinavia. Further, there are identifiable differences between and among Asian capitalisms: Chinese (including offshore amongst 'overseas Chinese' entrepreneurs), Indian, Japanese and so on. And finally, there may be emerging a mutant version in the former Soviet empire: mafia capitalism? But business studies and strategies also recognize features of contemporary capitalism that advance regionalisms such as logistics/supply-chains and brands/logos. The dramatic expansion of South African franchises and technologies into Africa over the last decade is but one example of a rather distinctive regional capitalism (Shaw and van der Westhuizen 2004).

Second, *analyses of mafias and militias* who have regional even global reach and who exploit global and regional infrastructures such as air-freight, cellphones, container lines and money-laundering may provide insights into informal regionalism. Such gangs have proliferated as more weak regimes have been created. And they complicate economic and political transitions towards liberalization as well as old-fashioned notions of 'peacekeeping'. As we note in the last paragraph of this section, new security entails treating new threats from global gangs as well as more familiar 'terrorists'.

Third, *oceans and seas* can be considered regions, such as, the Indian Ocean and South Pacific. Some archipelagos may be regions in their own right, like Indonesia; other island groups are institutionalized, such as the South Pacific Forum; and others have sector-specific regional arrangements, such as the North Atlantic Fisheries Organization. There are several different definitions of and debates among island types: vulnerable/small/developing, and so on (Commonwealth Foundation 2004, UNCTAD 2004b), in part reflecting different histories and interests, and in part a function of shifting state–non-state balances in the Small Island Developing States.

Fourth, *migration* or the voluntary and forced, economic and ecological movements of people is leading to diasporas in countries or communities or cities of settlement. At least initially, most such migration is across a border into a neighbouring state rather than to the North. Such diasporas typically send remittances home (e.g. via Western Union or Money Gram), which are now the largest source of foreign exchange in several economies of the South. Diasporas may also invest back home in houses, companies, technologies and so on. The case of successive waves of 'East Indian' migrants is instructive: they constitute the basis of the high-tech boom in outsourcing 'call centre' cities, like

Bangalore (Kobayashi-Hillary 2005). It is important to consider that many of these emerging transnational communities are operating within a regional (transnational) space and, again, reflects the informal side of regionalism.

And finally, fifth, *new security issues* which link security and development in both policy and practice also embrace a notion like the regionalization of conflict, as in Central and West Africa. As already noted, there has been a growing concern over the last decade about causes and consequences of conflicts, especially as they impact prospects for human development. This has generated conceptual and policy debates over, say, (human) security and development as reflected in DFID (2005). The range of issues is captured in a special issue of *Conflict, Security & Development* (December 2004) and a special section on 'What is Human Security?' in *Security Dialogue* (September 2004). Policy implications have been carefully considered and articulated in ICISS (2001) & UN (2004b) reports. There are regional as well as global to local dimensions of such conflicts as indicated in many of the preceding chapters by, for example, Amer, MacLean, Roald and Taylor.

We conclude this section by noting a possible conceptual or methodological development in this field. Indicators of 'development' have proliferated in the last quarter century along with debates over which are most accurate, functional, policy-relevant and so on. In turn, regions can be defined by whether they rank higher or lower on such indicators. Aside from early growth indicators like GDP per capita, among the most familiar indicator is the UN Human Development Index from the early 1990s which includes regional aggregates as well as national rankings, with Africa and South Asia usually coming last. The recent set of 'Facts and Figures' on 'Development and Globalization' from UNCTAD (2005a) divides the world into multiple overlapping regionalisms to compare character of economy and trade, commodities, financial flows, remittances, services, vulnerability, and so on, not just geographic regions but also Least Developed Countries (LDCs), Landlocked Developing Countries (LLDCs), Small Island Developing States (SIDS) and so on. Likewise, the newer Millennium Development Goals (MDGs) can be used to establish regional as well as national targets, with some regions like Africa unlikely to reach them by the target year of 2015 while other regions already exceed them (UN 2005: 3, 32–3). And regional development banks, UN Economic Commissions and UNDP are all advancing regional plans and discussions to effect MDGs. Finally, in terms of ocean regions, there are indicators of economic and ecological vulnerability developed by both the

Commonwealth and the UN (UNCTAD 2004b), with the South Pacific and then the Caribbean being ranked most vulnerable.

Rethinking regionalisms

As indicated in the final substantive section of our introductory overview, we suggest that there are at least four areas of theoretical development in the social sciences that have not yet contributed to the analysis of regionalisms. At the end of this collection, then, we return to the prospects of new insights taking into account the 'cultural turn'. In particular, we consider whether these are compatible with each other and the other factors already identified above and how they may contribute to our understanding of regionalism and regionalization.

As suggested in the introduction, regions serve as referents and imaginary constructs. They can provide the justification for policy formulation or even humanitarian interventions. In other words, the *imagined region* is an example of an imagined community and can form the basis for a construction of the public or common good and of shared responsibilities that go beyond the state. Regions can evoke a sense of belonging, which may stimulate people and policy makers to act in concert. It is, therefore, important to understand and analyse how regional spatiality is being constructed and how it relates to territoriality as well as the construction of boundaries and borders, both physical and fictive.

Such constructions cannot be done without sharing a common set of *ideas*, reflected in shared histories, culture and language and constructing identities which go beyond the local or national. To give an example, Mexican migrants in the United States tend to create new imagined regional communities which are reflected discursively: 'Puebla York' for those migrants living in the New (Nueva) York area who are originally from the state of Puebla in Mexico, or 'Oaxacalifornians' for Mexican migrants from the state of Oaxaca who are living in California. The interesting element of these constructions is that they reflect both region of origin and region of destination plus the transnational nature of the new community that they are representing. So a play on words implies multiple regionalities.

Another issue raised in the introduction is the question of *governance and governmentality*. Much has been said about governance, with emerging overlapping spheres of decision-making and sovereignties and it is clear that the regional level is increasingly becoming the site for regulation, in economic as well as security, environmental and migration issues. However, the discussions about regional regimes of governance have thus far not included the question of governmentality: for instance, how states are increasingly resorting to a form of biopolitics to monitor and regulate population flows and create a semblance of territorial sovereignty through such regulation.

Linked to these issues is the increasing presence of *networks*, so much so that it is referred to as the network logic (Castells 1996). As recent transformations have created new forms of organization, in particular networks, this affects how regions function, and are constituted, or embedded in larger patterns of interaction as well as how they are being reified. Moreover, informal networks such as (informal) trading networks in West Africa as well as (informal) migrant networks in, for instance, Central and North America, are often the constitutive element for informal regionalisms.

In short, it is not only important but imperative, to take these new dimensions, related to the discursive and cultural turn in the social sciences, into consideration if one wants to further our understanding of regions and regionalisms.

What futures for regions and regionalisms?

We conclude by recognizing that the field(s) of regional development/integration and regionalization, let alone new regionalism(s), are growing rapidly, so this collection is but a beginning. Nevertheless, we trust that we have advanced analysis somewhat through novel case studies and innovative perspectives. Hopefully, these will begin to be reflected by the second decade of the twenty-first century in novel curricula in a variety of regions, creative networks reflective of diverse regional experiences and ambitions, and responsive policies by state as well as non-state actors. As one of us, Morten Bøås, insisted in the conclusion to his collection with James Hentz (Hentz and Bøås 2003): the task is always to revise.

Bibliography

Abbot, Kevin and Duncan Snidal (2000) 'International Standards and International Governance', *Journal of European Public Policy*, vol. 8, no. 3, pp. 345–70.

Acharya, Amitav (1993) 'A New Regional Order in South-East Asia: ASEAN in the Post-Cold War Era', *Adelphi Paper*, no. 270, London: International Institute of Strategic and International Studies.

Acharya, Amitav (1995) 'Transnational Production and Security: Southeast Asia's Growth Triangles', *Contemporary Southeast Asia*, vol. 17, no. 2, pp. 173–85.

Acharya, Amitav (2001) *Constructing a Security Community in Southeast Asia. ASEAN and the Problem of Regional Order*, London: Routledge.

Africa Confidential (2002) 'Kraaling out of Trouble', vol. 43, no. 24, p. 3.

Africa News Service (26 September 1999) 'ZDF Chief in DRC Mining Ventures' (www.newsline.dialog.com).

Ajibewa, Ademeri Isola (1998) 'Myanmar in ASEAN: Challenges and Prospects', *The Indonesian Quarterly*, vol. 27, no. 1, pp. 28–36.

Alagappa, Muthia (1990) 'The Cambodian Conflict: Changing Interests', *The Pacific Review*, vol. 3, no. 3, pp. 266–71.

Alexander, Jocelyn (1991) 'The Unsettled Land: The Politics of Land Redistribution in Matabeleland 1980–1990', *Journal of Southern African Studies*, vol. 17, no. 4, pp. 581–610.

Al-Khalil, Samir (1989) *Republic of Fear. The Politics of Modern Iraq*, London: Hutchinson Radius.

Amer, Ramses (1994) 'The United Nations and Foreign Military Interventions. A Comparative Study of the Application of the Charter', *Report*, no. 33, Uppsala: Uppsala University.

Amer, Ramses (1996a) 'Vietnam and Southeast Asia Since the Fall of Saigon in 1975', *Sydostasien*, vol. 7, pp. 58–77.

Amer, Ramses (1996b) 'Indochinese Perspectives of the Cambodian Conflict', in Ramses Amer, Johan Saravanamuttu and Peter Wallensteen *The Cambodian Conflict 1979–1991: From Intervention to Resolution*, Penang: Universiti Sains Malaysia, pp. 63–117.

Amer, Ramses (1997) 'Territorial Disputes and Conflict Management in ASEAN', in Maria Lourdes Aranal-Sereno and Joseph Sedfrey S. Santiago (eds) *The ASEAN: Thirty Years and Beyond*, Quezon City: University of the Philippines Law Center, pp. 325–50.

Amer, Ramses (1998) 'Expanding ASEAN's Conflict Management Framework in Southeast Asia: The Border Dispute Dimension', *Asian Journal of Political Science*, vol. 6, no. 2, pp. 33–56.

Amer, Ramses (1999) 'Conflict Management and Constructive Engagement in ASEAN's Expansion', *Third World Quarterly*, vol. 20, no. 5, pp. 1031–48.

Amer, Ramses (2000) 'Managing Border Disputes in Southeast Asia', *Kajian Malaysia, Journal of Malaysian Studies*, vol. XVIII, no. 1–2, pp. 30–60.

Amer, Ramses (2001/02) 'The Association of South-east Asian Nations and the Management of Territorial Disputes', *Boundary and Security Bulletin*, vol. 9, no. 4, pp. 81–96.

Amer, Ramses (2003) 'Conflict Management within the Association of Southeast Asian Nations (ASEAN)', in Kamarulzaman Askandar (ed.), *Management and Resolution of Inter State Conflicts in Southeast Asia*, Penang: Southeast Asian Conflict Studies Network, pp. 111–31.

Amer, Ramses and David Hughes (1999) 'The Asian Crisis and Economic Cooperation: Implications for an Expanded ASEAN', in Mason Hoadley (ed.) *Southeast Asian-Centred Economies or Economics?*, Copenhagen: NIAS, pp. 113–36.

Amer, Ramses, Johan Saravanamuttu and Peter Wallensteen (eds) (1996) *The Cambodian Conflict 1979–1991: From Intervention to Resolution*, Penang: Universiti Sains Malaysia.

Aning, Emmanuel K. (1997) 'The International Dimensions of Internal Conflict: The Case of Liberia and West Africa', *Working Paper*, Copenhagen: Centre for Development Research.

Appadurai, Arjun (ed.) (2001) *Globalization*, Durham, NC: Duke University Press.

Ashby, Tom and Manoah Esipisu (2003) 'Commonwealth Extends Zimbabwe Suspension', *Reuters News Source*, published 7 December, www.zwnews.com/issuefull.cfm?ArticleID=8157.

AsianInt EIR (Sepember 2003) 'Assessing the Viability of East Asian Monetary Union', *AsiaInt. Reference Library, Economic Intelligence Review*.

Askandar, Kamarulzaman (1994) 'ASEAN and Conflict Management: The Formative Years of 1967–1976', *Pacifica Review*, vol. 6, no. 2, pp. 57–69.

Associated Press (25 August 1999) 'Uganda Explains Clash with Rwanda'.

Atkinson, Philippa (1997) 'The War Economy in Liberia: A Political Analysis', *RRN Network Paper* 22, London: Relief and Rehabilitation Network, Overseas Development Institute.

Bach, Daniel (ed.) (1999) *Regionalization in Africa: Integration and Disintegration*, Oxford: James Currey.

Bajo, Claudia Sanchez (1999) 'The European Union and Mercosur: A Case of Interregionalism', *Third World Quarterly*, vol. 20, no. 5, pp. 927–41.

Baker, James A. (1991) 'America in Asia: Emerging Architecture for a Pacific Community', *Foreign Affairs*, vol. 70, no. 5, pp. 1–19.

Bank of England (2002) 'News Release – Financial Sanctions: Zimbabwe', 17 September (www.bankofengland.co.uk/pressreleases/2002/098htm).

Baracyetse, Pierre (1999) *The Geopolitical Stakes of the International Mining Companies in the Democratic Republic of Congo (ex-Zaire)*, Buzet, Belgium: SOS Rwanda-Burundi.

Barrell, Howard (2000) Africa Watch – Back to the Future: Renaissance and South African Domestic Policy (www.iss.co.za/).

Barta, Armando (ed.) (2001), *Mesoamerica: Los Ríos Profundos. Alternativas Plebeyas al Plan Puebla Panamà*, D.F., RMALC/El Atajo Ediciones/Instituto 'Maya', A.C.: Mexico.

Batatu, Hanna (1978) *The Old Social Classes and the Revolutionary Movements of Iraq*, Princeton, NJ: Princeton University Press.

Bayart, Jean-François, Stephen Ellis and Beatrice Hibou (1999) *The Criminalisation of the State in Africa*, Oxford: James Currey.

BBC (14 March 2002) 'Africa Backs Mugabe Win'.

BBC (14 March 2002) 'Head to Head: Zimbabwe Election Observers'.

BBC (16 March 2002) 'Mbeki Issues Verdict on Zimbabwe'.

Beeson, Mark (1996) 'APEC: Nice Theory, Shame about the Practice', *Australian Quarterly*, vol. 68, no. 2, pp. 35–48.

Beeson, Mark (1999) 'Reshaping Regional Institutions: APEC and the IMF in East Asia', *The Pacific Review*, vol. 12, no. 1, pp. 1–24.

Beeson, Mark (2000) 'Mahathir and the Markets: Globalisation and the Pursuit of Economic Autonomy in Malaysia', *Pacific Affairs*, vol. 73, no. 3, pp. 335–51.

Beeson, Mark (2003) 'East Asia, the International Financial Institutions and Regional Regulatory Reform: A Review of the Issues', *Journal of the Asia Pacific Economy*, vol. 8, no. 3, pp. 305–26.

Beeson, Mark and Mark T. Berger (2003) 'The Paradoxes of Paramountcy: Regional Rivalries and the Dynamics of US Hegemony in East Asia', *Global Change, Peace & Security*, vol. 15, no. 1, pp. 27–42.

Bell, Coral (1999) 'American Ascendancy and the Pretense of Concert', *The National Interest*, Fall Issue, pp. 55–64.

Bello, Walden (May 2000) 'Regional Currency Swap Arrangement: A Step towards Asian Monetary Fund?', *Focus on Trade*, no. 50 (http://www.focusweb.org/).

Berdal, Mats and David Malone (eds) (2000) *Greed and Grievance: Economic Agendas in Civil Wars*, Boulder, CO: Lynne Rienner.

Berger, Mark T. (1999) 'APEC And Its Enemies: The Failure of the New Regionalism in the Asia-Pacific', *Third World Quarterly*, vol. 20, no. 5, pp. 1013–30.

Berger, Mark T. and Mark Beeson (1998) 'Lineages of Liberalism and Miracles of Modernisation: The World Bank, the East Asian Trajectory and the International Development Debate', *Third World Quarterly*, vol. 19, no. 3, pp. 487–504.

Berger, Mark T. and Douglas A. Borer (1997) 'Introduction – The Rise of East Asia: Critical Visions of the Pacific Century', in Mark T. Berger and Douglas A. Borer (eds) *The Rise of East Asia: Critical Visions of the Pacific Century*, London: Routledge, pp. 1–33.

Berger, Mark T. (2003), 'The New Asian Renaissance and Its Discontents: National Narratives, Pan-Asian Visions and the Changing Post-Cold War Order', *International Politics*, vol. 40, no. 2, pp. 195–221.

Berger, Mark T. (2004) *The Battle for Asia: From Decolonization to Globalization*, London: Routledge.

Bernard, Mitchell and John Ravenhill (1995) 'Beyond Product Cycles and Flying Geese: Regionalisation, Hierarchy, and the Industrialisation of East Asia', *World Politics*, vol. 47, no. 2, pp. 171–209.

Bevacqua, Ron (1998) 'Whither the Japanese model? The Asian Economic Crisis and the Continuation of Cold War Politics in the Pacific Rim', *Review of International Political Economy*, vol. 5, no. 3, pp. 410–23.

Bøås, Morten (2000) 'The Trade–Environment Nexus and the Potential of Regional Trade Institutions', *New Political Economy*, vol. 5, no. 3, pp. 415–32.

Bøås, Morten (2003) 'Weak States, Strong Regimes: Towards a "Real" Political Economy of African Regionalisation', in Andrew Grant and Fredrik Söderbaum (eds) *The New Regionalism in Africa*. Aldershot: Ashgate, pp. 31–46.

Bøås, Morten, Marianne H. Marchand and Timothy M. Shaw (eds) (1999) 'Special Issue: New Regionalisms in the New Millennium', *Third World Quarterly*, vol. 20, no. 5, pp. 897–1070.

Bøås, Morten, Marianne Marchand and Timothy M. Shaw (2003) 'The Weave-World – the Regional Interweaving of Economies, Ideas and Identities', in Fredrik Söderbaum and Timothy M. Shaw (eds) *Theories of New Regionalism*, Basingstoke: Palgrave Macmillan, pp. 197–210.

Bowles, Paul (2002) 'Asia's Post-Crisis Regionalism: Bringing the State Back in, Keeping the (United) States Out', *Review of International Political Economy*, vol. 9, no. 2, pp. 244–70.

Breslin, Shaun and Richard Higgott (2000) 'Studying Regions: Learning from the Old, Constructing the New', *New Political Economy*, vol.5, no. 3, pp. 333–52.

Brown, Paul (2004) 'GM Soya "Miracle" Turns Sour in Argentina', *The Guardian*, (16 April 2004).

Bull, Benedicte (1999) '"New Regionalism" in Central America', *Third World Quarterly*, vol. 20, no. 5, pp. 957–70.

Bull, Benedicte and Morten Bøås (2003) 'Multilateral Development Banks as Regionalising Actors: The Asian Development Bank and the Inter-American Development Bank', *New Political Economy*, vol.8, no. 2, pp. 245–61.

Bulmer-Thomas, Victor (1998) 'The Central American Common Market: From Closed to Open Regionalism', *World Development*, vol. 26, no. 2, pp. 313–22.

Business Day (27 September 1999) 'Private Firm to Aid Kabila's War', p. 4.

Business Day (18 April 2001).

Buzan, Barry (1991) *People, States and Fear: An Agenda for International Security Studies in the Post-Cold War Era*, Boulder, CO: Lynne Rienner.

Buzan, Barry, Ole Wæver, Jaap de Wilde (1998), *Security: A New Framework for Analysis*. Boulder, CO; London: Lynne Rienner.

Caballero-Anthony, Mely (1998) 'Mechanisms of Dispute Settlement: The ASEAN Experience', *Contemporary Southeast Asia*, vol. 20, no. 1, pp. 38–66.

Call, Wendy (2001) 'A Man, a Plan, Expansion: The Puebla–Panama Plan', *Institute of Current World Affairs*, 1 June.

Call, Wendy (2002a) 'Plan Puebla–Panama: Done Deal or Emerging Flashpoint?', Americas Program, Silver City, NM, Interhemispheric Resource Center, 9 April.

Call, Wendy (2002b) 'Resisting the Plan Puebla–Panama', Americas Program, Silver City, NM, Interhemispheric Resource Center, September.

Call, Wendy (2003) 'PPP Focus Moves South as Mexican Backing Loses Momentum', PPP Spotlight no.1, Americas Program, Silver City, NM, Interhemispheric Resource Center, 20 February.

Campbell, Horace (1999) 'From War to Peace in the Congo or Devastation and Militarism', unpublished mimeo.

Carmody, Pàdraig (2001) *Tearing the Social Fabric: Neoliberalism, Deindustrialisation and the Crisis of Governance in Zimbabwe*, Portsmouth, NH: Heinemann.

Carriére, Jean (2000) 'Biodiversity and Regional Cooperation', in CEDLA (ed.) *Fronteras: Towards a Borderless Latin America*, Amsterdam: CEDLA, pp. 141–47.

Castellano, Marc (18 June 1999) 'Internationalization of the Yen: A Ministry of Finance Pipe Dream?', *Japan Economic Institute Report*, 23A (www.jei.org/Restricted/JEIRArchive99.html).

Castellano, Marc (Feb. 11, 2000) 'Japan's Foreign Aid Program in the New Millennium: Rethinking Development', *Japan Economic Institute Report*, 6A (www.jei.org/Archive/JEIRArchive99.html).

Castells, Manuel (1996) *The Rise of the Network Society* (Volume 1 in trilogy on Information Age; second edition issued in 2000), Oxford: Blackwell.

Castro Soto, Gustavo (2002) 'Fortalezas Del Plan Puebla Panamá. Foda del PPP y Los Acuerdos de San Andrés', *Chiapas al Día*, no. 217, San Christobal de las Casas: CIEPAC.

CEO and TNI (2003) *Mercosur for Sale? The EU's FTAA and the Need to Oppose it*, Amsterdam: TNI.

Cerdas, Rodolfo (1998) 'Las Instituciones de Integración en Centroamérica', in Victor Bulmer-Thomas (ed.) *Centroamérica en Reestructuración: Integración Regional en Centroamérica*, San José: Flacso, pp. 245–76.

CFEOT (12 November 1998) 'Internationalization of the Yen (Interim Report)' (www.mof.go.jp/english/yen/itiran.htm).

CFEOT (20 April 1999) 'Internationalization of the Yen for the 21st Century – Japan's Response to Changes in Global Economic and Financial Environments' (www.mof.go.jp/english/yen/itiran.htm).

Chabal, Patrick (1994) *Power in Africa: An Essay in Political Interpretation*, New York: St Martin's Press.

Chabal, Patrick and Jean-Pascal Daloz (1999) *Africa Works: Disorder as Political Instrument*, Oxford: James Currey.

Chan, Stephen (2003) *Robert Mugabe: A Life of Power and Violence*, Ann Arbor, MI: University of Michigan Press.

Chin Kin Wah (1997) 'ASEAN the Long Road to "One Southeast Asia"', *Asian Journal of Political Science*, vol. 5, no. 1, pp. 1–19.

Chitiyo, Tapera Knox (2000) 'Land Violence and Compensation: Reconceptualising Zimbabwe's Land and War Veterans' Debate', *Track Two*, vol. 9. no. 1, p. 23.

Chubin, Shahram and Charles Tripp (1988) *Iran and Iraq at War*, Boulder, CO: Westview Press.

Cilliers, Jakkie (2002) 'NEPAD's Peer Review Mechanism' (www.iss.co.za/).

Clapham, Christopher (2001) 'Rethinking African States', *African Security Review*, vol. 10, no. 3, pp. 118–35.

Coetzee, David (2001) 'The New African Initiative'. Paper prepared for the Civil Society Planning Conference, 21–22 October, Ottawa.

Colitt, Raymond (2004) 'Mercosur and EU Revive Free Trade Aims', *Financial Times*, (20 January 2004).

Commonwealth Foundation (2004) *The Commonwealth Foundation and Small Island Developing States*, London: Commonwealth Foundation.

Conflict, Security & Development (2004) vol. 4, no. 3, pp. 217–562.

Contemporary Review (2003) 'African Leaders and the Crisis in Zimbabwe', vol. 280, no. 1637, pp. 344–8.

Cordesman, Anthony H. and Abraham R. Wagner (1990) *The Lessons of Modern War Volume II. The Iraq–Iran War*, Boulder, CO: Westview Press.

Cumings, Bruce (1999) *Parallax Visions: Making Sense of American–East Asian Relations at the End of the Century*, Durham, NC: Duke University Press.

Dashwood, Hevina (1996) 'The Relevance of Class to the Evolution of Zimbabwe's Development Strategy, 1980–1991', *Journal of Southern African Studies*, vol. 22, no. 1, pp. 27–48.

Dashwood, Hevina (2000) *Zimbabwe: The Political Economy of Transformation* (Toronto: University of Toronto Press).

Davidson, Basil (1994) *Modern Africa: A Social and Political History* (3rd edn), London: Longman.

Davies, Robert (1997) 'South Africa in the SADC: The Impact of Trade and Investment on Migration' (Briefing Paper), Pretoria, South Africa.

DFID (2005) *Why We Need to Work More Effectively in Fragile States*, London: DFID.

Dirlik, Arif (1992) 'The Asia–Pacific Idea: Reality and Representation in the Invention of Regional Structure', *Journal of World History*, vol. 3, no. 1, pp. 55–79.

Duffield, Mark (1998) 'Post-Modern Conflict: Warlords, Post-adjustment States and Private Protection', *Civil Wars*, vol. 1, no. 1, pp. 65–102.

Duffield, Mark (1999) 'Globalisation and War Economies: Promoting Order or the Return of History?', *Fletcher Forum of World Affairs*, vol. 23, no. 2, pp. 19–36.

Duffield, Mark (2001) *Global Governance and the New Wars: The Merging of Development and Security*, London: Zed Books.

Dynes, Michael (9 December 2003) 'Commonwealth Struggles to Show United Front as Summit Ends', *The Times* (www.zwnews.com/issuefull.cfm?ArticleID=8165).

Dwyer, Michael (22 September 1997) 'Japan Backs $133bn Asia Fund', *The Australian Financial Review* (http://www.afr.com.au).

Dwyer, Michael (17 September 2002) 'Asian Economies Fear "Friendly" Dragon', *The Australian Financial Review* (http://www.afr.com.au).

ECLAC (1994), *Open Regionalism in Latin America and the Caribbean*, Santiago: United Nations Economic Commission for Latin America and the Caribbean.

ECLAC (2000/2001) *Los Procesos de Integracion de los Paises de América Latina y el Caribe 2000–2001: Avances Retrocesos y Temas Pendientes*, Santiago: United Nations Economic Commission for Latin America and the Caribbean.

Economist (1997) 'Rumpus in Hong Kong', 27 September, p. 17.

Economist (1998) 'War Turns Commercial', 24 October, p. 88.

Economist (2005). 'Rebuilding Failed States: From Chaos, Order' 5 March, pp. 58–61.

El Cronista Comercial (27 July 1998).

EU (1999) *Community External Trade Policy in the Field of Standards and Conformity Assessment: Executive Summary*, Brussels: European Union.

EU (2001) *White Paper on European Governance*, Brussels: European Union.

Eurostat (no. 2, 1996).

Eurosur (no. 16, June 1997).

EU–Mercosur (2002) *European Commission Adopts Regional Programme in Support of Further Mercosur Integration*, Brussels: EU–Mercosur.

Farouk-Sluglett, Marion and Peter Sluglett (1987) *Iraq Since 1958. From Revolution to Dictatorship*, London: KPI Limited.

Financial Mail (Johannesburg), 15 January 1999.

Fontagne, Laurenz, Moris Freudenberg and David Unal-Kesenci (1996) *Analyse Statistique des Échanges ce des Produits Intermédiaires*, Luxembourg: Eurostat.

Foreign Press Center Japan (2000) 'ASEAN + 3 Finance Ministers Agree to Strengthen Currency Cooperation', 19 May.

Freeman, Constance (2000) 'The Three Economies of Africa', *African Security Review*, vol. 9, no. 4, pp. 66–81.

Frost, Frank (1991) 'The Cambodian Conflict: The Path towards Peace', *Contemporary Southeast Asia*, vol. 13, no. 2, pp. 119–61.

Funston, John (1998) 'ASEAN: Out of Its Depth?', *Contemporary Southeast Asia*, vol. 20, no. 1, pp. 22–38.

Gamble, Andrew and Anthony Payne (1996) 'Conclusion: The New Regionalism', in Andrew Gamble and Anthony Payne (eds) *Regionalism and World Order*. New York: St. Martin's Press, pp. 247–65.

Ganesan, Nansan (1998) 'Malaysia–Singapore Relations: Some Recent Developments', *Asian Affairs. An American Review*, vol. 25, no. 1, pp. 21–36.

Ganesan, Nansan (1999) 'Bilateral Tensions in Post-Cold War ASEAN', *Pacific Strategic Papers* 9, Singapore: Institute of Southeast Asian Studies.

Garnaut, Ross (1996) *Open Regionalism and Trade Liberalisation: An Asia-Pacific Contribution to the World Trade System*, Singapore: Institute of Southeast Asian Studies.

Gerschenson, Ana (2001) 'Una Nueva Apuesta a Favor del Mercosur' (www.clarin.com/diario/hoy/p-01301.htm).

Gillingham, John (2003) *European Integration, 1950–2003: Superstate or New Market Economy?*, Cambridge: Cambridge University Press.

Global Coalition for Africa (GCA) (www.gca-cma.org/emenu.htm).

Gowan, Peter (1999) *The Global Gamble: Washington's Faustian Bid for World Dominance*, London: Verso.

Gowan, Peter (2003) 'US Hegemony Today', *Monthly Review*, July–August, pp. 30–50.

Greenwood, Justin (2003) *Interest Representation in the European Union*, Basingstoke: Palgrave Macmillan.

Grubel, James (13 February 2003) 'Zimbabwe Suspension Extended', *The Australian* (www.zimbabwesituation.com/feb13a_2003.html#link2).

GTI (2001) Plan Puebla-Panmá: Iniciativas Mesoamericanas y Proyectos, Grupo Técnico Interinstitucioinal BCIE-BID-ECLAC con el apoyo del INCAE. San Salvador, El Salvador, 15 June.

Hamill, James (2003) 'South Africa and Zimbabwe', *Contemporary Review*, vol. 281, no. 1638, pp. 34–9.

Harvey, Neil (1998) *The Chiapas Rebellion: The Struggle for Land and Democracy*, Durham, NC: Duke University Press.

Hatch, Walter and Kozo Yamamura (1996) *Asia in Japan's Embrace: Building a Regional Production Alliance*, Cambridge: Cambridge University Press.

Hatcher, Peter and Michael Dwyer (27 September 1997) 'East versus West: How the Markets are Uniting Asia against the US', *The Australian Financial Review*, (http://www.afr.com.au).

Helleiner, Eric (1995) 'Explaining the Globalization of Financial Markets: Bringing States Back in', *Review of International Political Economy*, vol. 2, no. 2, pp. 315–41.

Helms, Christine (1984) *Iraq: Eastern Flank of the Arab World*, Washington, DC: Brookings Institution.

Hentz, James J. and Morten Bøås (eds) (2003) *New and Critical Security and Regionalism: Beyond the Nation-state*, Aldershot: Ashgate.

Heradstveit, Daniel (1987) 'Iran/Irak – Frå retorikk til pragmatikk', *Nupi-notat*, no. 374.

Herbert, Dieter (May 2000) 'Monetary Regionalism: Regional Integration Without Financial Crises', *CSGR Working Paper*, no. 52/00.

Herzog, Lawrence A. (ed.) (1992) *Changing Boundaries in the Americas: New Perspectives on the U.S–Mexican, Central American, and South American Borders*, San Diego, CA: University of California.

Hettne, Björn (1996) 'Globalization, the New Regionalism and East Asia'. Paper delivered at the United Nations University Global Seminar Shonan Session, Hayama, Japan.

Hettne, Björn (1999) 'Globalization and the New Regionalism: The Second Great Transformation', in Björn Hettne, Andreás Inotai and Osvaldo Sunkel (eds) *Globalism and the New Regionalism*. Basingstoke: Macmillan, pp. 1–24.

Hettne, Björn (2003) 'The New Regionalism Revisited', in Fredrik Söderbaum and Timothy M. Shaw (eds) *Theories of New Regionalisms: A Palgrave Reader*. Basingstoke: Palgrave, pp. 22–42.

Hettne, Björn and Fredrik Söderbaum (1998) 'The New Regionalism Approach', *Politeia*, vol. 17, no. 3, pp. 6–21.

Hettne, Björn and Fredrik Söderbaum (2000) 'Theorising the Rise of Regionness', *New Political Economy*, vol. 5, no. 3, pp. 457–73.

Hettne, Björn, András Inotai and Osvaldo Sunkel (eds) (1999) *Globalism and the New Regionalism*, Basingstoke: Macmillan.

Higgott, Richard (1998) 'The Asian Economic Crisis: A Study in the Politics of Resentment', *New Political Economy*, vol. 3, no. 3, pp. 333–56.

Higgott, Richard (2000) 'Regionalism in the Asia-Pacific: Two Steps Forward, One Step Back?', in Richard Stubbs and Geoffrey R. D. Underhill (eds), *Political Economy and the Changing Global Order*, New York: Oxford University Press, pp. 254–63.

Higgott, Richard and Richard Stubbs (1995) 'Competing Conceptions of Economic Regionalism: APEC versus EAEC in the Asia Pacific', *Review of International Political Economy*, vol. 2, no. 3, pp. 516–35.

Hiro, Dilip (1991) *The Longest War. The Iran–Iraq Military Conflict*, New York: Routledge.

Hoang, Anh Tuan (1994) 'Vietnam's Membership in ASEAN: Economic, Political and Security Implications', *Contemporary Southeast Asia*, vol. 16, no. 3, pp. 259–73.

Hoogvelt, Ankie (1997) *Globalisation and the Post-Colonial World*. Baltimore, MD and Boston, MA: Johns Hopkins University Press.

Hook, Glenn (1996) 'Japan and the Construction of Asia-Pacific', in Andrew Gamble and Anthony Payne (eds), *Regionalism and World Order*, London: Macmillan, pp. 169–206.

Hudson, Michael C. (ed.) (1999) *Middle East Dilemma: The Politics and Economics of Arab Integration*, New York: Columbia University Press.

Hughes, Christopher W. (2000) 'Japanese Policy and the East Asian Currency Crisis: Abject Defeat or Quiet Victory', *Review of International Political Economy*, vol. 7, no. 2, pp. 219–53.

Human Rights Watch Africa (1999) 'Between a Dream and a Nightmare'(http://www.hrw.org/hrw/worldreport99/africa/index.html).

Hurrell, Andrew (1995) 'Regionalism in the Americas', in Andrew Hurrell and Louise Fawcett (eds) *Regionalism in World Politics*, New York: Oxford University Press, pp. 250–82.

IBRD (2002) *The World Bank Group in Low-income Countries Under Stress (LICUS: A Task Force Report)*, Washington, DC: IBRD.

ICG (2000a) *Scramble for the Congo: Anatomy of an Ugly War*, Brussels: ICG.

ICG (2000b) *Uganda and Rwanda: Friends or Enemies?* Brussels: ICG.

ICISS (December 2001) *The Responsibility to Protect: Report of the International Commission on Intervention and State Sovereignty*, Ottawa: IDRC.

IDB (1998) *A Preliminary Estimate of 1998 Trade*, Washington, DC: IDB.

IDB (2001) 'A New Vision for Mesoamerica', *Americas*, Washington, DC: IDB, August, online version.

IDB (2002) *Beyond Borders. The New Regionalism in Latin America. Economic and Social Progress in Latin America. 2002 Report*, Washington, DC: IDB/Johns Hopkins University Press.

Iglesias, Enrique (1997) 'The New Face of Regional Integration in Latin America and the Caribbean'. Presentation at the Annual World Bank Conference on Development in Latin America and the Caribbean Trade: Towards Open Regionalism, Montevideo, Uruguay, 29 June–1 July.

ILO (2004) *A Fair Globalization: The Role of the ILO*, Geneva: ILO (Report to the World Commission on the Social Dimension of Globalization).

The Independent (31 October 1998) 'Congo Wealth Lures Africa's Power-players', p. 6.

International Monetary Fund (1997) *Interim Assessment of the World Economic Outlook*, Washington, DC: International Monetary Fund.

The Iraq Research and Documentation Project (IRDP-NIDS) (2003) 'The Iraq Research and Documentation Project. North Iraq Data Set' (http://www.fas.harvard.edu/~irdp).

Jenkins, Carolyn (2002) 'The Politics of Economic Policy-making After Independence', in Carolyn Jenkins and John Knight (eds) *The Economic Decline of Zimbabwe: Neither Growth Nor Equity*, Basingstoke: Palgrave, pp. 18–59.

Jessop, Bob (2003) 'The Political Economy of Scale: Globalization/ Regionalization'. Notes prepared for the cross-disciplinary PhD course: 'States and Regions: Exploring the Relationship'. Sole Hotel, Norway, 23–6 April.

Johnson, Chalmers (1998) 'Economic Crisis in East Asia: The Clash of Capitalisms', *Cambridge Journal of Economics*, vol. 22, no. 6, pp. 653–61.

Johnson, Chalmers (2001) 'Japanese Capitalism Revisited', *JPRI Occasional Paper*, no. 22 (http://www.jpri.org/).

Jones, Matthew (2002) *Conflict and Confrontation in Southeast Asia, 1961–1965: Britain, the United States, Indonesia and the Creation of Malaysia*, Cambridge: Cambridge University Press.

Jonquières, Guy de (2003) 'Mr. Zoellick Claims These Initiatives Can Offer a Quicker Way to Liberalise Trade than through Cumbersome and Long-winded WTO Negotiation', *Financial Times* (15 September 2003).

Jonquières, Guy de (2004) 'Exclusive Move to Kickstart Trade Talks', *Financial Times* (16 April 2004).

Kalele-ka-Bila (1993) 'Regionalist Ideologies', in Kankwenda Mbaya (ed.) *Zaire: What Destiny?* Dakar: CODESRIA, pp. 64–76.

Khadduri, Majid (1988) *The Gulf War. The Origins and Implications of the Iraq–Iran Conflict*, Oxford: Oxford University Press.

Kirby, Peadar (2003) *Latin America in a Globalized World*, London: Sage.

Kobayashi-Hillary, Mark (2005) *Outsourcing to India: The Offshore Advantage*, Berlin: Springer (2nd edn).

Kobrin, Stephen J (1999) 'Back to the Future: Neomedievilism and the Postmodern Digital World Economy', in Assem Prakash and Jeffrey A. Hart (eds) *Globalization and Governance*, London: Routledge (Routledge/RIPE Studies in Global Political Economy), pp. 165–87.

Koh, Tommy T. B. (1995) *The United States and East Asia: Conflict and Co-operation*, Singapore: The Institute of Policy Studies.

Krasner, Stephen (1999) *Sovereignty: Organised Hypocrisy*, Princeton, NJ: Princeton University Press.

Krauss, Clifford (2001) 'Economy Aide to the Rescue, as Argentina Fights Default', *New York Times* (www.nytimes.com/2001/03/30).

Kurus, Bilson (1993) 'Understanding ASEAN: Benefits and Raison d'Etre', *Asian Survey*, vol. 33, no. 8, pp. 819–31.

Kwan, C. H (2001) *Yen Bloc: Toward Economic Integration in Asia*, Washington, DC: Brookings Institution.

Lapper, Richard (2003) 'Latin-America Woos Europe as Counterbalance to US', *Financial Times*, 17 June 2003.

Lavergne, Real (ed.) (1997) *Regional Integration and Co-operation in West Africa: A Multidimensional Perspective*, Trenton, NJ: Africa World Press.

Lawrence, Susan V. and Murray Hiebert (24 October 2002) 'Sino-US Relations: Bending in the US Storm', *Far Eastern Economic Review*, pp. 32–6.

Leader, Robert (2003) 'The Real Reason for the Cancun Failure', *Financial Times*, (23 September 2003).

Lemarchand, René (1999) *Ethnicity as Myth: The View from Central Africa*, Copenhagen: Centre for African Studies (Occasional Paper).

Le Monde Diplomatique (October 1999) 'Carve-up in the Congo', p. 3.

Leys, Colin (1994) 'Confronting the African Tragedy', *New Left Review*, no. 204, pp. 33–48.

Linder, Staffan Burenstam (1986) *The Pacific Century: Economic and Political Consequences of Asian-Pacific Dynamism*, Stanford, CA: Stanford University Press.

Liu, Henry C. K. (12 July 2002) 'The Case for an Asian Monetary Fund', *Asia Times* (http://www.atimes.com/atimes/Asian_Economy/DG12Dk01.html).

Lo, Dic (1999) 'The East Asian Phenomenon: The Consensus, the Dissent, and the Significance of the Present Crisis', *Capital and Class*, no. 67, pp. 101–36.

Lockhart, James and Stuart B. Schwartz (1983) *Early Latin America. A History of Colonial Spanish America*, Cambridge: Cambridge University Press.

Lustig, Nora (1998) *Mexico: The Remaking of an Economy*, Washington, DC: Brookings Institution.

MacGaffey, Janet (1991) *The Real Economy of Zaire: The Contribution of Smuggling and Other Unofficial Activities to National Wealth*, London: James Currey.

MacGaffey, Janet and Remy Bazenguissa-Ganga (2000) *Congo–Paris: Transnational Traders on the Margins of the Law*, Oxford: James Currey.

MacLean, Sandra J. (2001) 'Ethnicity and Race in the Changing Political Economies of South Africa and Zimbabwe', in Sandra J. MacLean, Fahimul Quadir and Timothy M. Shaw (eds) *Crises of Governance in Asia and Africa*, Aldershot: Ashgate, pp. 67–81.

MacLean, Sandra J. (2002) 'Mugabe at War: The political economy of conflict in Zimbabwe', *Third World Quarterly*, vol. 23, no. 3, pp. 513–28.

Mahbubani, Kishore (1995) 'The Pacific Way', *Foreign Affairs*, vol. 74, no. 1, pp. 100–12.

Mail and Guardian (2 October 1998) 'Quiet African Push for Peace', p. 8.

Mail and Guardian (5 March 2004) 'Zim's Mining Sector Surges Amid the Gloom', p. 9.

Malik, J. Mohan (1997) 'Myanmar's Role in Regional Security: Pawn or Pivot?', *Contemporary Southeast Asia*, vol. 19, no. 1, pp. 52–73.

Mamdani, Mahmood (2001) 'Beyond Settler and Native as Political Identities. Overcoming the Political Legacy of Colonialism', *Comparative Studies in Society and History*, vol. 43, no. 4, pp. 651–64.

Maquila Solidarity Network (September 2001) 'Fox's Plan Puebla Panama Confronts Corridors of Resistance', Maquila Network Update (http://www.maquilasolidarity.org/resources/maquilas/planpuebla.htm).

Maquila Solidarity Network (2003) 'The Labor Behind the Label: How our Clothes are Made' (http://www.maquilasolidarity.org/).

Marchand, Marianne H. (2001) 'North American Regionalism and Regionalisms in the 1990s', in Michael Schultz, Fredrik Söderbaum and Joachim Öjendal (eds), *Regionalization in a Globalizing World. A Comparative Perspective on Forms, Actors and Processes*, London: Zed Books, pp. 198–210.

Marchand, Marianne H. and Morten Bøås (2004) 'Romanticising the Region: Governance and Change'. Paper presented to the ECPR Standing Group on International Relations Fifth Pan-European International Relations Conference, 9–11 September, The Hague.

Marcos, Sylvia (1995) 'Sacred Earth: Mesoamerican Perspectives', in Leonardo Boff and Virgil Elizondo (eds), *Economy and Poverty. Cry of the Earth, Cry of the Poor*, London: SCM Press, pp. 27–37.

Marr, Phebe (1985) *The Modern History of Iraq*, Boulder, CO: Westview Press.

Mbaya, Kakwarha (ed) (1993) *Zaire: What Destiny* (Dakar: CODESRIA).

Mbembe, Achille (1999) 'At the Edge of the World: Boundaries, Territoriality and Sovereignty in Africa', *CODESRIA Bulletin*, no. 3–4, pp. 4–16.

Mbiba, Beacon (2001) 'Communal Land Rights in Zimbabwe as State Sanction and Social Control: A Narrative', *Africa*, vol. 71, no. 3, pp. 426–48.

McElhinny, Vincent (2004) 'CAFTA: Few Benefits, Many Costs', Americas Program, Silver City, NM: Interhemispheric Resource Center, 29 January, revised 20 February.

McKinnon, R. I. (2000) 'The East Asian Dollar Standard, Life After Death?', *Economic Notes by Banca Monte dei Paschi di Siena SpA*, vol. 29, no. 1–2, pp. 31–82.

MEBF (2003) *Brasilia Declaration*, Brasilia: MEBF.

Midgley, John (ed.) (1986) *Community Participation, Social Development and the State*, London: Methuen.

Milner, Mark, Larry Elliot, Alex Bellos and Uki Goni (2001) 'Out Comes the Cavallo Knife', *The Guardian*, Friday 23 March.

Mittelman, James H. (1996) 'Rethinking the "New Regionalism" in the Context of Globalization', *Global Governance*, vol. 2, no. 2, pp. 189–213.

Mittelman, James (1999) 'Rethinking the "New Regionalism" in the Context of Globalization', in Björn Hettne, Andreás Inotai and Osvaldo Sunkel (eds) *Globalism and the New Regionalism*, Basingstoke: Macmillan, pp. 25–53.

Mittelman, James. H. (2000) *The Globalization Syndrome. Transformation and Resistance*, Princeton, NJ: Princeton University Press.

Mittelman, James H. (2004) *Whither Globalization: The Vortex of Knowledge and Ideology*, London: Routledge.

Molina, Ivan (2000) *El Pensamiento del EZLN*, Mexico, DF, Plaza y Valdés, S.A de C.V.

Moro, Braulio (December 2002) 'Puebla–Panama Plan Annexes Indigenous Resources: Central America's Jaguars Snarl', *Le Monde Diplomatique*, pp. 10–11.

Moyo, Sam (2001) 'The Land Occupation Movement and Democratisation in Zimbabwe: Contradition of Neoliberalism', *Millennium*, vol. 30, no. 2, pp. 311–30.

Mujaju, Akiiki (1999) 'How to Make Sense of the Events Taking Place in the Great Lakes Region', *Southern African Political and Economic Monthly*, vol. 12, no. 3, pp. 12–13.

Murphy, R. Taggart (1996) *The Weight of the Yen: How Denial Imperils America's Future and Ruins an Alliance*, New York: W.W. Norton & Co.

Murphy, R. Taggart (2000) 'Japan's Economic Crisis', *New Left Review*, no. 1, pp. 25–52.

Mwanasali, Musifiky (2000) 'The View from Below', in Mats Berdal and David Malone (eds) *Greed and Grievances: Economic Agendas in Civil Wars*, Boulder, CO: Lynne Rienner, pp. 137–53.

Nakash, Yitzhak (1994) *The Shi'is of Iraq*, Princeton, NJ: Princeton University Press.

Namibian (23 February 2001).

Narine, Shaun (2002) *Explaining ASEAN. Regionalism in Southeast Asia*, Boulder, CO: Lynne Rienner.

Nathan, K. S, (2002) 'Malaysia–Singapore Relations: Retrospect and Prospect', *Contemporary Southeast Asia*, vol. 24, no. 2, pp. 385–410.

Neuman, Iver B. (2003), 'A Region-building Approach', in Fredrik Söderbaum and Timothy M. Shaw (eds) *Theories of New Regionalism*, Basingstoke: Palgrave Macmillan, pp. 160–78.

New African (May 1999) 'Uganda's Congolese Treasure Trove', p. 10.

New Vision (18 April 1999).

Nguyen Vung Tung, (1993) 'Vietnam–ASEAN Cooperation in Southeast Asia', *Security Dialogue*, vol. 34, no. 1, pp. 85–92.

Nguyen Vung Tung (2002) 'Vietnam–ASEAN Cooperation in Southeast Asia', *Contemporary Southeast Asia*, vol. 22, no. 1, pp. 106–20.

Niemann, Michael (2000) *A Spatial Approach to Regionalisms in the Global Economy*, Basingstoke: Palgrave.

Nordhaug, Kristen (2002a) 'US Hegemony, Economic Integration and Monetary Regionalism in East Asia', Roskilde Universitetscenter, *IDS Working Paper*, no. 34.

Nordhaug, Kristen (2002b) 'The Political Economy of the Dollar and the Yen in East Asia', *Journal of Contemporary Asia*, vol. 32, no.1, pp. 517–35.

Okitakekumba, Longandjo (1993) 'State Power under MPR Control: An Interpretative Essay', in Kankwenda Mbaya (ed.) *Zaire: What Destiny?* Dakar: CODESRIA, pp. 35–55.

Oman, Charles (1994) *Globalisation and Regionalisation: The Challenge for Developing Countries*, Paris: OECD.

Osava, Mario (February 2003) 'Mercosur–Unión Europa: Un Juego con Pocas Cartas en la Mesa', *IPS*.

Ottaway, Marina (1998) 'Africa's "New Leaders": African Solution or African Problem?', *Current History*, pp. 209–13.

Pacific Rim Review (20 December 1997) 'Asian Crisis – Global Crisis'(http://pacificrim.bx.com/articles/12-20asian_crisis.htm).

Paribatra, Sukhumbhand (1994) 'From ASEAN Six to ASEAN Ten: Issues and Prospects', *Contemporary Southeast Asia*, vol. 16, no. 3, pp. 243–58.

Payne, Anthony (1998) 'The New Political Economy of Area Studies', *Millennium*, vol. 27, no. 2, pp. 253–73.

Payne, Anthony (ed.) (2004) *The New Regional Politics of Development*, Basingstoke: Palgrave Macmillan.

Perkmann, Markus and Ngai-Ling Sum (eds) (2002) *Globalization, Regionalization and Cross-border Regions*, Basingstoke: Palgrave Macmillan.

Prevost, Gary and Carlos Oliva Campos (2002) *Neoliberalism and Neopanamericanism: The View from Latin America*, New York: Palgrave Macmillan.

Quadir, Fahimul and Jaya Lele (eds) (2004) *Democracy and Civil Society in Asia* Vols. I and II, Basingstoke: Palgrave Macmillan.

Radelet, Steven and Jeffrey D. Sachs (1998) 'The East Asian Financial Crisis: Diagnosis, Remedies, Prospects', *Brooking Papers on Economic Activity*, no. 1 (http://www.cid.harvard.edu/cidpublications/hiid/asiacrisis.html).

Raftopoulos, Brain (2002) 'Briefing: Zimbabwe's 2002 Presidential Election', *African Affairs*, vol. 101, no. 404, pp. 413–26.

Ravenhill, John (2001) *APEC and the Construction of Pacific Rim Regionalism*, Cambridge: Cambridge University Press.

Ravenhill, John (2002) 'A Three Bloc World? The New East Asian Regionalism', *International Relations of the Asia Pacific*, no. 2, pp. 167–95.

Ravenhill, John (2003) 'The New Bilateralism in the Asia Pacific', *Third World Quarterly*, vol. 24, no. 2, pp. 299–317.

Reed, Ananya Mukherjee (ed.) (2003) *Corporate Capitalism in Contemporary South Asia: Conventional Wisdoms and South Asian Realities*, Basingstoke: Palgrave.

Reno, William (1996) 'The Business of War in Liberia', *Current History*, pp. 211–15.

Reno, William (1998) *Warlord Politics and African States*, Boulder, CO: Lynne Rienner.

Reno, William, (2000a) 'Clandestine Economies, Violence and States in Africa', *Journal of International Affairs*, vol. 53, no. 2, pp. 433–59.

Reno, William (2000b) 'Liberia and Sierra Leone: The Competition for Patronage in Resource-Rich Economies', in E. Wayne Nafziger, Frances Stewart and Raimo Vayrynen (eds) *Weak States and Vulnerable Economies: Humanitarian Emergencies in Developing Countries*, Volume 2, Oxford: Oxford University Press, pp. 231–59.

Reno, William (2000c) *War, Debt and the Role of Pretending in Uganda's International Relations*, Copenhagen: Center for African Studies, Occasional Paper.

Reuters (21 June 1999) 'France–Spain Clear Way for Mercosur Pact'.

Richards, Paul (1996) *Fighting for the Rain Forest: War, Youth and Resources in Sierra Leone*, Oxford: James Currey.

Risse-Kappen, Thomas (1995) *Bringing Transnational Relations Back In: Non-state Actors, Domestic Structures and International Institutions*, Cambridge: Cambridge University Press.

Roald, Ane M. (2004) 'The Iraqi Opposition. A Player in the Regional Game', Oslo: University of Oslo, (MA Thesis).

Robles, Alfredo C. (2004) *The Political Economy of Interregional Relations: ASEAN and the EU*, Aldershot: Ashgate.

Rotberg, Robert (2000) 'Africa's Mess, Mugabe's Mayhem', *Foreign Affairs*, vol. 79, no. 5, pp. 47–61.

Rowley, Anthony (1997) 'The Battle of Hong Kong', *Capital Trends*, vol. 2, no. 13 (www.gwjapan.com/ftp/pub/nrca/ctv2n13c.html).

Rowley, Anthony (2000a) 'Appetite for Asian Monetary Fund Grows', *Emerging Markets*, 6 May.

Rowley, Anthony (2000b) 'It's a Wrap: ASEAN Plus Three Sign Far-reaching Agreement', *Emerging Markets*, 7 May 2000.

Rüland, Jürgen (2002) 'Inter- and Transregionalism: Remarks on the State of the Art of a New Research Agenda'. Paper presented to the workshop Asia-Pacific Studies in Australia and Europe: A Research Agenda for the Future, Australian National University, 5–6 July 2002.

SAMP (2 October 2002) 'Extreme Brutality', *The Chronicle*, p. 13.

SAMP (7 October 2002) 'Mozambique/Zimbabwe Joint Commission to Discuss Border Controls', *Agencia de Informacao de Mocambique*, Maputo.

SAMP (13 October 2002) 'Botswana Government Probes Abuse Allegations Against Zim', *The Sunday Mirror*, p. 4.

SAMP (18 October 2002) 'Zimbabwe Nations Rush to Fix Their Refugee Status', *The Sowetan*, p. 6.

SAMP (31 October 2002) 'Commentary on State of Tourism in South Africa', *Business Day*, Johannesburg (www.queensu.ca/samp/news/2002/oct.htm #Regional).

Sandoval Palacios, Juan Manuel (2001) 'El Plan Puebla–Panamá Como Regulador de la Migración Laboral Centroamericana y del Sur-Surese de México', Foro de Análisis, Información y Propuestas Xela 2001 (http://usuarios.lycos.es./celaju/pronencia3-parte1.htm), pp.1–11.

Sandoval Palacios, Juan Manuel (2002) 'El Plan Puebla–Panamá y el Plan Colombia: Proyectos Geoestratégicos para la Conformaciónb de las Nuevas Fronteras Geopolíticas del Àrea de Libre Comercio de las Américas (ALCA)', *Tercer Congreso Europeo de Latinoamericanistas*, Amsterdam, 3–6 July.

Saravanamuttu, Johan (1996) 'The ASEAN Perspective and Role in the Cambodian Peace Process', in Ramses Amer, Johan Saravanamuttu and Peter Wallensteen (eds) *The Cambodian Conflict 1979–1991: From Intervention to Resolution*, Penang: Universiti Sains Malaysia, pp. 37–62.

Sberro, Stefan (2002) 'Une Alliance Stratégique entre l'Amérique Latine et l'Europe?' *Problèmes de l'Amérique*, no. 46–7, pp. 17–31.

Schmitter, Pierre C. (2001) *What is There to Legitimise in the European Union, and How Might this be Accomplished?*, Florence: European University Institute, Jean Monnet Paper no. 6/01.

Schraeder, Peter (2001) 'South Africa's Foreign Policy: From International Pariah to Leader of the African Renaissance', *The Round Table*, vol. 359, pp. 229–43.

Schwab, Peter (2001) *Africa: A Continent Self-Destructs*, New York: Palgrave.

Security Dialogue (2004) *Special Issue: What is 'Human Security'?*, vol. 35, no. 3, pp. 345–87.

Severino, Rodolfo C. (2001) 'The ASEAN Way and the Rule of Law'. Paper presented to the International Law Conference on ASEAN Legal Systems and Regional Integration (Sponsored by the Asia–Europe Institute and the Faculty of Law, University of Malaya) Kuala Lumpur.

Shaw, Martin (2003) 'The Global Transformation of the Social Sciences', in Mary Kaldor *et al.* (eds) *Global Civil Society*, Oxford: Oxford University Press, pp. 35–44.

Shaw, Timothy M. (2000) 'New Regionalisms in Africa in the New Millennium: Comparative Perspectives on Renaissance, Realism and/or Regressions', *New Political Economy*, vol. 5, no. 3, pp. 399–414.

Shaw, Timothy M. and Janis van der Westhuizen (2004) 'Trade and Africa: Transforming Fringe into Franchise', in Brian Hocking and Steven McGuire (eds) *Trade Politics*, London: Routledge (2nd edn), pp. 63–73.

Shearer, David (1997) 'Exploring the Limits of Consent: Conflict Resolution in Sierra Leone', *Millennium*, vol. 26, no. 3, pp. 845–60.

Simon, David (2001) 'Trading Spaces: Imaging and Positioning the "new" South Africa within the Regional and Global Economies', *International Affairs*, vol. 77, no. 2, pp. 377–405.

Simons, Geoff (1994) *Iraq: From Sumer to Saddam*, London: Macmillan.

Smillie, Ian, Lansana Gberie and Ralph Hazleton (2000) *The Heart of the Matter: Sierra Leone, Diamonds and Human Security*, Ottawa: Partnership Africa Canada.

Snitwongse, Kusuma (1995) 'ASEAN's Security Cooperation and Regional Order', *The Pacific Review*, vol. 8, no. 3, pp. 518–30.

So, Alvin Y. and Stephen W. K. Chiu (1994) *East Asia and the World Economy*, Thousand Oaks, CA: Sage.

Söderbaum, Fredrik (1998) 'The New Regionalism in Southern Africa', *Politeia*, vol. 17, no. 3, pp. 75–94.

Söderbaum, Fredrik (2002) 'Regionalism in Southern Africa', Gothenburg: Gothenburg University, (PhD thesis).

Söderbaum, Fredrik and Timothy M. Shaw (eds) (2003) *Theories of New Regionalism: A Palgrave Reader*, Basingstoke: Palgrave Macmillan.

Stiff, Peter (2000) *Cry Zimbabwe: Independence – Twenty Years On*, Alberton, South Africa: Galago.

Stiglitz, Joseph (2002) *Globalization and Its Discontents*, London: Allen Lane.

Stubbs, Richard (2002) 'ASEAN Plus Three: Emerging East Asian Regionalism?', *Asian Survey*, vol. 42, no. 3, pp. 440–55.

Sucesos Mercosur (21 July 1998) (sucesos@intermedia.com.ar).

Sum, Ngai-Ling (2002) 'The Material, Strategic and Discursive Dimensions of the "Asian Crisis" and Subsequent Developments', in Pietro Masina (ed.), *Rethinking Development in Asia: From Illusory Miracle to Economic Crisis*, London: Curzon Press, pp. 53–78.

Sunday Independent (8 November 1998) 'Kabila Mining Deal Seen as "Payment" for Mugabe Forces', Johannesburg.

Swyngedouw, Eric (1997) 'Neither Global nor Local: Glocalization and the Politics of Scale', in Kevin R. Cox (ed.) *Spaces of Globalization. Reasserting the Power of the Local*, New York: Guilford Publications, pp. 137–66.

Szeftel, Morris (2000) 'Between Governance and Under-development: Accumulation and Africa's Catastrophic Corruption', *Review of African Political Economy*, no. 84, pp. 287–306.

Taylor, Ian (2002) 'Commentary: The New Partnership for Africa's Development and the Zimbabwe Elections: Implications and Prospects for the Future', *African Affairs*, vol. 101, no. 404, pp. 403–12.

Thomas, Nick (2002) 'From ASEAN to an East Asian Community? The Role of Functional Cooperation', *Working Paper Series*, No 28, Southeast Asia Research Centre, Hong Kong (http://www.cityu.edu.hk/searc/WP.html).

Treat, Jonathan (2002) Plan Puebla–Panama's Merida Summit. Americas Program, Silver City, NM, Interhemispheric Resource Centre, 24 July.

Tripp, Charles (2000) *A History of Iraq*, Cambridge: Cambridge University Press.

Tussie, Diane (1998) 'Emerging Regionalism in Latin America', in Walter D. Coleman and Geoffrey Underhill (eds) *Regionalism and Global Economic Integration: Europe, Asia and the Americas*, London: Routledge, pp. 93–114.

UN (1996) *Report of the International Commission of Inquiry*, New York: UN.

UN (2001) *Report of the Panel of Experts on the Illegal Exploitation of Natural Resources and Other Forms of Wealth of the Democratic Republic of Congo*, New York: UN.

UN (2004a) *Report of the Panel of Eminent Persons on UN–Civil Society Relations ('The Cardoso Panel')*, New York: UN.

UN (2004b) *High Level Panel on Threats, Challenges and Change Addressed to the Secretary-General*, New York: UN.

UN Millennium Project (2005) *Investing in Development: Overview Report*, New York: UN.

UNCTAD (2004) *Development and Globalization: Facts and Figures,* Geneva and New York: UNCTAD

UNCTAD (2004) *Is a Special Treatment of Small Island Developing States Possible?* Geneva: UNCTAD.

Vasconcelos, Arturo de (2003) 'Back to the Future: Strengthening EU–Mercosur Relations and Reviving Multilateralism' (www.chairemercosur.sciences-po.fr/negaciations).

Vatikiotis, Michael and Murray Hiebert (1998/1999) 'Help Yourself', *Far Eastern Economic Review*, 31 December/7 January, pp. 12–13.

Veiga, Motta P. (1995) 'Mercosul: a Agenda da Concolidacao e os Dilemas da Ampliacao', in J.P. dos Reis Velloso (ed.) *Mercosul e NAFTA: o Brasil e a Integracao Hemisferica*, Montevideo, Uruguay: Mercosur, pp. 14–26.

Vries, Da'oud (29 March 2004) 'Does Namibia Opt for Land Expropriation?' *New Era* (Windhoek), p. 4.

Wade, Robert (1999) 'Gestalt Shift: From Miracle to "Cronyism" in the Asian Crisis', *IDS Bulletin*, vol. 30, no. 1, pp. 134–50.

Wade, Robert (2000) 'Wheels Within Wheels: Rethinking the Asian Crisis and the Asian Model', *Annual Review of Political Science*, vol. 3, pp. 85–115.

Wade, Robert (2001) 'The US Role in the Long Asian Crisis of 1990–2000', in Arvid J. Lukauskas and Fransisco L. Riviera-Batiz (eds) *The Political Economy of the Asian Crisis and Its Aftermath: Tigers in Distress*. Cheltenham: Edward Elgar, pp. 195–226.

Wade, Robert H. (2003) 'The Invisible Hand of the American Empire', *Open Democracy Network* (www.opendemocracy.net/themes/article-6-1038.jsp).

Wade, Robert and Frank Venoroso (1998a) 'The Asian Crisis: The High Debt Model Versus the Wall Street – Treasury – IMF Complex', *New Left Review*, no. 228, pp. 3–22.

Wade, Robert and Frank Venoroso (1998b) 'The Gathering World Slump and the Battle over Capital Control', *New Left Review*, no. 231, pp. 13–42.

Wain, Barry (2002) 'A Questionable Strategy', *Far Eastern Economic Review*, 31 January, pp. 48–52.

Wallace, William (2000) 'Regionalism in Europe: Model or Exception?', in Louise Fawcett and Andrew Hurrell (eds), *Regionalism in World Politics: Regional Organization and International Order*, Oxford: Oxford University Press, pp. 201–27.

Weatherbee, Donald E. (1995) 'The Foreign Policy Dimensions of Subregional Economic Zones', *Contemporary Southeast Asia*, vol. 16, no. 4, pp. 421–32.

Webber, Douglas (2001) 'Two Funerals and a Wedding? The Ups and Downs of Regionalism in East Asia and Asia-Pacific after the Asian Crisis', *The Pacific Review*, vol. 14, no. 3, pp. 339–72.

Weinstein, Jeremy (2000) 'Africa's "Scramble for Africa": Lessons of a Continental War', *World Policy Journal*, vol. 17, no. 2, pp. 11–20.

White, Michael (8 December 2003) 'Mugabe Quits Commonwealth', *The Guardian*, p. 15.

Wiener, Antje and Thomas Diez (2004) *European Integration Theory*, Oxford: Oxford University Press.

Wrong, Michaela (2000) *In the Footsteps of Mr Kurtz: Living on the Brink of Disaster in the Congo*, London: Fourth Estate.

www.africa2000.com/UGANDA/introdgeopolitique.html 'Corporate Pirates and Other Scoundrels in the Congo War'.

Yahoo! (2000) 'Japanese Experts Call for Yen-Based Imports from Asia', *Yahoo! Asia News*, 29 May.

Zapata, Francisco (2003) 'Crisis en el Sindicalisimo en América Latina?' (unpublished mimeo.).

Index